Christian Heresy, James Joyce, and the Modernist Literary Imagination

NEW DIRECTIONS IN RELIGION AND LITERATURE

This series aims to showcase new work at the forefront of religion and literature through short studies written by leading and rising scholars in the field. Books will pursue a variety of theoretical approaches as they engage with writing from different religious and literary traditions. Collectively, the series will offer a timely critical intervention to the interdisciplinary crossover between religion and literature, speaking to wider contemporary interests and mapping out new directions for the field in the early twenty-first century.

Series editors: Emma Mason and Mark Knight

ALSO AVAILABLE IN THE SERIES:
The New Atheist Novel, Arthur Bradley and Andrew Tate
Blake. Wordsworth. Religion, Jonathan Roberts
Do the Gods Wear Capes?, Ben Saunders
England's Secular Scripture, Jo Carruthers
Victorian Parables, Susan E. Colón
The Late Walter Benjamin, John Schad
Dante and the Sense of Transgression, William Franke
The Glyph and the Gramophone, Luke Ferretter
John Cage and Buddhist Ecopoetics, Peter Jaeger
Rewriting the Old Testament in Anglo-Saxon Verse, Samantha Zacher
Forgiveness in Victorian Literature, Richard Hughes Gibson
The Gospel According to the Novelist, Magdalena Mączyńska
Jewish Feeling, Richa Dwor
Beyond the Willing Suspension of Disbelief, Michael Tomko
The Gospel According to David Foster Wallace, Adam S. Miller
Pentecostal Modernism, Stephen Shapiro and Philip Barnard
The Bible in the American Short Story, Lesleigh Cushing Stahlberg and Peter S. Hawkins
Faith in Poetry, Michael D. Hurley
Jeanette Winterson and Religion, Emily McAvan
Religion and American Literature since the 1950s, Mark Eaton
Esoteric Islam in Modern French Thought, Ziad Elmarsafy
The Rhetoric of Conversion in English Puritan Writing, David Parry
Djuna Barnes and Theology, Zhao Ng
Food and Fasting in Victorian Religion and Literature, Lesa Scholl

FORTHCOMING:
Marilynne Robinson's Wordly Gospel, Ryan S. Kemp and Jordan M. Rodgers
Weird Faith in 19th Century Literature, Mark Knight and Emma Mason
The Economy of Religion in American Literature, Andrew Ball

Christian Heresy, James Joyce, and the Modernist Literary Imagination

Reinventing the Word

Gregory Erickson

BLOOMSBURY ACADEMIC
LONDON • NEW YORK • OXFORD • NEW DELHI • SYDNEY

BLOOMSBURY ACADEMIC
Bloomsbury Publishing Plc
50 Bedford Square, London, WC1B 3DP, UK
1385 Broadway, New York, NY 10018, USA
29 Earlsfort Terrace, Dublin 2, Ireland

BLOOMSBURY, BLOOMSBURY ACADEMIC and the Diana logo are trademarks of
Bloomsbury Publishing Plc

First published in Great Britain 2022
This paperback edition published 2023

Copyright © Gregory Erickson, 2022

Gregory Erickson has asserted his right under the Copyright, Designs
and Patents Act, 1988, to be identified as Author of this work.

For legal purposes the Acknowledgments on pp. xvii–xix constitute
an extension of this copyright page.

Cover design: Rebecca Heselton
Cover image: Stained Glass window depicting a heretic, in the Cathedral of Saint Rumbold
in Mechelen, Belgium / Aurelian Images / Alamy Stock Photo

All rights reserved. No part of this publication may be reproduced or transmitted
in any form or by any means, electronic or mechanical, including photocopying,
recording, or any information storage or retrieval system, without
prior permission in writing from the publishers.

Bloomsbury Publishing Plc does not have any control over, or responsibility for,
any third-party websites referred to or in this book. All internet addresses given
in this book were correct at the time of going to press. The author and publisher
regret any inconvenience caused if addresses have changed or sites have
ceased to exist, but can accept no responsibility for any such changes.

A catalogue record for this book is available from the British Library.

A catalog record for this book is available from the Library of Congress.

ISBN: HB: 978-1-3502-1275-6
PB: 978-1-3502-1279-4
ePDF: 978-1-3502-1276-3
eBook: 978-1-3502-1277-0

Series: New Directions in Religion and Literature

Typeset by Integra Software Services Pvt. Ltd.

To find out more about our authors and books visit www.bloomsbury.com
and sign up for our newsletters.

To Angelina

To Catie

To my students

To Mittens and Ñoñita

and to all the wonderful Joyceans, modernists, historians, artists, and religious studies scholars I've met along the way

Contents

List of Figures	viii
Preface	ix
Acknowledgments	xvii
Abbreviations for Works by James Joyce	xx
1 Christian Heresy, James Joyce, and the Modernist Imagination	1
2 Five Moments of Schism: A Selective History of Heresy	25
3 Reversals of History: From Gnostic Heretics to James Joyce and Back Again	53
4 Arius and the Anxiety of Vampiric Creation	87
5 Joyce, Medieval Heresy, and the Eucharist: Fragmented Narratives of Doubt	113
6 Alternative Reformations: Iconoclasm and *Finnegans Wake*	139
Epilogue: Heretical and Sacred Reading Strategies: The Book of Mormon and *Finnegans Wake*	173
Fin Again: Writing and the Practice of Heresy	191
Bibliography	202
Index	215

Figures

1. Tring Tiles: Apocryphal images of Jesus as child "tile," near 1330, artist unknown, within The Tring Tiles Series © The British Museum, 1997. Reproduced with the permission of The British Museum — 37
2. Death of Arius in a public lavatory "St. Nicholas and Arius the Heretic," 1665, artist unknown, located at the Smolinsky Convent, Moscow © Prof. Michael Fuller, 2006 — 101
3. Elevation of the Host "Corpus Christi," early 1400s, The Ranworth Antiphoner, contributors unknown © St. Helen's Church Ranworth. Reproduced with the permission of the Broadside Benefice, Parishes of Ranworth and Panxworth, Woodbastwick, South Walsham, and Upton and Fishley — 119
4. Squint at Church of St. Thomas of Becket — 133
5. Medieval Man of Sorrows painting with Reformation era text "Christ the Man of Sorrows," undated, text added 1539, 1525, 1535, contributors unknown © St. Mary and the Holy Cross Binham. Reproduced with the permission of the Rector and the Church Council of St. Mary and the Holy Cross Binham — 144
6. Recovered sculpture of the Trinity in Kilkenny parish church — 162
7. Original cover page of the Book of Mormon — 181
8. Grandin building in Palmyra, New York: Print shop where the Book of Mormon was first printed — 188
9. Images and graffiti on church wall in Saint George's in Cappadocia — 193

Preface

In the summer of 2007, I participated in a six-week National Endowment for the Humanities (NEH) faculty seminar on James Joyce's *Ulysses* in Dublin, led by Kevin Dettmar. It was my first trip to Ireland, my first intensive study of Joyce, and my first post-graduate school seminar. I had recently finished a book on modernism and religion which looked at a late Henry James novel, the work of Marcel Proust, and the music of Arnold Schoenberg through what I identified as postmodern theologies of absence. I was looking for a new project where I could continue to think about religion and literature, this time with an eye on doing something more historical. The NEH seminar was transformative, as it introduced me to new ways of reading and thinking about *Ulysses* and to the inspiring intellectual, and social, world of Joyce scholars. These six weeks were also, although I did not know it at the time, the genesis of this project.

Much has happened in the thirteen years since, and when I revisit my journey of reading, writing, teaching, traveling, and—more than anything—learning, I find that all of it is in this book. At the Dublin Joyce seminar, I felt slightly out of place: I was not a Joycean, nor was I a modernist in the way that most of the participants were. Everyone seemed to have such focused projects, and were working with specific archives, manuscripts, and editions. This kind of material research was new to me. But I discovered that I liked thinking about objects, texts, and spaces, and my burgeoning interest in Christian history and heresy seemed like a good reason to see (and travel) more. In addition to the expansion of my academic interests, this book represents my slow process of becoming a specialist on James Joyce, a process aided by multiple Joyce classes, conferences, and reading groups—experiences both joyful and illuminating.

Why Heresy? Why Joyce? And Why Now?

The late-twentieth and early-twenty-first centuries have seen various "returns of" and "turns to" religion, both within academia and public discourse. While modernist studies—perhaps because it has often defined itself in relation with a process of secularization—has been a little slow to acknowledge and address these various returns of religion, recent books and conference seminars indicate developing moves in this direction.[1] Because of my focus on Joyce, modernism, the Western literary tradition, and the concept of heresy, I will stay within—and occasionally on the blurry edges of—specifically Christian traditions. In his *Modernism and Christianity*, Erik Tonning argues that modernist studies should be "rethought in accordance with the insight that the role of Christianity is intrinsic to any coherent account of Modernism" (2014: 1). Within the world of Joyce studies, there has also been a recent boom in re-examining his relationship to Christianity.[2] For Tonning, Joyce is important to this discussion because his "case suggests that for some Modernists at least, the church and not modernity per se remained the principal adversary" (2014: 7). From my perspective, however, it is not the church-as-adversary or Christianity-as-other that I am interested in. I will instead focus on locating the others and adversaries *within* Christian traditions and at how these interactions have shaped literary thinking.

Part of what is encouraging these new approaches to literature and religion are engagements with new definitions and methodologies in the field of religious studies. Religious studies—long linked, particularly in the United States, to a confessional, usually Christian, and often Protestant-based methodology—has moved in new directions that question longstanding foundational terms such as "divine," "scripture," and even the concept of "religion" itself, especially in de-emphasizing belief and doctrine in favor of lived practices. Finally, within the general public, books from Elaine Pagels's *The Gnostic Gospels* to Dan Brown's *Da Vinci Code* have reinvigorated interests in religious history and in marginalized sects and non-canonical texts. While modernist literature has traditionally been understood as representing a decline in religious faith (with certain exceptions, such as T.S. Eliot), the modernist and postmodernist questioning of epistemological and physical certainty is also inescapably contained *within* the theological fabric of Western thought. In other words, we do not have to see modernism as denying, resisting, replacing, or even re-inventing a formerly stable and now lost religiosity; instead we can see it as a continuation of longstanding, and often destabilizing, interactions between art, literature, and religion that go back to the second century.

---

1 Several recent titles that offer new methodologies or paradigms for thinking about religion and modernist literature include *Religious Experience and the Modernist Novel* by Pericles Lewis, *Angels of Modernism* by Suzanne Hobson, and *Blasphemous Modernism: The 20th-Century Word Made Flesh* by Steve Pinkerton. Five recent Modernist Studies Association Conferences (2011, 2013, 2014, 2016, 2019) have included seminars on modernism and religion, all of which I have participated in and learned from.

2 For example, *Joyce's Misbelief* by Roy Gottfried, *Help My Unbelief: James Joyce and Religion* by Geert Lernout, and *James Joyce and Catholicism: The Apostate's Wake* by Chrissie Van Mierlo.

Religious studies scholar Tyler Roberts is in line with my book when he argues for a more *humanistic* study of religion. He cites scholars such as Amy Hollywood who, without "obvious allegiance to Christianity," still think *with* religious thinkers and,

> contribute to our knowledge of religion by cutting against the grain of traditionally secular scholarship to view traditions of religious thought not just as objects of study but also as sources of analytic categories.
>
> (2013: 16)

In my construction of these analytic categories in concert with reading Joyce, I have tried to balance three intersecting historical narratives:

1. A broad and complex history of Christianity, reflecting more on the history of *how* it has been imagined, than making any sort of claims for what it actually was.
2. A historical moment captured in the works of James Joyce and the early-twentieth-century culture in which he wrote.
3. A history of shifting religious and literary attitudes in the late-twentieth century and in the first two decades of the twenty-first.

In addition, perhaps a fourth historical narrative would be the decade-long history of my evolving approaches within and to this project. This book, then, both is and is not a sweeping history of heresy or a critical interpretation of the works of Joyce. I will be looking at theological and religious debates and issues through the lens of modernist literature, and I will be thinking about Joyce and his texts through a sequence of theological movements in Christian history. The focus of this book will be the novels of Joyce read through and alongside "heretical moments" in the history of Christianity from second-century Gnostics and early Christological debates to Joseph Smith and the Book of Mormon. The book is an exploration of the ways that literature and theology are linked through writing and the imagination, intersections that we—as readers and thinkers, students and scholars, believers and atheists—continue to grapple with today.

Chapter Overview

This book is organized chronologically, moving from second-century heresies to the nineteenth and twentieth centuries, and each chapter will link the ideas and history of a specific heretical movement or debate with ideas and passages from

Joyce's works. While the beginning chapters will touch on Joyce's early works, the focus will be primarily on *Ulysses* and *Finnegans Wake*. First, however, Chapter 2 will sketch a historical background by presenting brief overviews of the five examples of schism or heresy that will organize the rest of the book: Gnosticism, Arius and early Christology, debates over the medieval Eucharist, the Reformation and iconoclasm, and the Book of Mormon. The chapter presents the basic ideas behind each heresy for readers with little background in religious history as well as highlights new knowledge and understandings of these historical examples that have developed in the late-twentieth and twenty-first centuries. Most significantly, it asserts that each heresy can be seen as a clash over how to read, write, and interpret written texts in ways that both influence and echo our current literary practices.

Chapter 3 will examine how some of the earliest Christian theologians—the Gnostics of the second century—were engaged with issues of reading, interpretation, and the book. Although Joyce rarely mentions Gnosticism in his works, the ways in which he challenged modes of reading, the relationship of his books to prior texts, the idea of canonical scriptures, and the possibility of the unity of a book itself, echo Gnostic ideas and early Christian debates. This chapter will discuss how new discoveries about Gnosticism in the twentieth century changed the ways we tell Christian history. This radical act of revisionist history belongs partly to the worlds of religious studies and archeology, but also partly, I argue, to modes of reading and understanding that come out of the challenging literature of modernist authors like Joyce. The final part of the chapter examines Gnosticism after the dramatic 1945 discovery of ancient Gnostic texts in Egypt, which gradually led to a radical redefinition of Gnosticism and an expanded conception of Christian scriptures that had been anticipated and perhaps prepared for by works like *Finnegans Wake*, which had already taught us new ways to "read" both history and scripture.

Chapter 4 will focus on the fourth-century bishop Arius, the heresiarch mentioned most often in *Ulysses*. Arius's heresy was that Christ, like humans, was also created, that he too came from nothing, a conception that forced thinkers to theorize the act of divine and human creation. This chapter looks at several episodes from the first half of *Ulysses* to read Joyce's connection to the Arian. Joyce seems to have found in Arius's rebellion a model for a radical rethinking of the role of literature and its connection to how we think not only about concepts like divinity and the Trinity, but also about the act of artistic creation itself.

In the context of the history of Christian heresies, the Eucharist sits at the exact middle of my book; it is an answer to Gnostic and Arian concerns, on the edge of the Reformation, and yet still exists as a theme, a reality, a metaphor, and a debate for Joyce and contemporary Christians. Chapter 5, which is part memoir, part art criticism, and part literary analysis, makes the claim that Joyce's use of the Mass in *Ulysses* can open our eyes to a different kind of medieval: one that is about the movement of bodies through incomplete or disrupted spaces, and the fragmented movement of texts and objects through time. This chapter complicates how scholars of modernism have engaged with and employed medieval Eucharistic metaphors, especially in the formal and stylistic experimentation of Joyce's *Ulysses*.

Chapter 6 takes us from damaged Catholic devotional art in England and Ireland to the Joyce archives in Buffalo, New York to tell a story of the Reformation, iconoclasm, and modern literature. Joyce's *Finnegans Wake*, in particular its incomplete drafts, word fragments, notebooks, and puns, can be read as a text that has lived through and been changed by the Middle Ages and the Reformation. Reformation debates over words and images provide a useful example of the power of art and poetry to negotiate and dramatize this religious conflict. My reading of *Finnegans Wake* and Joyce's handwritten *Finnegans Wake* Notebooks adopts a method viewed through Reformation iconoclasm—one that is always simultaneously aware of tradition, changes, and decay, both literary and material—and existing on the border between legacy and finitude, memory and amnesia.

In the epilogue, I turn to heresy in the so-called New World, specifically within the Book of Mormon. In shifting my focus to more modern comparisons, my goal is to help identify ways that literature is a part of how we conceive of, create, and recreate scripture—and how this is related to how we process and read historical and literary narratives. In comparing the Book of Mormon and *Finnegans Wake*, I return to some of the themes of writing history from chapters three and four; yet, instead of recreating a modern text out of ancient Gnostic texts, here I find two very different modern texts re-imagining themselves as an ancient Other.

*　*　*

[Bloomsday: June 16, 2021, New York City]
Bloomsday, as readers of Joyce know, is a celebration of the novel *Ulysses* that happens every year, on June 16: the day that the novel is set and the anniversary of Joyce's first date with his partner, Nora, in 1904. Celebrations in streets, theaters, classrooms, and pubs across the world bring together Joyce scholars with passionate amateurs, professional actors with curious drinkers—costumes,

pints of Guinness, Irish music, and enthusiastic public readings can be found in cities and towns around the world. Before the idea of being a literature professor had even occurred to me, I used to attend the marathon Bloomsday readings at Symphony Space on Broadway in New York City, fascinated and perplexed by the language of a novel I had yet to read. Since 2008, I have usually spent Bloomsday buried in the middle of the National or International Joyce Symposium, and the day is spent in panels and seminars, followed by a reception. This year, 2021, was different. The previous year's conference—scheduled to be held in Trieste—had been canceled, and the rescheduled 27th International Joyce Symposium was being held remotely due to Covid restrictions. I had presented a paper on the morning of the first day of the conference, but, other than that, I had mostly been occupied in making final addition and edits to this book, which was due to the publisher a few weeks later, on July 1. I found myself stuck in the familiar but uncomfortable space of balancing final edits, writing a preface, and facing the existential insecurity that always comes with finishing a book.

Like I advise my graduate students, I saved the writing of this preface until the end in order to have a sense of the ending at the beginning—to be able to write from a position of at least tentative completeness. In the writing, however, I was constantly reminded of philosophers who wrote on the "question of the preface," who argued for its impossibility, for how it, in Gayatri Spivak's terms, "harbors a lie" (1976: x). The lie works in many ways—most familiarly, in the fiction that the preface *introduces* a project which is usually (as in my case) at the very edge of being finished. But a preface also tends to assume the presence of a single book produced by a single person. Not only is one of the arguments of this book that a book is not a single, self-contained entity, but I have never felt more strongly that a single person did not write it. Not only have I leaned on, learned from, borrowed from, and written with numerous colleagues and friends, but I am not the "I"—the same person—who began writing this book almost a decade ago. A progression of different authors, at different times and places, have written this book. A traditional preface tends to assume a single space between writing and reading, and—to quote Spivak again—"merely enacts what is already the case: the book's repetitions are always other than the book" (1976: xii). There are many authors and many versions of this book. Which version or author am I assuming this preface addresses?

An old-fashioned Bloomsday celebration seemed a good way to both avoid and perhaps address these doubts, so when my friend and colleague Jonathan Goldman invited me to an outdoor pub celebration on the Upper West Side, I agreed. I wrote most of the day, dropped into a few remote Joyce panels, watched a YouTube Joycean walking tour of Trieste, and then headed to Dive 106 on Amsterdam Avenue, the first, large, in-person event I had attended since Covid. I took the 1 train uptown, my copy of *Ulysses* under my arm. The subway stalled due to a door malfunction—which felt almost nostalgic—so I got off to walk from the 96th street station, a stop that always reminds me of Bloomsday on Broadway at Symphony Space in the 1990s. Walking up Amsterdam—thinking about an unfinished book, a remote conference, a city coming to life on a beautiful spring day, and the problems of the preface—I found the bar, but, not feeling quite ready for a group of Joyceans yet, stopped to look at a nineteenth-century church on the corner. I was already thinking about time and history—fifteen months of Covid, a decade writing a book, twenty-five years of Bloomsdays, 100 years of *Ulysses*—and a little smartphone-research on the West End Presbyterian Church's official website showed that it stood on that corner in 1888, when the pastor described it as "little less than a howling wilderness, inhabited mostly by shantyites and goats." By 1904, when James was meeting Nora over in Dublin, an article in the *New York Herald* stated, "The [West End] Church … was organized only sixteen years ago with 69 members, and now numbers 1,864 communicants." Much of my book is about the idea of "events" in the philosophical sense—how we understand a moment that changes everything that happens after: the crucifixion or the discovery of the Nag Hammadi Gnostic texts. The West End church had stood almost empty this past year for the first time since 1888, while, like most churches in the world, holding online services. What would be standing here in 100 years?

The well-known "Mookse and the Gripes" section of James Joyce's *Finnegans Wake* is thinking through something similar. The episode is a retelling of the "Fox and the Grapes" fable, with multiple references to various religious schisms, rifts, and heresies woven in, there is suddenly a shift in tone and we read of a "broken-arched traveller from Nuzuland … " (*FW* 156.29–30). These words refer to a passage in Leopold von Ranke's 1840 *History of the Popes*, in which Ranke imagines a traveler from New Zealand standing on the "broken arch of London Bridge to sketch the ruins of St. Paul's" (1847: 209). While Ranke is imagining the possible "undiminished vigour" of a still powerful Roman Catholic Church, Joyce's look into the future of a crumbling London finds in the ruins of St. Paul's an echo of past spaces, religions, and texts lost to time.

At the bar, I was warmly greeted, sat next to a couple of friends, and listened to reader after reader recite their favorite sections. Asked to read near the end of the evening, I choose the first sixty-three lines, or the "Overture," of chapter eleven of *Ulysses*, the "Sirens" chapter written in and through various musical styles. I introduced my selection by explaining that it was these exact lines—back when I was still a struggling classical musician, reading *Ulysses* for the first time—that were perhaps the beginning of my more serious academic career. These opening lines offer an initially incomprehensible and random-seeming selection of the chapter's language, words, sounds, and plot. Not comprehending them at all, I spent hours reading and researching this chapter to understand how it worked. I began to understand that *Ulysses* is not just a book to be read, but that it is to be heard, seen, remembered, forgotten, and reread. I began to read—reread, in fact—out loud:

> * Bronze by gold heard the hoofirons, steelyringing.
> Imperthnthn thnthnthn. (*U* 11.1–2)

"Imperthnthn thnthnthn" or "impertinent insolence" indeed. What does it mean to read what might seem incomprehensible? What is that space between the spoken and written word, and where does reading out loud fit into it? These are questions of Christian history and Christian heresy as well, and some other version of a preface to my book might very well address them.

I kept reading. I could hear the noise of Amsterdam Avenue around me: buses, taxis, motorcycles, and bicycles went past, blending in with the words. A person walked through the tables blasting rap music. I (unwisely) tried to time my reading to the music, a strong 4/4 time, emphasis on beat 2 and 4.

> Clap. Clipclap. Clappyclap.
> Goodgod henev reheard inall (*U* 11.28–9)

Back in my musician days, these sixty-three lines had opened up my ears to literature, to the intersection of sound, word, image, and meaning. The beginning of my life as a serious Joyce reader. Now the end of my book. A preface, too, is both beginning and ending. I read on, nearing the end.

> Then not till then. My eppripfftaph, (*U* 11.61)

I was hearing the re-awakening city, imagining a Dublin or a New York in 1904, and looking forward to feeling and hearing them again in 2022.

> Done.
> Begin! (*U* 11.62–62)

Acknowledgments

I am a different person now than I was when I started this book. I like to think that I am a better person, a better teacher, and a better colleague. If that is true, then the communal experience of writing this book has been part of those changes. I decided somewhere along the line that if I was going to write scholarly books then I was going to do it communally. The names on this page are some of my best friends, and some of the best people I know. It has been, for the most part, a joyful experience, and I hope some of that comes through on the pages.

This book would not exist without three National Endowment for the Humanities Faculty seminars in which I participated. The first—during which I read *Ulysses* in Dublin for six weeks with Kevin Dettmar and an amazing group of scholars—not only made it possible for me to read, teach, and write about Joyce, it literally literally changed my life in ways I cannot begin to express here. A second NEH seminar on the study of religion, with Charles Mathewes and Kurtis Schaeffer, introduced me to new patterns of thinking and writing about religion that I am still processing today. A third NEH seminar in York, on medieval devotional art, led by Laura Gelfand and Sarah Blick, allowed me to play medievalist for a month, but also inspired several chapters in this book. Each of these seminars—and sadly the NEH no longer funds faculty seminars abroad—introduced me to a community of scholars, teachers, and colleagues that opened my mind to new ways of thinking and made me a better teacher and a better scholar. A fourth seminar in which I participated at the Folger library with Brad Gregory on Renaissance constructions of the human was also central in giving me new perspectives on the Reformation. There is not room here to thank all the amazing participants in these seminars, but I want to give special shout outs to Julia Perratore, Steve Rozenski, Elisa Foster, Greg Winston, Maria McGarrity, Joe Kelly, Erin Templeton, Janine Utell, Clayton Crockett, and Kathy Foody.

Much of this material was presented at many conferences over the years—the International and National Joyce Symposiums, the International Society for Heresy Studies, and the Modernist Studies Association. Thank you to everyone who attended, presented, and commented. Thank you to my amazing students at New York University's Gallatin School of Individualized Study especially those students in the three seminars I taught on "Interdisciplinary Joyce" and the two on "Reading and Performing *Finnegans Wake*." Many of these students are still a big part of my life and still inspire me every day. Also, a big thank you to Susanne Wofford and the Gallatin School for the generous support I have received over my years of teaching and research. I would also like to thank the Folger Library, the Conference on Christianity and Literature, and the University of Buffalo Humanities Institute, for financial and research support, as well as Binham Priory Church and the Church of St Helen, Ranworth, for permission to use images.

Thank you to Richard Santana, my writing partner since graduate school, who listened to me explain an early version of this book and responded, "I think you may have something there." Since then I have written and workshopped many of these pages at his upstate home, fortified by good food and scotch. Thanks to Eugene Vydrin, who, after participating in a friendly workshop of an early (i.e., long) version of a single chapter, said, "I want to read all the chapters." I took him up on that in the later stages, sending him a 120,000-word document and asking for his help reducing it to 80,000. Thank you to Catie Piwinski, former graduate student, then research assistant, now editor, colleague, and close friend. Catie has been along on every step of the last part of this journey, reading every chapter multiple times, encouraging me, correcting and clarifying my prose, and giggling at my comma placement. We didn't always agree on what should be in here. "It's not a Joyce book," I would respond to her comments asking me to cut or rephrase a section, and then she would explain to me why it was. "Why is this here?" she would ask, and I would try to explain, to then realize that I needed to write that very thought. She was usually right. She doesn't know it yet, but she will someday also write a "Joyce book," and I look forward to reading it. Thanks to Tess Brewer, Tanya Radford, Bob Royalty, Bernard Schweizer, Jennifer Lemberg, Suzanne Hobson, Ross Edwards, Finn Fordham, Jonathan Goldman, Craig Bernardini, Colleigh Stein, Sasha Sharova, Eugenia Kisin, Ryan Leas, Andy Romig, and my parents Ray and Lavina Erickson. You all deserve more than a single mention here, and you all helped make this a better book.

And special thanks to Angelina, who read very little of this, but without whom it would have been impossible. I promise to take a little time off now.

* * *

While most of this manuscript is previously unpublished, earlier versions of several sections have appeared in articles and chapters that have been revised and reinscribed into the context of this book. Antecedent versions of these can be located in the following publications, which are used with permission:

"James Joyce's *Ulysses* and the Medieval Eucharist: Fragmented Narratives of Doubt and Creation," *Devotional Interaction in Medieval Britain and Its Afterlives*, 347–71, Foster, E. A., J. Perratore, and S. Rozenski, eds. (2018), Leiden: Brill Publishers.

"Arius and the Vampire: Figures of Heresy and Disruption in James Joyce's *Ulysses*," in *Religion and the Arts*, (2016) 20 (4): 442–58.

"Epilogue: Heretical Unmaking," Reading Heresy: *Religion and Dissent in Literature and Art: Selected Essays from the 2014 Conference of the International Society for Heresy Studies*, Erickson, G. and B. Schweizer, eds. (2017), Berlin: De Gruyter.

Abbreviations for Works by James Joyce

D   James Joyce, *Dubliners*

FW   James Joyce, *Finnegans Wake*

The page number is followed by the line number.

P   James Joyce, *A Portrait of the Artist as a Young Man*

U   James Joyce, *Ulysses: The Corrected Text*

The chapter number is followed by the line number.

L1   James Joyce, *Letters*, Volume 1

L2   James Joyce, *Letters*, Volume 2

L3   James Joyce, *Letters*, Volume 3

SH   James Joyce, *Stephen Hero*

CW   James Joyce, *The Critical Writings*

VI.B.3   James Joyce, *The Finnegans Wake Notebooks at Buffalo: VI.B.3*

VI.B.6   James Joyce, *The Finnegans Wake Notebooks at Buffalo: VI.B.6*

VI.B.7   James Joyce, *The Finnegans Wake Notebooks at Buffalo: VI.B.7*

VI.B.14 James Joyce, *The Finnegans Wake Notebooks at Buffalo: VI.B.14*

1

Christian Heresy, James Joyce, and the Modernist Imagination

"Bibelous hicstory and Barbarassa harestary."

(*FW* 280.5–7)

Ulysses and the Heretical Imagination

Readers of James Joyce's works, particularly *Ulysses*, have long debated its relationship with religion and particularly to Catholic theology and practice. While many find Joyce's treatments of Catholicism primarily subversive, blasphemous, or parodic, others have made the opposing claim that Joyce's depiction of Catholic themes expresses an admiration for aspects of Catholicism. Critics on both sides often seem most concerned with addressing the question by looking to Joyce's biographical relationship to confessional belief. On the surface, Joyce's relationship to the Catholic Church and religion is a story of antagonism. After considering the priesthood as a young man, by his early twenties, Joyce wrote that he had "left the Catholic church hating it most fervently" and that he would "make open war upon it by what I write and say and do" (*L* 2:48). Geert Lernout's recent book, *Help My Unbelief: James Joyce and Religion*, makes the claim that we can *only* read Joyce's works properly if we understand that Joyce was an unbeliever throughout his entire writing life (2010: 2). Other works on Joyce and religion focus on the historical backgrounds of Catholic doctrine and liturgy, or on cataloguing the religious elements, themes, figures, and scriptural quotations in his work.[1]

---

1 Among many examples are James Atherton's *The Books at the Wake: A Study of Literary Allusions in James Joyce's Finnegans Wake* in the 1950s, Frederick Lang's *Ulysses and the Irish God* in the 1990s, and Steve Pinkerton's *Blasphemous Modernism: The 20th Century Word Make Flesh* in 2017.

Joyce biographer Richard Ellmann influentially wrote that Joyce's "Christianity evolved from a religion into a system of metaphors" (1983: 66). This anachronistic idea—that because of and through modernism we have "evolved" past a "primitive" type of religious faith—still often implicitly (and sometimes explicitly) shapes readings of Joyce. As Roy Gottfried and others have pointed out, "Ellmann betrays, of course, the secular view that Joyce moved on to more complicated ideas than those found in religion" (2008: 48). In recent decades, beginning with Frederick Lang's 1996 *Ulysses and the Irish God*, and more recently in Gottfried's 2008 *Joyce's Misbelief* and Chrissie Van Mierlo's 2017 *James Joyce and Catholicism: The Apostates Wake*, critics have begun to explore how serious engagements with religion can move beyond historical influence or the biographical and can be studied in the style, structure, and themes of Joyce's fiction. Reading Joyce through these dialogues reveals unstable boundaries between belief, unbelief, heresy, and blasphemy that raise questions resonating throughout literary, theological, and religious history.

As readers, we always balance our own definitions of what it means to be religious or non-religious, or anti-religious, with our understandings of the definitions available at the time of the writing. To read in this way is to constantly be aware of at least two historical horizons: the time when the work was written and the time when one is reading it. In this book, I will build on this idea by adding a third historical horizon. What I intend to show throughout this book is how both Joyce's novels and earlier moments in the history of Christian heresy are grappling with many of the same issues. Debates over origin, book, interpretation, author, body, and text are continually reinvented across the history of theological debate and become defining aesthetic issues in modernist literature. Juxtaposing the history of heresy and the works of Joyce can point to and create these networks that can sometimes appear as antagonistic and other times as dialectical—a process that dismantles and deconstructs stable theological elements at the same time that it can confirm them. The history of heresy, then, intersects with modernist literature and the writings of James Joyce in very literal ways: by reading Joyce through the lens of heresy, and reading heresy through the lens of Joyce, we find—in the margins and traces, in the metaphors, paradoxes, puns, shadows, and non sequiturs—elements of the theological and the literary that are surprising and revealing.

* * *

Heresy, blasphemy, and theology are inescapable from the beginning of *Ulysses*, as the opening pages thrust readers into a world clearly shaped by and yet also challenging an orthodox religious past. Even my students new to Joyce, entering the novel without preconceptions and finding themselves on a tower on the outskirts of Dublin looking over Dublin Bay, understand that religion and theology are important themes. On top of the tower is Buck Mulligan, mocking the Catholic Mass and the holiness of Christ by holding a bowl of shaving lather aloft and issuing a call to the altar, offering blessings, and joking about the process of transubstantiation of wine into blood. The second character on the roof is Stephen Dedalus—the reader may know him (or a version of him) from Joyce's earlier *A Portrait of the Artist*—a Jesuit-educated, young poet wearing black in mourning for his mother. Downstairs, and also living in the tower, is the Englishman Haynes, who has annoyed Stephen during the night by raving in his sleep about a black panther.

We will return to this opening chapter and all its provocative details of blasphemy, theology, mythology, mockery, and religion later, but I here want to examine an early passage that offers a list of heresies and heretics. In one of Stephen's first extended flights of imaginative association, thoughts of bells, a choir, and a fragment of the Nicaean Creed lead to a vision of the "vigilant angel of the church militant disarmed and menaced her heresiarchs" and then a "horde of heresies fleeing," and a short catalogue of famous heretics:

> Photius and the brood of mockers of whom Mulligan was one, and Arius, warring his life long upon the consubstantiality of the Son with the Father, and Valentine spurning Christ's terrene body, and the subtle African heresiarch Sabellius who held that the Father was Himself His own Son.
>
> (*U* 1.650–62)

The paragraph packs together sound, memory, ritual, orthodox dogma, and several heretics known for questioning aspects of God or Christ's nature— especially relationships of the Son to the Father, human to the divine, and body to soul. All of these heresiarchs challenged church orthodoxy by redefining and reframing the ontology and materiality of the God-idea, debates over creation and creator that also redefine the role of the author, the idea of the book, and theories and practices of reading and interpreting scripture.

In this passage, as my students find with a quick in-class Google search, each heretic is identified with the theological trait they are most associated with. Arius, perhaps the most important heretic in *Ulysses*, argued that Jesus was *created* by the Father and was in this way not eternal or identical to God.

Sabellius, whose Christology advocates the opposite of Arius, saw Christ as fully divine, and therefore not fully human (in other words, a figure who could not truly suffer and die on the cross). Valentine (or Valentinus) was the most important Christian Gnostic, and believed in a fully spiritual Christ who could not, by definition, embody a truly physical human form. Photius was a central figure in the split between Eastern and Roman orthodoxy, partly because of arguments over the source of the Holy Ghost. As we will see in subsequent chapters, these figures and their ideas are woven into the complexities of reading Joyce's works and in parsing out the ways that Christian debates are embedded into the aesthetics of modernist literature and our reading experience.

Each of these heresies also implicitly asks us to rethink what we mean by the concept of the "real." James Joyce's three main characters in *Ulysses* (Stephen, and Leopold and Molly Bloom) will each spend at least part of the day pondering, in their own ways, the nature of reality, and wondering if and why we assume it is real. Although they may not say it in these words, and although only Stephen is thinking with a theological vocabulary, they are all struggling against the received ideas of their culture, the buried *orthodoxies* of their religious educations and upbringings, and their received cultural assumptions. The fourth main character—the city of Dublin itself—will also serve as a space of heretical reflection, offering an intersection of myth, religion, storytelling, and occultism that puts Homer, Shakespeare, Swift, Blake, the Bible, and a cast of Dublin pub drinkers, writers, priests, and workers into a very unorthodox conversation.

To what extent Stephen (or Joyce) was aware of the role of heresy in their acts of writing and thinking about literature is indeterminable. And while this is not a question I will spend my time with, it certainly continues to be an active debate among Joyce scholars.[2] Within the content of *Ulysses*, Stephen's theological knowledge of the heretics he mentions is not deeply explored. Although the Jesuit-educated Stephen is clearly well versed in theology and also deeply skeptical of the Church, when it comes to each of these heretics, as Gottfried claims "it is their historical identities as real persons that matters most to Stephen who focuses as much on the actors as on their ideas" (2008: 109). For Gottfried, Stephen's main point is to "emphasize the details of their lives, which otherwise would have been erased by authoritative power" (2008: 110). Clearly, power and erasure are important themes in thinking

---

2 For example, the focus of Christopher David Laws' recent (2017) dissertation, *James Joyce and His Early Church: The Art of Schism and Heresy*, is to highlight hitherto unidentified sources from which Joyce drew his understanding of Arius and Photius.

through issues of heresy and literature, but if we just look at our list of heresiarchs as anti-authoritarian figures whose actions threatened to erase them from history, we miss an opportunity of using *Ulysses* as a tool to think about issues of heresy more broadly. My purpose in this book is not just to better understand Joyce's work, but to use his texts to explore patterns of thinking and reading, especially in reimagining the relationship of literature to religion. Recent books, like Mathew Mutter's *Restless Secularism: Modernism and the Religious Inheritance*, find the "religious" in modernist literature as not opposed to secularism, but as part of it. For Mutter, modernist literature can serve to "disentangle the religious from the secular and see what each entails for language, aesthetics, emotion, ethics, and the body" (2017: 8). The idea of literature that emerges in this formulation can simultaneously stand for a desire for unity and structure and, at the same time demonstrate its impossibility, a paradox that stems from literature's relationship to religion, concepts of the divine, and definitions of the "book." Heresy allows us to more clearly see how the creation of art plays a contradictory, paradoxical, and subversive role within Joyce's works, and how these works, in turn, force us to rethink our current models of thinking about religious history.[3]

* * *

My core assumption—shared, I think, by Saint Augustine, Buck Mulligan, Stephen Dedalus, and James Joyce—is that theological claims are never just about God, but also include beliefs about self and world, mind and matter, and art and literature. Debates over defining orthodox doctrine are not only about theology, but also about the relationship between language and identity, civic power and the individual, and creative thinking and intellectual traditions. Studying heresy is a way both to break away from modes of thinking cemented as "normal" by Christian orthodoxy and to acknowledge how Western metaphysical and critical thought are linked to patriarchal Christian theology. Heresy then—even strictly Christian heresy—can be political, social, philosophical, and ethical, as well as theological. But, for the sake of this book, heresy will primarily be framed as theological debates over how to read and write. This book's first heretical figures are the Gnostics, who were heretical in large part because of their deconstructive reading of the Book of Genesis and the Hebrew Bible. This book's final heretical

---

3   Joyce, of course, was not the only modernist writer to see the potential of using the history of Judeo-Christian heresy as a way to comment on more contemporary aesthetic and philosophical concerns. Other examples would be Thomas Mann's *Doctor Faustus*, George Bernard Shaw's *Saint Joan*, Arnold Schoenberg's opera and libretto *Moses und Aron*, and T.S. Eliot's *Murder in the Cathedral*.

figure, Joseph Smith, was heretical because he added to these same texts. Joyce's *Ulysses* and *Finnegans Wake* are only recent examples of literature thought and written through books of scripture and theology.

Religious heresy may be repressed, erased, or disguised, but the ideas and debates never disappear, and are instead folded into the tensions and instability of orthodox practices and doctrines. Temporarily domesticated, hidden, and veiled, heretical ideas are embedded within church doctrine and energize the art and literature that develop around its margins. Influential theorists of comparative religion, such as Mircea Eliade, often stressed the role of religion in overcoming chaos and establishing order. In this formulation, myth and ritual are defined by retellings and reenactments that, through repetition, maintain order over chaos. But other religion scholars—from J.Z. Smith to Tyler Roberts—claim that ultimately myths never overcome chaos, and that chaos persists through religious figures such as tricksters, shamans, and prophets (Roberts 2013: 26). As late-twentieth-century theory taught us, ordering always has a remainder; heresy, hidden in the margins, tucked into the hesitations and ambiguities of orthodox doctrine, and speaking to us from both the distant and the recent past, is another way to get at these remainders and to question how we continue to organize knowledge. Readers, authors, and literary critics may or may not be able to discuss how the writing of the Nicaean creed was a reaction to Arius, they may not know the difference between Chalcedonian and non-Chalcedonian Christianity, they may not know why Mormons must be re-baptized if they convert to Catholicism, but the tensions that accompany each of these religious issues come out of familiar passages in the Bible or out of political events in late-antiquity or the Middle Ages that have been influential to the development of Western art and thought. In other words, even if the arguments over heresy and orthodoxy are not well known, they nonetheless inform works and interpretations into the present day.

In early Christianities, we repeatedly encounter the questions of how to read and interpret the Hebrew Scriptures. For many within Gnostic traditions, the Hebrew Scriptures may have been inspired not by the one true God, nor by the devil, but by some *other* divine being. For our purposes, what is most interesting is how this shows the need for intermediaries between God and the world and between sacred text and the written commentary—in other words, literally a kind of guided reading. This idea of an intermediary finds a voice in modernist literature and reading practices that give us models of how to break apart the imagined unity of a text and return it to the collage of competing styles, genres, and voices from which it is made. Literature like *Ulysses* or *Finnegans Wake*, and the (often collaborative) acts of reading these difficult texts, can provide non-scriptural ways of imagining beyond traditional discourse and beyond standard definitions of belief, faith, and worship.

Although these tenuous borders of faith and belief are underexplored in literary criticism, radical and postmodern theological and philosophical thinkers have often developed these themes using literary works such as Dostoyevsky's novels of dialogic debate, Kafka's claustrophobic short stories, Stevens's aphoristic poems of searching agnosticism, and Beckett's dramas of existentialist drifters. I will talk more about the idea of "radical theology" in upcoming chapters, and how these radical theologians find these authors as paths that can use be used to move away from reductive definitions of concepts such as God, faith, and scripture, and create new approaches to meaning-making. This kind of theology and this model of "God" (a god who is often absent, non-existent, dead, or beyond being) represent a response to and a reversal of the classical ontotheological understanding of total presence, and unquestioned origins and meanings. Throughout this book, I will build on and use modern heterodox philosophers or theologians such as Thomas J.J. Altizer, Mark C. Taylor, Amy Hollywood, Thomas Carlson, and Slavoj Žižek who often use modern literature to build their deconstructive readings of scripture. But I am equally interested in how readers of modernist literature can similarly look to heretical ideas and figures as models of reading and thinking about texts.

These theories and theologies of absence may seem far from traditional Christian doctrines, but they can be found in the central question of early Christianity—the question that spawned much of what would later be labeled heretical thought: How does the earthly (Jesus) become divine (Christ)? This question can be translated into literary terms: How does the text gain meaning? Or, how does an idea become a book? These questions open a space between being and not being, imagination and reality that is, at its core, theological. For example, the fourth-century creedal decisions that embrace the full divinity *and* humanity of Jesus as well as the thirteenth-century proclamation about the real presence of the Host *also* affirm something about reality; they suggest that the real is embodied in time and space, and therefore that the world and its history are real rather than illusory or imagined, as we might find in other religious or artistic traditions. This position is not an obvious conclusion, nor is it one that is held across all culture or even all of Christianity, but it is one that is important to

Western literature as well as theology. The history of Church doctrine, however, is not so definitive as history often suggests, and heretical counter-narratives to these positions suggest that these assumptions may be unstable, temporary, or arbitrary.

From God to Human to Book

Early Christians gathered and recorded their new writings not on scrolls, like the Hebrew Scriptures or other ancient writings, but in a codex, resembling a modern book. The early Christian insistence that the new sacred writings were foretold in the Old made it significant that readers and writers could now flip easily between one text and another. One could read the Christian Gospel and then a Hebrew prophesy. Or prophesy and then Gospel. Or prophesy then Gospel and then a theologian who explains the connection. Readers could move easily back and forth from small book to small book and from page to page. This changed the whole concept of what it was to read or interpret a text.

Almost every Christian theological argument—heretical, orthodox, or other—claims to base its position on some kind of reading or interpretation of a book (the Bible) and a body (Jesus). From the New Testament to *Finnegans Wake*—as well as hundreds of texts from the centuries in between—the borders between such concepts as book, text, body, and divinity are conflated and blurred in ways that define much of Western art, literature, and religion. The Bible itself is not at all clear on the relationship between Christ's human and divine nature. In fact, the Bible is not clear about whether Jesus is divine at all, much less whether he is somehow equal to or the same as God the Father. Jesus says "I and the Father are one" (John 10:29-30), and "Anyone who has seen me has seen the Father" (John 14:8-9). On the other hand, in the same Gospel he also says, "The Father is greater than I" (John 14:28). To read the Christian scriptures is to discover a main character who suffers, weeps, bleeds, gets angry, questions his fate and God's plan, and who *dies*. What does that *mean*? Does God weep? Does God die? Later Christians asked more cosmic questions: Was there a reason God had to create Jesus? Was something lacking before? Or was somehow Christ—or the Word—there from the beginning? For most (but not all) Christians throughout history, Jesus is equally God and Man. And while Christianity, and the people who practice it, has changed in dramatic ways, what has not changed is the instability of this formulation—an instability that has influenced how we think about subjects from politics to literature to law and from music to computers. This basic belief in Jesus Christ as some sort of God/Human requires combining two essentially different categories of being—one spirit and unimaginable and the other material and familiar. Many (perhaps most) modern Christians could not explain this contradiction in a way that would not be considered a grave heresy by the early church theologians.

In the early centuries of Christianity, as the preferred technical term for the divine in Christ came to be "Logos" (or Word) instead of "Spirit," the connection between Christ and the act of God speaking in Genesis was strengthened. This connection was very literally an act of literary interpretation, as these profoundly important connections were established between words existing in different languages, books, and cultures. The Gospel of John's "in the beginning was the word" was taken to refer unambiguously to Christ, yet never loses its association with language, a language that will always already be written as well as spoken. If God, in the book of Genesis, begins everything by speaking, then, for Christians, Christ is also present and literally *is* that first great speech act that begins time and creation, and that will become *real* in the presence of a book. "In the beginning was the word" is perhaps simultaneously the most orthodox and the most radical statement in the Christian scriptures: John's "Word" is actually the Greek *logos*, which he borrows from a tradition older than Jesus. Logos means more than simply "word," and it is a good place for us to begin exploring the long-complicated relationship between Christianity, the Bible, and modernist literary traditions. Logos means not a single particle of speech, but "the whole act of speech, or the thought behind the speech ... its meanings spill outwards into conversation, narrative, musing, meaning, reason, report, rumour" (MacCulloch 2011: 19)—a definition that might also define the modernist collage that is *Finnegans Wake*. Then John tells us that the "Word was made flesh, and dwelt among us" (John 1:14) and that his name was Jesus Christ, a name that is already a tangle of opposing Aramaic, Greek, and Hebrew languages and thought, or, as we read in *Ulysses*: "Jewgreek is greekjew. Extremes meet." (*U* 15.2097–8).

Despite generations of theological exegesis, perhaps no thinker has more successfully deconstructed this phrase than Joyce, when, in *Finnegans Wake*, he writes "in the buginning is the woid" (*FW* 378.29). The phrase combines "word" and "void" into "woid," and thereby suggests both the cyclical passage of history and creation from Genesis to Gospel and back again, as well as a reading of absence at the heart of language and the Christian narrative. Joyce's version gives us creation from a *void* where there should be a *word*; it linguistically presents doubt at the very origin of the Christian myth. As Christine van Boheemen-Saaf writes, "in Joyce, origin is a void of absence, and the Word is always already voided" (1999: 77). Like any good pun or metaphor, the meaning here is unstable, oscillating between one meaning and the other, and finally creating something new, a Word which literally is also an absence, or, a loss that is also God.

Heresy in Theory

In the same years that Joyce was writing *Stephen Hero*, an early abandoned version of what would later become *A Portrait of the Artist*, the Englishman G.K. Chesterton—most popularly known today as the author of the Father Brown mysteries—published a book of essays entitled *Heretics* (1905), to be followed by *Orthodoxy* (1908). Both books were written when Chesterton was an Anglican, although his definition of his own "orthodoxy" moved him to convert to Catholicism in 1922, the same year *Ulysses* was published. While Chesterton's writings are arguments for a traditional orthodoxy and against what he saw as an increasingly secular modernism, he was also known for his use of deception and paradox; his novel, *The Man Who Was Thursday* (also published in 1908), is an example of a theological novel that is open to a heretical reading.

The basic plot depicts a secret anti-anarchist police force that recruits a poet to infiltrate an anarchist organization. Ultimately, the novel reveals that *all* of the leaders of the organization are undercover and that their mysterious leader ("Sunday") is also the head of the secret police department and a force for good and order (perhaps God himself) who ends the novel by claiming to suffer more than all mortals, as he quotes Jesus: "can ye drink of the cup that I drink of?" (Mark 10:38–9). While *The Man Who Was Thursday* is often read for its Christian allegory and as a defense of orthodoxy and a critique of nihilism, for the philosopher Slavoj Žižek, it suggests just the opposite. While Žižek acknowledges Chesterton's aim in this novel as a characteristic move to show that "order is the greatest miracle and orthodoxy the greatest of all rebellions," he finds instead an unintended dramatization of a divinity that deeply doubts even himself, in other words, a model of a Christian atheist or a radical theologian (2009: 43). Žižek's reading of Chesterton is an example of the kind of postmodern, negative, or radical theology that, broadly interpreted, often shapes my interpretations of Joyce and heresy. It is significant that Žižek's subversive theological statement returns to the early-Christian debates over just what happened on the cross, a scene I will also return to in almost every chapter. For Žižek, the ultimate lesson to be learned from the divine incarnation and subsequent death of Christ is that "the finite existence of mortal humans is the only site of the Spirit, the site where Spirit achieves its actuality" (2009: 60). In other words, it is only in the finitude of life and the absoluteness of death that we find the sacred. Žižek finds no transcendence or resurrection in the crucifixion, but instead "Christ's death on the Cross just means that we should immediately ditch the notion of God as a transcendent caretaker who guarantees the happy outcome of our acts, the guarantee of historical teleology" (2009: 60) or, in other words, Zizek's interpretation suggests we are on our own now, the fullness of life is up to us.

The crucifixion has been revisited and revised by religious thinkers from the Gnostics to Joseph Smith and also in modern works of fiction such as Nikos Kazantzakis' 1955 novel *The Last Temptation of Christ*. In Kazantzakis' novel, Jesus cries out "*Eli, Eli,*" then passes out on the cross and has a vision or dream of a normal life with a wife, children, and grandchildren. In the dream, his aged disciples visit him late in his life; Paul claims he can create Christianity with just history regardless of what Jesus actually does, while Mathew laments that all of his writings will be forgotten. Judas accuses Jesus of betraying them all and labels him a coward. Jesus then awakes, calls out "*lama sabachthani,*" adds "It is accomplished," and dies as the novel's final words proclaim this moment as the true beginning of everything.[4] This scene and the book emphasizes the role of writing and story and leans on Jesus's human side in a way that might be labeled heretical. But the book was written from a Greek Orthodox perspective, and is an almost orthodox reading of the human side of Christ that was capable of being tempted and of suffering. A more obviously blasphemous example is found in Philip José Farmer's *Jesus on Mars* (1979) in which people are resurrected through technology and Jesus returns on a spaceship, or in James Morrow's *Towing Jehovah* (1994) in which a two-mile-long dead body of God is found floating off the coast of Africa and is towed to the Artic where the body will be better preserved by the cold. Whatever the intentions of these novelists—Kazantzakis was devoutly Greek Orthodox, Farmer an eccentric Joyce-reading agnostic, and Morrow an outspoken atheist—the themes would be familiar to a second-century debate between the competing Christianities of

---

[4] The Stephen of *Stephen Hero* listens to a Good Friday sermon and, half asleep, also thinks on these final words of Jesus, but hears competing translations: "It is ended. It is accomplished… consummated…achieved… finished… concluded… " (*SH* 120).

the proto-orthodox Irenaeus and the Gnostic Valentinus. Both these second-century theologians and the modern novelists are asking whether God can have a material body, and just what is at stake in that question. If God can be material, then it follows that the matter has to come from somewhere, and that it is likely the same matter that makes up our bodies. In that case, how are we defining our God? If, on the other hand, God cannot be material, it raises question as to reality and being. Traditions tell us to look for these answers in our scriptures, but that suggests many of the same questions of difference and being as between divinity and human. How is a book of holy scripture different than other books? Is the material that makes up a divine being the same material that makes up a sacred book? What I will be demonstrating throughout *this* book is that historical heresies and their debates over text and authority, body and mind, reality and imagination, still resonate today, both inside and outside of any religious or theological context and through our modern art, literature, and philosophy.

Žižek, for example, builds his reading of Christianity upon a heretical interpretation that can only be fully understood within Christological debates. Žižek's heresy is that "the Son was not present in the God prior to Incarnation, sitting up there at his side. Incarnation is the birth of Christ, and after his death, there is neither Father nor Son, but 'only' the Holy Spirit" (2009: 33). For Žižek, the crucifixion represents a unique moment where "God does not believe in himself," and "what dies on the cross is ... God himself, the very transcendent God of beyond" (2009: 60). A similar sentiment of divine self-doubt is expressed in Joyce's *Portrait*, when Stephen is asked if he had even considered that maybe Jesus was not what he pretended to be. Stephen answers that "The first person to whom that idea occurred ... was Jesus himself" (*P* 263). Both Joyce and Žižek are pointing to a scripture that depicts a God who doubts, a God who knows weakness.

This heresy finds us without a fully present and Christian God or, to put it in the language of literary theory, without Jacques Derrida's "transcendental signifier" of stable linguistic meaning. Instead of a God-like transcendent meaning, Derrida uses concepts such as "trace," a word that suggests meanings that fade, decay and are hidden instead of enacting linguistic mastery. Gayatri Spivak defines Derrida's trace as the "mark of the absence of a presence ... of the lack of the origin" (1976: xvii), or, in other words, everything is in the process of being erased. For Derrida, "there is no such thing as an eternal unerasable presence. An unerasable trace is not a trace, it is a full presence, an immobile and uncorruptible substance, a Son of God" (Derrida 1978: 339). But the Son of God as negotiated by early Christian heretics like Sabellius and Arius is already a Son and God with elements of absence and with murky origins, more of a trace in the Derridean sense than a full presence. From the point of view of Christian orthodoxy, this may seem radical, contradictory, or atheistic, but these views are not unique or even particularly modern if viewed from the perspective of the study of early heresy. Žižek's "Son who was not present" prior to his birth echoes the fourth-century heretic Arius and his idea of a created Christ. Žižek's death of God on the cross also can be found in literary versions of the apocryphal death of Arius—shamefully bleeding to death in a public latrine—that may also symbolize the end of Arius' concept of Jesus Christ. In Žižek, as in much modern popular religion, we find a Christianity more Arian than orthodox. Arius' Jesus—more human than god—is on the one hand always dying, and on the other, will never die, but instead resurfaces again and again throughout a Christian history that desires immanence as much as transcendence, flesh as much as mystery, and revels in the story of a man who became a god.

The central questions of early Christianity—questions that spawned what would be labeled heretical thought—are essentially still with us, even if we express them outside of any confessional context. Yet these very concepts of spirit and body as argued within early Christianity demonstrate the impossibility of unification as much as they do a desire for it. When Richard Ellmann claims that the message of *Ulysses* is "that we are all members of the one body, and the one spirit" (1972: 176), it is a clear statement of modernist orthodoxy. Ellmann predicted that future critics of *Ulysses* would "pull the book together rather than apart" (1975: 1118), and although we can argue the level to which he was wrong or right, the tension between unity and fragmentation is still significant. Within the world of Joyce scholarship, Ellmann can be seen as standing for a type of orthodoxy rooted in the idea of unified books and a unified biographical sense of the author as singular person. More recently, less orthodox Joyce scholars have embraced ideas of fragmentation and see both texts and author, not as stable material objects or ideas, but as construction, as plural, as still in process, and as an unstable and constantly emerging set of meanings that take place between images and words, and across times, texts, and readers.

Telling "Another Story:" *A Portrait of the Artist as a Young Man*

I want to begin with a moment of the making and unmaking of religion that can be found in Joyce's first published novel, the semi autobiographical *A Portrait of the Artist as a Young Man*. The novel is broken into five chapters—taking the protagonist from childhood to young adulthood—each of which can be seen as a developing writer's struggle to come to terms with his changing ideas of God, religion, art, and language. In the famous first section, the young Stephen Dedalus enters the confusing world of language, as words heard, spoken, imagined, and written turn around in his head and off his tongue. In the process, he explores the gap between signifier and signified, asking and searching for something material to give weight or meaning to the mere sounds of words. As we will see in the next chapter and throughout this book, the act of defining words, or theorizing the relationship between the verbal and visual sign and object, is central to the interwoven connections between heresy and literature. The young Stephen ponders the words "belt," "suck," and "kiss" and notices the ambiguity and multiplicity of meaning, trying them out and playing with them in his head: "That was a belt round his pocket. And belt was also to give a fellow a belt" (*P* 5). Joyce develops each of these words into themes by exploring their different meanings throughout the novel, often in ways that weave religion into his psychological "portrait" and that play a role in influencing Stephen's development as a writer. Stephen will experience "kiss" as a kiss from his mother, a kiss from a prostitute, and as the feel of the Host on his tongue, all experiences that are both physical and spiritual. A few pages later, Stephen thinks about the word "God:"

> God was God's name just as his name was Stephen. *Dieu* was the French for God and that was God's name too; and when anyone prayed to God and said *Dieu* then God knew at once that it was a French person that was praying. But though there were different names for God in all the different languages in the world and God understood what all the people who prayed said in their different languages still God remained always the same God and *God's real name was God*.
>
> (*P* 13, my emphasis)

When Stephen says "*Dieu* was the French for God and was God's name too," he opens the possibility for an interpretation of God the pun-conscious, multilingual Joyce would have appreciated. As philosophers of religion Emmanuel Levinas and Hent de Vries point out, the very pronunciation of God's name in French captures God's contradictory nature: it is a movement toward God—*à dieu*—and, at the same moment, an *adieu*, a farewell to and taking leave of the very God it seemed to address (de Vries 1999: 70). This pun on the space between *à dieu* and *adieu* simultaneously suggests the name of God, a desire for God, a dismissal of God, and also a non-God in much the same way that we see a devotional stained-glass window in which the Father and Son have been meticulously removed by Protestant Reformers—we see the divine shapes in their absent image—a removal, a fear, and a desire for God contained in the same visual gesture.

Young Stephen desires to bridge the gap between word and meaning and between text and reality. He believes that nothing means anything *real* except for God who, despite different names, has a "real name." God alone can assure true linguistic *presence*; for Stephen, he must be the origin or center of all meaning: a transcendental signifier. And yet, as the literary language of the rest of Joyce's career shows, divine language is always treacherously unstable and plural. Stephen's search for a single definition is also a search for a specific kind of God who stabilizes meaning rather than challenges it, which is perhaps, as all Joyce's books demonstrate, a futile quest. As Christine van Boheeman-Saaf writes, "the linguistic signifier 'God' anchors the hierarchy of difference and identity; it lends stability to Stephen's own identity and name. Only provisionally, however … " (1999: 48). Like the early Gnostics, who resisted any single or reductive definition of "God," and instead acknowledged the pluralities and inconsistencies of scripture and story, Stephen and the novel are tentatively expressing a distrust of inherited language and religious traditions, a distrust that will increase throughout the novel and into *Ulysses* and *Finnegans Wake*.

Although the first prayer that we see Stephen offer is "addressed neither to God nor saint" (*P* 92), later, after attending a terrifying religious retreat focusing on damnation and the end times, he temporarily turns his guilty conscious over to God: "It was true. God was almighty" (*P* 134). Stephen prays desperately for forgiveness, goes hungrily to offer his confession, and plans a pious life. He even considers becoming a Jesuit priest, but, in a shift most dramatically shown in the famous "epiphany" or "secular baptism" scene where he watches the "bird girl" wade in the water, he feels the call to the worldly pursuit of art, to instead, "recreate life out of life!" (*P* 186). He appears in this scene to separate the material from the spiritual, to embrace the "earth that had borne him" and to see the heavens as only a "vast indifferent dome" (*P* 187). But while this scene is often read as art replacing religion, it also demonstrates the opposite. If this Stephen is the Stephen of *Ulysses*, then he is never able to completely let go of religion and belief, and they will continue to occupy his mind and structure his writing. In this way, he is a model for modernism itself, which—despite the claims of many critics—was also unable or unwilling to replace religion with art. Modernism was not as Suzanne Hobson writes, "so fastidious about avoiding religious languages as has sometimes been claimed" (2011: 9). Instead, the church—in all of its orthodoxies and heresies—always finds a way into the language of art. But while Stephen ultimately rejects the church's God, defiantly claiming that he will not poison himself by paying "false homage to a symbol behind which are massed twenty centuries of authority and veneration" (*P* 265), he still replaces him with an artistic, creator god. Absent and present, this is the god of the modernist artist. Like many modernist thinkers, Joyce and Stephen are tempted to replace one center with another, without disturbing the base of the scaffolding. No longer does it/he have a "real name," but a divine creative force still looms over artistic creation and controls through linguistic presence.

While this process gets more complicated in *Ulysses* and *Finnegans Wake*, it is in this literary tension between the tearing down and re-creation of the god-idea where we find echoes of heretical arguments that go back many centuries. As we just saw, the event of the crucifixion both destroys and creates, and the biggest gap in biblical writings is the resurrection itself, which remains forever undescribed. The New Testament is indeed, as Diarmaid MacCulloch writes, a "literature with a blank at its centre" (2011: 94), but despite, or because of, this blank, this gap receives the most intense focus in art, theology, and worship. How would Christianity and Western Literature have developed if a single detailed description of the resurrection had come down as sacred and canonical? Heresy, as we will see over and over again, is often about how we read, write, and think about spoken and written language and the incomprehensible gaps in between. In *Portrait*, Stephen's quest for a controlled stable text is also the reader's, and both are theological quests conducted through desire for a determinate god and stable linguistic meaning, a battle we will also see in the competing god ideas of early Christianity. This stable god of presence and unity can also be found in the older Stephen's Aquinas-influenced aesthetic theories, where he proclaims that one must "apprehend the [aesthetic image] as one thing. You see it as one whole" (*P* 230), a theory that Joyce's later books, as we shall see, take pleasure in dismantling. In this proclamation of unity, Stephen, like his younger self, seeks a force to check the endless chain of deferred meaning and substitute representation. This force, this god without the name of God, manifests its monotheistic presence as a singleness of vision and a faith in a coherent and unified text, an image that orthodox Christians have insisted upon since the second century in debates with the heretical Gnostics and their more plural God that was harder to contain.

The second chapter of *Portrait* focuses on Stephen growing up surrounded by the decay and decline of his family's situation. At one point, while at a school play, Stephen has a "sudden memory" of being accused of committing a heresy in an essay written for school. The accusing teacher, Mr. Tate, points to the offending passage:

> —Here. It's about the Creator and the Soul. Rrm … rrm … rrm … Ah! *without a possibility of ever approaching nearer*. That's heresy.
> Stephen murmured:
> —I meant *without a possibility of ever reaching …*
> —O … Ah! *ever reaching*. That's another story.
>
> (*P* 83–84)

Most Joyce scholars read this scene by beginning with Don Gifford's explanation that the "orthodox position is that each soul is granted sufficient grace to approach that communion. Stephen's heresy resides in the implication that the soul has not been granted sufficient grace" (2008: 167). Most critics also seem to feel that Stephen corrects his heresy in his revised wording, but that it also has a lasting impact on how he understands himself as a writer. This impact, however, is an uneasy and instable one that persists throughout the novel and into *Ulysses*. As Sheldon Brivic writes, "the attack, like all threats, generates unanswered questions and forces Stephen to rearrange the figuration of his identity" (2008: 47). This "identity" is, as we have seen, is also associated with words and their heretical and sacred potential. For Vincent Cheng, Stephen here has a "growing sense of himself as a revolutionary of the word" (1995: 72). The multifaceted connection to in this scene plays out through the complex juxtaposition of Stephen's memory of "heresy" and his present experience of performing in a Whitsuntide play, and especially in how it is superimposed onto ideas of writing, revision, and narrative. Heresy, as we will continue to see, is woven into ideas of how we tell the story, how we remember it, and how we learn to re-tell it differently. What Stephen is being taught here is, as Steven Morrison writes, that "it is not just another story, it is the *right story*" (2000: 67, my emphasis). Since every scene in the novel can be read as a portrait of the *artist*, each detail is necessarily part of the development of a literary mind, and in this scene Stephen is getting a strong message of literary orthodoxy which he will later rebel against.

As much as *Portrait* is about questioning the orthodox meanings of religion that Stephen grapples with, this is the only scene in the novel where the word "heresy" appears. Gottfried sees this scene as prefiguring the young Stephen's (and Joyce's) embrace of literature—and of seeing literature as a form of religious heresy: "It is heresy to which this episode and the two memories it evokes return … and in each case, heresy is intimately connect to the power of literature" (2008: 11). Gottfried points to how this scene indicates Joyce's sense that form and style in literature itself create "freedom" and "possibility." For him, the "repetitions, variations, and wordplays" can serve as a form of heresy in the way that "religion can be opened up and turned" and that the repetition of synonyms for schism in *Portrait*—"ripping," "split," "cleft," "torn"—offers this freedom and possibility (2008: 13–14). In other words, "Schism is the unstated, primary concern of the heresy scenes, where religious choice resides in literary gesture. And for Joyce, schism is the very means by which art is made" (Gottfried 2008: 14). If "religious choice resides in literary gesture" and "schism is the very means by which art is made," then there is a powerful link between religious heresy and literary creation through which both influence the other. Although this scene—like most of the novel—is presented without authorial comment, the implied questions are clear: Is there a right way to tell a story and who makes that determination? What is the role of literature and language in bridging the gap between Creator and Soul (or author and text)? What do these questions do in the mind of a writer? Stephen's silent pondering of the role of heresy in the education of the modern writer gives us an implicit link in the history of Christian heresy with reading Joyce. Morrison helps us make this connection by pointing to Joyce's style of writing in this scene:

> What makes this passage unusual is that there is no change of voice on the part of the narrator, nor even a change of tense… By means of this retention of a common narrating instance, the subject of heresy is tied directly to the larger section of the chapter which surrounds it.
>
> (2000: 66)

In other words, the themes, voice, and origin of the novel itself contain elements of heresy along with the modernist *bildungsroman*. As the rest of novel continues to follow Stephen struggling to make sense of language and religion, the focus on gods, fathers, authors, and authority leaves the reader grasping for a textual origin that is constantly asserted and negated, a dialectical process that will be expanded and complicated in *Ulysses* through a more modernist picture of the author figure.

It is common in Joyce criticism to comment on his conflation of God and author, or to say, as Cheng writes, that for Joyce, "artist and god were equivalent" (2015: 140). One of the most cited examples from *Portrait* is Stephen's "God of creation" speech: "The artist, like the God of the creation, remains within or behind or beyond or above his handiwork, invisible, refined out of existence, indifferent, paring his fingernails" (*P* 233). As often quoted as it is, this passage more or less copies Gustave Flaubert's also well-known statement that "the artist in his work must be like God in creation, invisible and all-powerful; you can sense him everywhere but you cannot see him" (1997: 247–8). The question here is whether it is Joyce or Stephen who is doing the plagiarizing, which also again points us to issues of author and authority, God and creator, and the gaps between matter and spirit, human and divine. Joyce's framing of author and God is particularly challenging to classical ideas of creation when understood through Joyce's writing style of borrowing, translating, and copying and pasting.

Western literature and theology can be interpreted through the idea that God's word (by definition perfect) must somehow be transmitted and translated into human words (by definition imperfect). Art and theology, then, both grapple with how to negotiate this gap and what kind of artistic or religious language can best make this translation. How do we construct imperfect metaphors of perfection? Jesus Christ's ontological status as a God/man is one solution to this problem; the elevation and the consuming of the Host in the Mass is another; gazing at devotional iconic images is yet another—in each case they present a paradoxical relationship of divine/human and word/image, and are surrounded by debates of heresy and orthodoxy. One person's transcendence is another's blasphemy; the effectiveness of theological concepts perhaps lies partly in this instability.

One of the most well-known and most unstable concepts in Christian history is the Eucharist, which, depending on your point of view can stand for absolute presence, total absence, empty ritual, or superstitious magic. Instead of creating God from the Host, Stephen will focus on "transmuting the daily bread of experience into the radiant body of everliving life" (*P* 240). Garry Leonard points to the importance of Joyce's word "everliving" instead of "everlasting," writing that the "soul of the artist may not be immortal, but the daily bread of experience it manages to transmute into everliving life will live on" (2015: 12). While Stephen, and probably Joyce and Leonard, is being romantically idealistic about the role of art, this interplay of language and theology as a way of challenging the orthodox borders of religion is an entry point into the subjects I will be exploring in this book. All of these ideas as they are presented in *Portrait*—the overlapping of human and divine creation, the language of heresy as a way to reshape religious ecstasy, and the use of religious language to challenge literary ideas—will be further developed in *Ulysses* and *Finnegans Wake*.

Heresy may be in the background throughout most of *Portrait*, but in *Ulysses* and *Finnegans Wake*, heresy enters literary and artistic texts in more direct ways. These works often directly refer to a heretic or a heresy, or they can directly or indirectly address a theological or doctrinal issue that has traditionally occupied a border between the orthodox and the heretical. Again, it is important to locate the heretical in the form as well as the content. While the idea of heresy is commonly acknowledged as being central to the theme of Stephen's search for a father figure in *Ulysses*, it is not only the presence of Stephen's heretical thoughts, but the structure and style of *Ulysses* itself that explore questions of origin, author, and fatherhood. By shifting styles and parodying and borrowing multiple literary sources, *Ulysses*—like *Finnegans Wake* after it—deconstructs the idea of language or literature as stemming from a single source. Like the heretical "created" Christ of Arius, like Stephen himself, like the idealized author or book, the original source of creation and meaning is always on the other side of true presence. When Stephen remarks that the church is founded upon the mystery of fatherhood—"upon incertitude, upon unlikelihood" (*U* 9.842)—it can be taken as expressing doubt in every aspect of artistic creation and meaning. Do artists create something from nothing, or do they merely rearrange material into a new ordered text? These ideas and questions subvert the orthodox/romantic notion of a single divine/genius creator and the unified scripture/text.

Continuity and Disruption

To begin thinking about how ancient heretical or theological thought can be a tool to read Joyce and modernist literature, we can start with the figure of Marcion—the "hereticalist Marcon" in *Finnegans Wake* (*FW* 192.1)—a second-century Roman and early heretic who questioned the possibility that a good, all-knowing, and all-powerful God could be in charge of history. Marcion could not accept that such a figure could have permitted the deception and fall of man. His solution was that there must be two Gods, one good and one evil, one the Creator of the imperfect world, and one the Father of Jesus Christ. In order to separate Christ from the imperfect human, Marcion attributes the creation of Christ to the one True God. Marcion's Christ is not of a woman, not of a human body, and only appeared to have a body of flesh and blood. Humans, alternatively, come from the lesser Creator God and are therefore flawed and corrupt.

What is significant for my project is that Marcion's positions represent an alternative theory of reading, history, authorship, and language. For Marcion and many of the like-minded Gnostics who followed him, a literal reading of the Hebrew scriptures led to the conclusion that its main character must be inferior to the True God. The Hebrew God was weak and flawed: he changes his mind, he seems unable to find Adam in the Garden, and he makes immoral choices.

For the anti-Gnostic Tertullian, on the other hand, these passages of God's indecisiveness or emotions were to be read figuratively and not literally. But reading practices as a way of dividing orthodox from heterodox is not reliable or consistent; this orthodox insistence on "figurative" reading was only occasional, as other early orthodox writers often argued that it was the Gnostics who were reading too figuratively and needed to read passages literally.

New historical appreciations of second-century Christianity now see it as a "time rich in discontinuities, when straightforward development is difficult to trace or to predict, and as a time of experimentation, when ideas, structures, and patterns of behaviour are being explored" (Lieu 2015: 1). It was also a time of learning to write, read, and edit in new ways. Theologians and church leaders were forced to return time and again to passages of the Hebrew scriptures or the new (not yet canonical) Christian writings; they had to argue over proper ways of reading, whether to privilege author intent; whether to read symbolically, allegorically, or literally; how much to use words and concepts from other languages and cultures. Marcion was both a writer and an editor, composing a now-lost commentary on the Bible, in which he made his argument that the God of the Hebrew Bible was not the Father of Jesus, and an edited collection where he established a canon of Christian scripture far in advance of the established New Testament. In his Scriptures, Marcion—like Luther and Thomas Jefferson centuries later—removed passages that went against his theological positions; in Tertullian's words, he interpreted the scriptures "with a pen knife" (Ehrman 2003: 108). Marcion continually stressed discontinuity: between the Hebrew Bible and the new Christian scriptures, between creation and salvation, between law and gospel, between Creator and Father, and between humans and Christ. The Christian interpretive practice of typology—a strategy of continuity that reads the Old Testament through the New—was rejected by Marcion, who denied the Hebrew prophecies could refer to Jesus, instead insisting on their literal meaning. The influential nineteenth-century theologian Adolf Harnack, who famously labeled Marcion the "first reformer," described Marcion as reading the book from left to right instead of from right to left. In other words, by reading linearly from past to present he "incorrectly" removes Christ and the Christian God from his reading of the Hebrew Bible. As we see in Marcion—and as we will see in the early chapters of this book—early Christian heresies can always be seen as coming out of and reflecting different styles of reading and writing, including practices of archiving and organizing history.

I will spend the rest of this book thinking about the role of reading and how Joyce's works and these early heretics and heretical debates can illuminate each other. One point that I will often return to is that experiments in writing—whether texts of history, theology, or fiction—continually comment on and change how we read other texts. Marcion was changed forever by Luther and then by the nineteenth-century theologian Harnock and is changed again through the new ideas and styles of modernist fiction. When, in *Finnegans Wake*, Joyce refers to that "hereticalist Marcon" with his "two scissymaidies" (*FW* 192.1–2), it seems to be a reference to Marcion sinning with young women (although we can also read "scissymaidies" as schismatics). But, as John Gordon points out, "Marcon" also echoes Marconi, father of wireless telegraphy, or another form of experimental writing, in this case where the text's meaning and presence are sonic as well as visual.

Joyce's *Finnegans Wake*—his final and most difficult novel—is written in a largely idiosyncratic language filled with multi-lingual puns, invented portmanteau words, literary allusions, dream associations, lists, and what seems an almost total abandonment of narrative conventions. The novel is also, as much as it can be said to be "about" anything, about myths and stories of death and resurrection. The *Wake* can serve as a literary example that joins together many of the themes of literature and theology that figured in the twentieth-century philosophical writings of thinkers like Thomas Altizer, Mark C. Taylor, Hent de Vries, and Richard Kearney, who—building on thinkers like Jacques Derrida, Martin Heidegger, and Jean Baudrillard—combined literature and continental philosophy with what is often called "radical theology." Altizer and Taylor point to a modernist "death of God" as a crisis that changed our sense of history, identity, and writing. This crisis of doubt and thought, and modernity and art, provides an entry point in rethinking our view of the relationship between James Joyce and Christian heresy. Each of these three elements—writing, identity, and history—is intertwined with creating and perceiving art, and our understanding of time, plot, narrative, and the purpose of art. These doubts characterize much twentieth-century thought, not only in philosophy, but also in literature, art, and music. Philosophers and literary theorists after the "death" of God must recognize that—whatever we claim about God's reality or existence—we, as a culture and as meaning-making individuals, must still grapple with the possible absence of and the unfulfilled desire for God. Modern literature and modern literary criticism, in their very essence, dramatize the tensions surrounding issues of origin, autonomy, transcendence, presence, and authority that define the borders of orthodox religion.

The *Wake*, like *Ulysses*, like *Portrait*, is full of religious allusions and references to scripture, and it underscores Joyce's understanding that a book like the Bible does not have a single universal meaning, but is instead subject to moods, polyphony, and cycles that are inseparable from our religious and literary imaginings. The radically displaced reader of the *Wake* must rethink the relationship of words to ideas and also experience an entirely remixed chronology and sense of time and history where the past and present influence each other in both directions. In the *Wake*, the early histories of the central character HCE, for example, are layered across time, within sacred and classical texts, street gossip, and electronic media, with other voices representing the people's history or the "four old men" (the four Evangelists) representing the academic and the orthodox. When writing ecclesiastical history, Joyce seems to suggest, there is always "another story."

2

Five Moments of Schism: A Selective History of Heresy

"A horde of heresies fleeing"

(*U* 1.656)

Part I: Reading and Writing Heresy

Before continuing our reading of Joyce and heresy, it is worth briefly reviewing and defining the five moments in the history of Christianity that will organize this book. Since my purpose is to explore how these debates over orthodoxy and heresy inform how we read, write, and think in the twentieth and twenty-first centuries, my choices reflect debates that continue to influence and fascinate modern writers. I have also selected heresies that, by their very nature, were debates over writing, text, interpretation, and language. From the very beginning, Christian heresy was connected to words and how to interpret them. The early-Christian theologian Tertullian (ultimately declared a heretic himself) writes that "heretics either wrest plain and simple words to any sense they choose by their conjectures, or else they violently resolve by a literal interpretation words which … are incapable of a simple solution" (Pelikan 1971: 61). These debates also tended to focus on how these words were presented and dispersed. Even in the earliest centuries of Christianity and with the first codices of scripture, orthodox statements began to emphasize the written over the spoken, a process that led to a canonical Bible. This chapter is my history of putting books into often unfinished and misunderstood conversation with other books: old books, new books, famous books, obscure books—a microcosm of the way heresy works and how it remains always on the edges of the human literary imagination.

"Heretics," wrote the third-century theologian Origen, "all begin by believing, and afterwards depart from the road of faith and the truth of the church's teaching" (Pelikan 1971: 69). Over the long Christian tradition, most orthodox and heretical thinkers have believed in one truth, one doctrine, and one set of sacred texts. Both the heretical and the orthodox (or "proto-orthodox") were insistent that their positions were the correct ones.[1] As early as the second century, the Bishop Irenaeus wrote that "heresy" stood for a "deviation from the standard of sound doctrine" (Pelikan 1971: 69). Later, Augustine would separate heretics who hold "false opinions regarding God" and therefore do "injury to the faith itself," from schismatics, who "in wicked separation break off from brotherly charity, although they may believe just what we believe" (Pelikan 1971: 69). Such definitions assume a single faith and a single opinion on doctrine, either right or wrong. Heresy is not, though, an *intentional* snubbing of church doctrine, ritual, or faith. Although the twentieth century, as Chesterton noted, saw people who made proud rebellious claims of being a heretic, the term as I use it, and as it has been historically employed, no heretic would think of themselves as a heretic.

However distant these debates may appear to modern sensibilities, they all involve vital themes that would split apart the Christian world in later eras. From the Reformation through the Victorian era to our own time, some of these same debates play out in the conflicts between faith and education, issues of the quest for authority, the relationship between church and state, the proper ways of reading and interpreting scripture, the ethics and conduct demanded of Christians, and the means of salvation. They also continue to shape how we believe, doubt, read, and think outside of our religious practices. Gnosticism offers subversive reading practices and alternative approaches to history, while Arius questions the idea and role of creation and creative material. In the Middle Ages, we find doctrinal, material, and visual answers to some of these questions only to see them radically challenged by the words, books, ideas, and writings that explode out of the Reformation and the Renaissance. Finally, in the nineteenth-century Book of Mormon, we find a simultaneously ancient and modern literary take on many of these issues—creating, rewriting, and challenging the ideas and origins and authority of scripture where it all began in the second century.

---

1 The term "proto-orthodox Christianity" or "proto-orthodoxy" is used by the popular New Testament scholar Bart Ehrman to describe early Christian movements which would only later be established as orthodox.

Revising the History of Scripture

In the early Christian centuries, there was not yet an official Christian Bible or "New" Testament. When Paul refers to "scripture," he means the Hebrew Bible, as the Gospels were written decades after the death of Jesus by anonymous authors who never met him. Without exception, the first Christians were Jews, and their new faith was initially assumed to be continuous with their old. Then, as now, there was not an official orthodoxy in Judaism and ideas about God varied according to the individual or the group. It was only after the fall of Jerusalem in 70 AD that a rift developed between Hellenistic Jews and Hellenist Jewish-Christians, which then spread to Christian and Jewish thought. As more new Jesus followers begin to come from pagan or gentile backgrounds the lineage shifted: "For Jewish Christians," Pelikan writes, "the question of continuity was the question of their relation to their mother; for Gentile Christians, it was the question of their relation to their mother-in-law" (1971: 14). This struggle over the authority of the Hebrew Scriptures and over the continuity between Judaism and Christianity is central to early debates over orthodoxy and heresy. These issues of authority, origin, and influence would never be definitively settled and continue to emerge throughout Christian history.

There was never a single and definitive "original" Christianity. Scholars such as Bart Ehrman point out that ancient Christianity may have been even more diverse than the plurality of Christianities in the modern world (2003: 1). One explanation for this variety is the absence of a single stable and authoritative text. While all of what would *become* the *New* Testament had been written by the second century, there was not yet any *canonized* scripture. Books of what we now know as the New Testament existed and were read alongside other Christian texts, many of which have been lost or exist only in fragments, and some of which have resurfaced only in the modern era. For most of the history of Christianity, scholars and writers have unquestioningly accepted the versions told by the branches of Christianity that emerged as orthodox. But although the idea was unthinkable for centuries, and has been recently resisted even in the face of growing evidence, scholars now know that, in various times and places, many of these now non-canonical books were also thought of as divinely inspired, sacred, prophetic, or scriptural.

These early Christian works of literature—gospels, tracts, sermons, poems, myths, songs—were dispersed, copied, forged, falsified, altered, destroyed, and preserved in ways that were never neutral, as the resulting variations often privileged one point of view over another or required different strategies of reading. As Ehrman points out, one of the most distinctive features of early Christianity was its literary character, as "no other religion of the Roman empire was so rooted in literary texts" (2003: 203), and the "struggles for dominance in early Christianity were in no small measure carried out on literary battle fields" (2003: 201). In many cases, the early heretics of the first and second centuries did not actually reject the validity of what would become orthodox doctrine, but interpreted them in ways that they felt were deeper and more insightful (2003: 185). In essence, they claimed they were better readers.

What is most significant theologically is not that the categories of orthodoxy and heresy are invalid, but that "true faith" must be determined on the basis of some criteria other than origin. What if we were to somehow determine, for example, that a Gnostic text gave a more historically authentic version of the life and words of Jesus than the four canonical gospels do? What would the relationship be between historical and theological truth claims? These questions are not only important to theologians and believers. It is provocative and challenging to imagine Western art, music, and literature had Christianity not become a religion of both Testaments. Most demonstrably, there are the images, stories, and songs that entered the Christian traditions and shape later genres. These early Christian literary genres have direct links to the modern literary genres: from the drama of the Catholic Mass to medieval mystery plays to Joyce's Black Mass in "Circe" in *Ulysses*; from the spiritual autobiography of Augustine's *Confessions* to Stephen's concluding diary in *A Portrait of the Artist*; from the Christian epic of *Paradise Lost* to the deconstructed epic of *Finnegans Wake*. Furthermore, the reading practices of allegory, metaphor, and typology that had to be perfected within Christian apologetics are reading strategies that still dominate literary criticism. Finally, it is provocative to think about how concepts of history and narrative would have evolved with a stronger sense of rupture, rather than continuity—if we had always had a sense of unwritten, erased, and unremembered origins and gap-ridden histories, rather than the fantasy of true origins and a single teleological plot line.

Two significant and defining sets of questions—both characterized by rupture—emerged for the early Christians. First: What does it mean that our leader is dead? What meaning can we take from his death and who was, or is, he? How do we tell this story and how do we continue on through memory and practice? Second: Are we still Jewish? Do we worship the same God? What meanings do the pre-existing laws and scripture have for us? How do we tell *this* story? Despite disagreement and discontinuities, the eventual acceptance of Jewish traditions, the Jewish God, and the Jewish scriptures also set up an apparently linear tradition on which future generations of Christians would base their art and writing. Milton's *Paradise Lost*—although it has its own heretical elements, or the "hearasay in paradox lust" (*FW* 263.4)—assumes a Christian interpretation of the Hebrew Adam and Eve story (apples and falls, Satan and free will) that few readers would even question. The constructing of the beginnings of this tradition, however, involved major debates and efforts: literary, philosophical, and theological. As Pelikan points out, "Virtually every major Christian writer of the first five centuries either composed a treatise in opposition to Judaism or made this issue a dominant theme in a treatise" (1971: 15).

While many Gnostics denied the authority of the Jewish or Hebrew scriptures, the proto-orthodox found a way to shape these scriptures to their own use. In other words, not just as a book of Jewish history, but as an essentially Christian book whose full meaning can only be revealed through the events and language of the Christian writings. This involved a model of reading and meaning-making known as "typology," which became an influential model of reading across texts and across history. A "type," according to this way of reading, is a person, event, or thing in the Hebrew bible which foreshadows a person, event, or thing (the "antitype") in the Christian Bible. Typology contains within it a theory of time and of narrative: the "antitype" completes and fulfils the "type" and reveals the meaning hidden in it. For example, the Israelites wandered forty years in the desert, Christ fasted in the desert forty days; Adam brought death into world, Christ brings life. To read, as centuries of Christians have, that Eve and Mary are literally joined thematically, theologically, and historically is simultaneously a theory of reading, of time and history, and of the ontology of the human body. Mary, who gave birth to God and human salvation, was the opposite of Eve, whose indiscretion brought about the fall of man. Yet Mary and her divine son are not possible without Eve and her expulsion from the Garden. Stories, legends, myths, and history therefore blur as both a textual strategy and as a theme for poets and painters who conflate images of Mary and Eve. The "Fortunate Fall," in which Eve enables Mary, is a repeating theme in *Finnegans Wake*, which also develops its own typological theory of history where times can exist simultaneously and where the ancient legend of Eve is also a modern woman married with children in a suburb of Dublin, a river, and a medieval Irish princess.

Throughout the early centuries of Christianity—and arguably ever since—Christian believers and practitioners have employed many strategies of interpretation to resolve problems of scripture and logic, body and spirit, practice and belief. Different sects, writers, and scholars varied the stress they placed on Jesus's humanity or his divinity, and they would often find specific biblical passages to support their opinions. For some, Christ is so fully divine that he basically ceases to be human. He looks like a human, he can be touched, but it is only a disguise. Others see him as a great man whom God has given power and wisdom. Centuries of Christian artwork, children's tales, and Christmas nativity scenes would suggest that he was clearly divine from the beginning, but that is not so clear from the biblical text, and many early thinkers had other views. Much Christian writing would seem to suggest that it happened at the moment of his baptism. Some Gnostics understood the idea of "word becoming flesh" as a thirty-year-old man materializing in the wilderness ready to take on his divine mission. Read this way, we could then read the crucifixion as the moment when the baptism and the God-power of Christ abandon the man Jesus.

The central and essentially irresoluble problem here—which we will return to throughout this book—focuses on Jesus' suffering and death. If Jesus is God, then who is it that speaks *"Eli, Eli, lama sabachthani?"* (Father, Father, why hast thou forsaken me?) (Mathew 27:46). This line presents one of the most complex paradoxes in the Christian Bible; from the perspective of a reader, it might suggest a character crying out to an author, or perhaps an author crying out to themselves. To understand the importance of asserting a single correct opinion within the Church (instead of, as we might see today, agreeing to form separate denominations) is a matter of understanding the central controlling metaphor of the Church as the undivided body of Christ—a move that can be seen as reversing the pluralities of Gnosticism. Just as all limbs and organs form one complete unified human body, the perfect church would be made out of different parts formed perfectly into a whole. For a body to be perfect—and Christ had to be both body and perfect—it had to be united; to *not* be united was to be deformed and imperfect, and not God. Contained within this metaphor are ideas of Christ as body and as divine and the idea of completeness as perfection, all philosophical ideas that we will revisit and question through twentieth-century literature and thought. This link between body and book—as both self-contained, complete, and unified with clearly defined boundaries—is a link that is constantly made and unmade in the ongoing history of religion and literature.

Part II: Early Christians and the Gnostics: Body and Text

For many readers, the history of heresy begins with a group known as the Gnostics. There is, however, no single "Gnosticism." Gnosticism is a modern name for a variety of ancient religious ideas and systems, originating in Judeo-Christian traditions of the first and second century CE. Gnosticism, in the most general sense, has historically been used to refer to varieties of early Christianity that denied their connection to Judaism, or, more broadly, any outside contamination of "pure" early Christianity. More specifically, Gnosticism's theological characteristics may contain features such as anti-cosmic dualism, the consubstantiality of the human and the divine, salvation by knowledge (rather than by faith or grace), and the separation of a true God from a flawed, or evil, creator God. Most Gnostics, while they represented an array of theological positions, believed that the material world was created by an emanation of the highest God, trapping a sort of divine spark within the physical human body. This divine spark could be liberated by the right kind of "knowledge" or *gnosis*. Gnosticism can therefore be defined as a "system which taught the cosmic redemption of the spirit through knowledge." Standing on the "borders between heretical Judaism and heretical Christianity" (Pelikan 1971: 82–3), Gnosticism is a further exploration of the ideas of authority, text, body, and unity that we saw dialectically developed in the proto-Gnostic Marcion in chapter one, and that we will find dramatically staged in the writing of Joyce.

After the second century, Gnosticism persisted as an undercurrent within Christian culture, re-appearing most visibly in the Renaissance as forms of esotericism or in the early-twentieth century as forms of theosophy or occult magic. More than anything else, the legacy of these early Christian debates can be found in perceptions of the human body and the relationship between body and text. The Gnostic views on the sinfulness of all materiality led to very different views on who or what Christ was, what happened on the cross, and the nature of resurrections—views and questions about mind, body, soul, and autonomy, that survive into our time, embedded in poetry, art, laws, and literature. Because they rejected the world of matter, most Gnostics denied that Christ had a physical body, that he had been born of a woman, or that he had suffered or died. The Gnostic "Gospel of Thomas" offers an alternative perspective to the four canonical gospels through 114 sayings of Christ, none of which either confirm or deny his divinity, and which are not as concerned with belief or proof of his divinity. The Gospel of Thomas is a Gospel without a cross, without a death, no last days of Jesus, and no physical miracles. Accepting the body as proof—an essentially orthodox move—is a tricky wager: no body is permanent proof of anything. Bodies rot, decay, and disappear back into earth and dust. The Gnostic documents found in the Egyptian desert near Nag Hammadi in 1945 were reportedly found next to the buried and forever muted remains of a human—

only the texts could tell their story, and even that story is partial. If the ineffable and transcendent God is always on the edge of not existing, of disappearing into subjectivity or pure spirit, then conversely the earthly Jesus is always in danger of becoming merely mortal, purely material, everyday flesh and blood, immanent instead of transcendent, temporary instead of eternal. These ideas present a particular set of problems for Christians throughout history, including the modern era.

Another text discovered at Nag Hammadi, the Valentinian "Gospel of Truth," echoes much of the language from the New Testament, but also shows the influence of the Gospel of Thomas, Gnostic myth, and Greek philosophy. In this sermon, our fallen material world is the result of ignorance—it is not even "real." Jesus represents the true knowledge we need for salvation, a salvation that is knowledge both of the True God and of ourselves. The text draws a metaphorical line from the tree that Jesus died on to the tree of knowledge in the Garden, but reverses the book of Genesis in characterizing the knowledge as beneficial and not as the path to the Fall. Further emphasizing the act of eating, the Gospel uses Eucharistic imagery to locate the salvation in the crucifixion. The crucifixion, like Christ, then, is *knowledge*, a point which we see demonstrated in another metaphor in the Gospel of Truth where the author describes the crucifixion as a text or a book, where the death on the cross literally "publishes" the book containing the knowledge to escape the material world and return to the Father.

Although one can still find paranoid rejections of "Gnostic" belief systems on evangelical websites, much of today's popular Christianity also teaches that our bodies are evil and urges Christians to turn away from the material and the flesh and place all hopes in heaven—ideas more from Gnosticism than from the New Testament. In thinking about issues of the body—particularly those issues of fluidity and ontology that we face in the twenty-first century—it is useful to consider the various perspectives offered by orthodox and heretical branches of Christianity. The orthodox view of resurrection—that a dead man comes back physically to life—can be seen to promote the idea that human life is inseparable from bodily experience. Gnostic Christianity, on the other hand, seems to have dismissed the idea of bodily resurrection and saw bodily actions (sex, birth, etc.) as either unimportant or disgusting. The resurrection, they claimed, was not a unique event *in* history. Instead, it symbolized how Christ's presence could be experienced in the present. This is not unknown to Catholic Christianity either, and the drama of the Mass—which we will be looking at through the lens of Joyce's *Ulysses* and the heresies of the Reformation—is at least in part about recreating the resurrection in the present.

Gnostic thought highlights many theological issues that early Church Fathers were perhaps hesitant to address, including human alienation from an unreachable God. If we identify poetry and mysticism as existing in the gap between humans and God, to be developed in the knowingly impossible task of traversing a gap that is beyond language and beyond imagination, then these gaps—which Gnosticism calls attention to—are spaces of creation and anxiety. They are not only where poetry and heresy meet, but also where modernism meets theology—worlds of dreams, surrealist images, dada objects, monsters, and invented words that make us question where our ideas come from and make us work together to invent new ways of seeing and thinking. These new ways of seeing in the twentieth century in the West were shaped by new archeological discoveries, Einsteinian physics, existential philosophy, and Freudian psychoanalysis, all of which chipped away at a sense of certainty. In the first edition of his book on Gnosticism and existential philosophy, the twentieth-century philosopher Hans Jonas opens with a romantic "what-if" flourish: "Out of the mist of the beginning of our era there looms a pageant of mythical figures whose vast, superman contours might people the walls and ceilings of another Sistine Chapel" (1958: xxxi). The Sistine Chapel may be the most famous artistic representation of the gap between human and God; the fingers of God and Adam remaining forever separate in a 500-year-old dramatization of the idea that artistic creation only exists in our inability to touch the divine—it seems we can only point. What might "another" Sistine Chapel—perhaps one depicting a fallen God—have looked like? What would a Gnostic history of art and literature be?

1934 and Modernist Gnosticism

Despite what centuries of Church historians had claimed, modern historians now understand that in the second century there was not a clear definition of "orthodoxy" and "heresy." As Karen King writes, "constructing a heretical other simultaneously and reciprocally exposes the partial, mutable, and irregular character of orthodoxy" (2003: 26). In just a few short years, Gnosticism moved from being defined in a nineteenth-century Webster's Dictionary as a "sect of philosophers … who pretended that they were the only men who had a true knowledge of the Christian religion" and in the 1909 Catholic Encyclopedia as a "fungus at the root" of true Christianity, to a 1934 text by Christian historian Walter Bauer in which he categorized Gnosticism as not "heresies" at all but "only forms of the new religion"—or, in his words, "simply Christianity." Bauer's paradigm-challenging *Orthodoxy and Heresy in Earliest Christianity* called for an abandonment of the master narrative of Christian origins or the "ecclesiastical position," which insisted on a pure doctrine stemming directly from Jesus himself that was always fated to triumph. "Even today," Bauer writes, "the overwhelmingly dominant view still is that for the period of Christian origins, ecclesiastical doctrine already represents what is primary, while heresies, on the other hand, somehow are a deviation from the genuine" ([1934] 1971: xxiv). The original publishing date of Bauer's book, 1934, is a pivotal year in thinking about reassessments of Gnosticism. It is also the same year that *Ulysses* was on trial for obscenity in the United States, and Martin Conboy, a former lawyer and president of the Catholic Club of New York, showed a truly Gnostic-like disgust for the body and bodily functions by testifying that *Ulysses* was an "obscene book" that "begins with blasphemy, runs the whole gamut of sexual perversion, and ends in inexpressible filth and obscenity" (*New York Daily News*).

Bauer's book was not translated into English until 1971, so much of the English-speaking world—in an echo of the deferred historical understanding of Gnosticism itself—was only aware of his work through the refutations of his opponents. (This same process of deferred meaning is also reenacted in *Ulysses*, published in 1922, but not openly available in Ireland until the 1960s.) Although some of Bauer's specific conclusions have been questioned by more recent research and discoveries, his basic claims—that we need to rethink how we narrate the history of Christianity and that writing the history backwards through the lens of later ecclesiastical and theological positions distorts the narrative—are generally accepted. In essence, he made the same decision many of the Gnostics made in not reading the Jewish scriptures as a form of Christian writing: to not read the past through the present, but to read from left to right. Bauer's work parallels, echoes, and anticipates the literature and literary theory of the twentieth century in its resistance to universals, origins, and continuity. It is the same impulses that will see Joyce not as the universal modernist claimed by early critics and supporters like Eliot and Pound, but as an Irish writer engaging with specific times and places. Bauer's decision to not take the New Testament as the starting point of Christian history, and his attention to what the Gospel writers and church fathers did *not* say as much as to what they *did*, is similar to modernists who continually find the poetic in the unsaid and the non-linear.

Also in 1934, philosopher Hans Jonas published Volume One of *Gnosis und spätantiker Geist*, a work which would become his much-read *The Gnostic Religion* in later English translation. For the young Jonas, Gnosticism could be understood as an anticipation of existentialist philosophy and its themes of alienation and the individual. For Jonas, Gnostic thought "knocks at the door of our Being and of our twentieth-century Being in particular" (1958: xxv). As a Jewish-European philosopher in the 1930s, Jonas would understandably agree with the Gnostic view that the material world is made of ignorance and suffering, and salvation can come only by escaping it. Although from today's perspective, Jonas's work used limited primary resources, it remained the most known and read work on Gnosticism long after its English translation in 1958. Jonas turned away from the available historical sources and instead asked where the Gnostic mind or imagination originated. In other words, he saw the Gnostics as reacting to and creating a worldview that combined a pessimistic or existentialist attitude toward the human condition with a strategy for self-transcendence—a worldview that would speak to his post-War readers. His point in writing the book as a philosopher was not to give a "record of its history" but instead to "bring us face to face with one of the more radical answers of man to his predicament and with the insights which only that radical position could bring fourth" (1958: xxxiv–xxxv). Jonas's work was the "only extensive study of Gnosticism that did not take up the question of the relationship to Christianity as a decisive starting point or goal" (King 2003: 133). While his views on Gnosticism turned more negative over the course of his career, and although much of his work still focused on the idea of "correctly" locating the origins of Gnosticism, Jonas saw Gnosticism as a "living force" instead of "merely a sponge sopping up whatever traditions lay at hand" (King 2003: 116), and found its "deepest religious impulses and feelings rooted in existential alienation and revolt" (King 2003: 135). As a living force, then, Gnosticism was able to be seen as inventing its own symbols and by extension, could be used to offer new perspectives on later philosophy and literature. If heretical thought has never really disappeared, but has been discursively and dialectically worked into mainstream religion, philosophy, and language, then it is in the spirit of Jonas that various heretical movements can be revisited to understand our attitude toward existence as it continues to shift and change.

For Jonas, as for Joyce, creativity is part of one's relationship to the self and world, but too much creativity can lead to "heretical" thinking in any era. According to their contemporary detractors, Gnostics believed in a link between creative authorship and spiritual experience. Irenaeus intends it to be dismissive when he complains that Gnostics are inventors of "imaginative fiction" and that they "generate something new every day ... no one is considered initiated among them unless he develops some enormous fictions" (*Against Heresy* I.18.1). This kind of creativity in writing and interpretation produced a variety of ideas and beliefs that the orthodox saw as deviation from a single, stable apostolic tradition. Every Gnostic, according to Tertullian, "modifies the traditions he has received, just as the one who handed them down modified them" (Pagels 1979: 23); he then goes on to accuse them of adding writing to the Scriptures or challenging orthodox interpretations. In essence, these 1934 works by Jonas and Bauer changed the landscape of the study of Gnosticism and, in a way, created the opportunity for studies like mine, which emphasize that the Gnostic heresies are as much a part of the twentieth-century imagination as they are a part of ancient Christian history. If modern literature has its roots in these early debates over texts and reading practices, we see here some of the beginnings of later tensions over creativity, inspiration, and authority that readers find in the pages of *Ulysses* and *Finnegans Wake*.

Part III: Arius and Fourth-Century Christology

Following the debates over Gnosticism, Christianity seemed to have developed several stable tenets: Jesus is divine, God is one, and the God of the Hebrew Bible is also the God of the Christian Gospels and letters. But three hundred years after the death of Jesus, a central question persisted: Just what was he? The idea that he had somehow transcended death and that the crucifixion was central to the practice of the religion was probably agreed upon by most—but how did this work and just what did it mean? Late-nineteenth- and early-twentieth-century thinkers in particular returned to these questions in their reframing of Christian history. In his late-nineteenth-century book of lectures on heresy, Unitarian Edward Hall writes that fourth-century Christians had "learned to call Christ God, but had as yet gone no further" (1891: 48). The Gnostic texts had separated the person of the Christ and the physical pains described in the canonical Gospels. Although these Gnostic forms of Christianity were ultimately ruled heretical, the challenges they offered the Church, especially as to the nature of God and Christ, did not go away, and led to the great councils of the fourth and fifth centuries.

Although it was Gnostic-related thought that prompted Christians to articulate a concept of heresy, it was at the beginning of the fourth century that Christianity experienced its most famous heresies. The Gnostic belief that Christ's human body was essentially an illusion was not confined to Gnostics and other heretics, but was sufficiently widespread within the churches to evoke the repeated warnings of early Christian writers (Pelikan 1971: 174). Yet, the accepted position that he was divine posed difficult problems when combined with his humanity. For many of the first Christians, Jesus had perhaps just two stages of existence: his life on earth and his eventual triumphant return. But other questions soon suggested themselves: Where was he before he was born? Where would he be hanging out between resurrection and return? And if, as Paul had suggested, Jesus was with God before his birth (Phil. 2:6–10), then not only had he voluntarily gone to the cross, he had perhaps also willingly submitted to being human. Many Christians of the time would agree with Stephen Dedalus when he says that "Jesus is more like a son of God than a son of Mary" (*P* 264). A Jesus more God than human is a persistent figure in folk and apocryphal traditions. Stories found in Gnostic texts such as the Infancy Gospel of Thomas describe a supernatural child Jesus who performs miracles such as killing his playmates and then bringing them back to life for fun. These stories remained popular for centuries, even if ruled heretical, and are represented in art works such as the medieval Tring Tiles in the British Museum.

For Christians to accept the idea of Christ's divinity, there were three basic options for doctrine, although more marginalized branches of early Christianity offered more radical interpretations: (1) Father and Son are the same divinity; they just appear differently to humans; (2) Father and Son are both divine, but are somehow different; (3) Father and Son are somehow both identical and

Figure 1 Tring Tiles: Apocryphal images of Jesus as child "tile," near 1330, artist unknown, within The Tring Tiles Series © The British Museum, 1997. Reproduced with the permission of The British Museum.

different, which resolves problems but requires a complicated act of logic and language through which God exists, but is not a thing among other things. It is the gray area of the "somehow different" that is the birth of theology. Each of these claims involves types of reading and thinking about texts that we can see being negotiated and performed in the twentieth and twenty-first centuries. "Somehow different" becomes, to put it in more modern terms, an unstable space of difference, on the edge between chaos and order, and a site of emergent creativity that we find in the modernist questioning of borders and certainty.

Although central to much Christian doctrine, the Bible itself says very little about Jesus as God, and Jesus himself never clearly claims to be equal to or equivalent with God the Father. However, the idea of Jesus as divine (not necessarily equal to the Father God) was established quite early. One of the oldest surviving Christian sermons after the New Testament (a text sometimes called 2 Clement from the early-second century) opens with "we ought to think of Jesus Christ as of God," and the oldest surviving pagan report about the church describes Christians "singing a hymn to Christ as though to [a] god" (Pelikan 1971: 173). Perhaps the first complication—and one that continues to produce alternative and heretical positions today—comes from reconciling Christ's suffering with his divinity, which brings us back to the central question of the cross. Answers to this impossible question would define one of the main lines between orthodoxy and heresy for centuries. This is a central question of Christian theology, of course, but also one that occupies modern philosophers from Hegel to Žižek: the death on the cross, taken outside of any orthodoxy, becomes the death of God himself, a gap in meaning that needs to be filled, and, in a sense that we will continue to explore, a source of imaginative writing.

Arius's heretical position was that there was a time when Christ did not exist and that he must therefore have been "created" (hence the wording of the anti-Arian Nicaean Creed, that Christ was "begotten, not made").[2] This creation and subordination of Christ was accepted by many Christians in Arius's time, and the debate forced Christian thinkers to more clearly address and define paradoxical issues regarding the nature of Christ. Due, in part, to the sackers of Rome who had adopted a form of Arius's version of Christianity, Arius would be remembered not just as a dissenting theological voice, not just as a heretic, but a "kind of Antichrist among heretics" whose "spirituality cloaked a diabolical

---

2 The distinction, as most Christians understand it, is that when you beget, you beget something of the same kind as yourself. When you make, you make something different from yourself. One could analogously ask if a poet *makes* or *begets* a poem?

malice" (Williams 1987: 1). Arius's apocryphal death, bleeding to death on a public latrine—a famous scene that reflected this hatred not only in its graphic nature, but also in its echoing of the death of Judas in the Book of Acts—is a much written, told, and visually depicted story.

For Arius, the emerging idea that Christ the Son of God was—like God the Father—eternal and unchanging was wrong. Arius claimed that the Father, as the one true God, was fully and totally unique and that the Son had to have been created by him: "If the Son is a true Son, then the Father must have existed before the Son; therefore, he was created." For Arius, Christ was, indeed, God, but only because God had willed him to be. According to contemporaneous figures, like Gregory of Nyssa, this debate was not just held among educated bishops and theologians, but was argued among bath-attendants and bakers. A popular song in Alexandria even contained the Arian slogan line: "There was a time when the Son was not." While Arius taught that the Son had been created in time, Athanasius, the ultimate source of orthodoxy on this matter, insisted that the Son was begotten eternally—a battle of concepts and of words that negotiated the borders between *creating* and *begetting* and between *time* and *eternity*.

Like the debates over Gnosticism in the second century, the Arian controversy forced leaders in various parts of the Christian world to clarify and develop just what it was they should teach and believe. To do so, they turned to biblical exegesis and philosophy, and to issues of reading, writing, and literary interpretation. At the same time, they were forced to preserve traditions, doctrine, and worship practices that had been established as orthodox or normative. Some of the essentially literary questions that were revisited and re-evaluated included deciding the limits of allegorical interpretation and the factual acceptance of the Hebrew Scriptures. For example, were both the Hebrew and Christian Scriptures the words of Christ? Many church historians point to the Arian controversy as playing out over the exegesis of Proverbs 8:22-31. The passage begins:

> The Lord created me at the beginning of his work, the first of his acts of long ago. Ages ago I was set up, at the first, before the beginning of the earth. When there were no depths I was brought forth, when there were no springs abounding with water.

Although this passage was written hundreds of years before Jesus, it was read typologically by theologians such as Irenaeus to "prove" that the Son was always with the Father. But the passage also clearly points to "creation" and, that being a creature, he did not exist before he came into being (Pelikan 1971: 192). In a famous letter, Arius quoted Proverbs 22-3 to show that "before he was begotten or created or ordained or established, he did not exist" (Pelikan 1971: 193). The reading that later creeds would rely upon was that the phrase "created me," in Proverbs 8:22, was speaking only of the created humanity of the incarnate Christ.

These debates point to the importance of critical language; no longer were the arguments just about scriptural language, but now the important terms became those of philosophers and theologians, translators, and poets. As Philip Jenkins writes "By the end of the fourth century, theologians drew subtle yet critical differences between a number of words that earlier had been thrown around in far vaguer terms" (2010: 55). The most important thinkers at this point would be those who could effectively use a language that was both more precise in argument and yet allowed for flexibility and ambiguity. As these terms play out through theological, philosophical, and literary history, it also becomes important how they move between languages, for example, "ousia" (οὐσία) in Greek becomes "essential" (*essentialis*) in Latin and "being" in English. Or the Greek *physis* is translated in Latin and English as "nature." However, as theories of translation show, there are no true equivalences between languages, and each of these terms comes with its own philosophical and literary history, its own "trace." And, even as these words become canonical, they still left rifts, gaps, and aporias. Like modern writings from Joyce and Derrida, these texts dramatize the shifting meanings of words over time, and create and reinterpret words for new purposes. The critical point becomes not the search for a stable definition, but the slippage between words.

Although there is little evidence that Joyce undertook any serious study of Arius or Arianism, there was a shift in English language studies of Arianism in the nineteenth century largely due to the writings of Cardinal John Henry Newman, whose writing Joyce greatly admired. In *Portrait*, the young Stephen Dedalus argues that Newman was the greatest writer of prose (*P* 84) and Joyce himself would make this claim in the mid-1930s (*LI* 366). In 1833, Newman's *The Arians of the Fourth Century* represented a more modern model of Christian intellectual thought and history. While Newman's book does present a more objective re-evaluation of the history of Arius and Arianism, he was still an orthodox Christian scholar in his ultimate condemnation of the heresy of Arianism. The Anglican Rowan Williams criticizes Newman's "harsh polemic" and his "Arianism as other" position, although Williams recognizes them as views of the time (1987: 22). Still, Newman's book placed an Arius that was not simply an evil anti-Christ into nineteenth-century intellectual conversations that would be in the air in the early twentieth century.

For Christians facing suffering, it was important to believe that Christ had indeed suffered on the cross. For some, the changeable Christ of Arius meant that it was possible that Christ could turn evil or could even cease to exist, return to nothingness. For others, a Christ without a human mind or human bones feels too unconnected to humanity. Believing that Christ is both human and divine changes forever what it means to be human, but also what it means to imagine a god. Changing what it means to be human and god shifts the experiences of art, and what it means to tell, remember, and forget stories, and to interact with the fragility and impermanence of daily life—central themes for the characters in *Ulysses*, walking through Dublin on a typical day in 1904, and for all the various voices and storytellers in *Finnegans Wake*.

One, Two, or Three: Unity or Plurality?

The defeat of Arius after Nicaea seemed to settle the important theological issues. The orthodox position was that Christ was outside of time—eternal, uncreated—was both fully human and fully divine, and was God in every way—they were of the same "substance" (*ousia*). But what exactly did this solve? What does it mean to say "substance" when we talk about a divinity? The Father is not a tree, a rock, a book, or skin and bone, so what "substance" is he made of? Again, the central issues involved the reading and defining of words. When Jesus narrates a parable or makes a pronouncement, it is not clear whether these words come directly from God or not. Conversely, when he questions God's plans or the need for his own upcoming death, it is hard to imagine these are God's words. How do we read the scenes in the Christian scriptures where Jesus prays to God? How were Father and Son literally of the same substance, but not identical? And what was the Holy Spirit, an entity that had been mostly neglected in the Nicaean Creed, but had been around and important since the early days of the Church?

These questions created the next great Christian theological challenge. The answer came out of Cappadocia, Turkey in the idea that God was one *ousia* but three *hypostases*, another fine distinction that that relied heavily on Greek language and Platonic philosophy, but also represented new metaphors for being and creating. The solution, as it was ultimately worked out, is an example of how theology and, by extension, the future of Western thought and literature were inevitably issues of reading, interpretation, and language. Many Christian leaders had been uncertain about the use of the word *ousia*. What eventually allowed them to agree to a creed was bringing in a different Greek word—*hypostasis*—which also meant essence or substance, but now spinning it slightly differently so that the Trinity was framed to consist of three equal *hypostasis* in one *ousia*: three equal "Persons" sharing a single essence. This orthodoxy accepted by the Roman Empire and passed on ever since to the majority of Christians, Protestant, Catholic, or Orthodox—although many denominations, especially recently, have begun to deviate from this formulation— was established in 451 CE at the great council at Chalcedon. The radical nature of this statement was that it refused to compromise either on the Christ as man or god, in the process essentially creating a new philosophy of being. Christ's two natures co-existed "without confusion, without change, without division, without separation." For centuries, Church historians presented the conclusions of the great council as inevitable, and conclusive.

As many modern historians have pointed out, Chalcedon was "not the only possible solution, nor was it an obvious or, perhaps, even logical one" (Jenkins 2010: xi). One important fact that the Christological debate brings out is that each new argument over heresy often points to problems in the previous orthodoxy. It is this pattern that keeps heresy alive and significant. While the doctrine of the Trinity somewhat clarified the relationships among Father, Son, and Spirit, it left another issue unexplained—the relation between the human and the divine in Christ. For Stephen in *Ulysses*, the Trinity seems to be a strategy to reconcile the eternal conflict between father and son—a conflict that Stephen demonstrates through Hamlet's relationship to his own ghost father and Claudius, his stepfather. As we will continue to see, these other points of view, representing different ways of thinking, may be repressed, but never go away either. History seen this way is not what we remember—is not what gets written in a book—but is a messy, marginal, and confusing muddle, a process better represented in a text like *Ulysses* or *Finnegans Wake* than any more formal history of heresy.

Part IV: Medieval Eucharist: The Heresy Solution

Arius may be the archetypal heretic, but if you asked a person on the street what they know about heresy, odds are they would think of something stereotypically medieval in character. Inspired by film and television from the silent *Joan of Arc* to *The Name of the Rose* to Monty Python, the word "heresy" invokes images of the inquisition, drowning witches, blind evil monks, and burning and torture. But understanding the historical, social, and theological significance of heretical movements in the Middle Ages is a slippery task, and one that—like the study of early Christianity— has changed its focus in recent decades. Once reductively characterized as the "Age of Faith," the Middle Ages were thought to represent (depending on your confessional position) either the height of Catholic spirituality or the depths of Christian superstition and ecclesiastical corruption. Protestant-influenced scholars established a historical interpretation of medieval Christianity as decayed, corrupt, and incoherent, dominated by magical rites surrounded by relics, miracles, and fables, and ruled over by fraudulent institutional practices, such as selling indulgences. In the 1980s and 1990s, scholars such as Christopher Haigh and Eamon Duffy influentially challenged these views, arguing instead for flourishing and robust medieval devotional and Catholic theological traditions that continued into the Reformation.

Although Christian debates, schisms, and controversies over orthodoxy never stopped, alternative forms of Christian belief and practice around the year 1000, represented by movements such as the Bogomils, "signaled the revival of heresy through Latin Europe for the first time since late antiquity" (Frassetto 2007: 22). The new millennium saw new concepts of church and world that fostered a climate for new marginal movements and power struggles. The official Church deemed many of these emerging movements heretical, and the eleventh century saw the first officially authorized execution for heresy since antiquity. The most famous medieval heretical movements come from the twelfth and thirteenth centuries, a time that saw rapid urban growth and an expansion of trade and manufacturing. These shifts led to a new class of people, people whose power and wealth were not based on inherited wealth or ecclesiastical bounty, but on money through business. The growing merchant and manufacturing class exhibited a rising literacy that resulted in both an increased presence and an easier circulation of biblical and theological texts, but that also created challenges to the Church, oftentimes resulting in heresy. The "return" or "revival" of heresy included such groups as the Waldensians, the Cathars, the Hussites, and the Beguines, groups who challenged the organization and ideas of the Church particularly around issues of dualism, Christology, apostolic poverty, and gender.

Rather than focus on any one or several of these medieval heresies, I will instead look at the role of the medieval Eucharist—a powerfully orthodox idea and practice, but one that rests uneasily in relationship to heresies and schisms ancient, medieval, and modern. In the context of the arc of Christian heresies, the medieval Eucharist sits at the exact middle of our story of heresy and modernism—an answer to Gnostic and Arian concerns, on the edge of the Reformation, and still existing as a theme, a reality, a metaphor, and a debate for Joyce and contemporaneous Christians. As Pelikan notes, perhaps the clearest medieval contrast with the earlier patristic period is the "identification of the Eucharist rather than of baptism as the most important sacrament in the church" (1978: 2–3). The rise of Eucharistic culture is a prime example of how debates over orthodoxy and heresy create powerful new theological tropes of unity, which are then appropriated and adapted by creative artists. The images of Christ on the cross, the crucifix, or the rood were ubiquitous in the European medieval world, most prominently as the centerpiece of every church, large or small, many of which were themselves constructed in the shape of a cross. These churches, crucifixes, and rood screens communicate a central message about art, materiality, and the sacred: like the Incarnation itself, the sacred could exist in space and could take material form. These ideas are also communicated through the Mass, where God becomes truly and physically present. If the roots of Western art can be found in the spaces between humans and the divine, the medieval Eucharist gave this position a more tangible specificity. As Miri Rubin writes, "whereas early Christianity looked to holy men and early medieval society turned to saints to affect the connection between God and humankind through prayers of intercession, a different order was now emerging" (1991: 13). This different order, by creating a precise material and definable object and action that serves to connect man to the divine, lends itself more directly to artistic and poetic representations and analogies. Rather than "charismatic and exemplary figures," the Eucharist is a "neatly defined mystery" that becomes a visible moment of change or a moment of action which one could attempt to represent or imitate in art (Rubin 1991: 13). Although often rooted in the everyday, we might think here of Joyce's "epiphanies" or Virginia Woolf's "moments of being" as modernist examples of a kind of identifiable action that links the human and the beyond.

Perhaps surprisingly, despite centuries of ritual, the philosophical issues surrounding the Eucharist had "remained only loosely formulated until the eleventh century" (Rubin 1991: 14). In 1215, the Fourth Lateran Council declared doctrine that what is consumed during the Mass, while it may still look and taste like bread, has actually become the body of Christ. In the words of the Council "the body and blood are truly contained in the Sacrament of the Altar under the outward appearances of bread and wine, the bread having been transubstantiated into the body and the wine into the blood." The Council, at least temporarily, fulfilled the Gregorian aim of ensuring a true uniformity of belief: the Eucharist was now to be experienced at least once a year, and more importantly, there was an emphasis that the faithful should *understand* the Eucharist. Transubstantiation was an explanation for the "Real Presence" of the body and blood of Christ in the bread and the wine. This was also about the same time that the elevation of the Host became common practice, which literally gave the theater of the Mass a visual high point and a narrative climax.

By the early-thirteenth century, the Eucharist had become the main space or tool for affirming what Western theologians thought they believed, taught, and confessed (Pelikan 1978: 5). Or, as Eamon Duffy more poetically puts it:

> Christ himself, immolated on the altar of the cross, became present on the altar of the parish church, body, soul, and divinity, and his blood flowed once again, to nourish and renew Church and world.
>
> (1992: 91)

We can also see how earlier heretical debates are directly or indirectly addressed and are, in a sense, "answered" by this newly elevated sacramental act. The Mass was, as Peter Marshall writes, "a conduit of communication between worlds" (2018: 9). In the act—specifically, the raising and ingesting of the Host framed by visual art of altar, screen, and stained glass—were negotiated issues of Christ's divinity and humanity, the relationship between clergy and layperson and divinity, the meaning of the sacrifice on the cross, and the explanation of Christian art, architecture, and relics. The Eucharist materialized a relationship between body/divine and it further negotiated the anxiety over creation that we saw in the Arius section; it gave a narrative that further clarified the relationship to Hebrew Scriptures; it emphasized the authority of the priest and the presence of magic and miracles in objects and language. The Eucharist ritual, along with the theology, texts, images, culture, objects, and architecture that surrounded the Host, is perhaps the best lens through which to view the relationship between theology, history, and art in the European Middle Ages as well as their legacies. Conversely, within Christian (particularly Catholic) theology, to proclaim the existence of the creator through the central act of the Eucharist is to feel absolute presence—and to feel presence is to sense or perform the word and voice of the creator. For Joyce, author also means God and God also means author. Therefore, to question the creator is to question the very idea of the absolute. Joyce, the fallen Irish Catholic, trying to reinvent the English language novel—and arguably the idea of the English Christian epic—explores these spaces and relationships in ways that echo heresies of the past and negotiate how we read our heretical futures.

Part V: The Reformation: Destruction and Words

While the complicated multi-media presentation of the Host—with its interior and exterior dramatization of the connection and mystery between human and divine—was in some ways the medieval answer to questions left over from Gnostic or Arian debates, it was also soon shown to be an unstable solution. From Jan Hus and the Hussites in Bohemia and John Wycliffe and the Lollards in England to the more successful and recognizable Reformations of Luther and Calvin, the various heretical reform movements attacked—among other aspects—the relationship between word and image that made the medieval drama of the Mass possible. Furthermore, they also attacked *with* words: books, literature, sermons, pamphlets, and graffiti. The Reformation is often framed as a word-based religion replacing an image-based religion: rood screens and altars became pulpits, painted images of saints were whitewashed and covered with biblical texts, stories told in stone and stained glass were related in sermons. Stuart Clark has noted that, during the Reformation, "vision became the subject of fierce and unprecedented confessional dispute" (2007: 161). While late-medieval piety gave the visual perception of devotional objects a "virtually tactile quality," in which just seeing the elevated Host was considered a form of touching, Luther famously countered by saying that Christians should put their "eyes in their ears."

To even call the Reformation a heresy is a somewhat unusual move. But, on the other hand, it is a narrative in which we can see—for the first time in Christian history—the triumph of a form of heresy, a story in which heresiarchs become founding fathers, and heresies are turned into orthodoxies. More than the other heresies discussed so far, ideas associated with the Reformation are still with us in plain sight. Ideas such as *sola scriptura* ("by scripture alone," or the idea that scripture is the sole source of Christian authority) and the priesthood of all believers have—especially in the United States, but also across Europe and beyond—been woven deeply into our national consciousness and politics. This being said, recent writers have urged us not to automatically associate the Reformation with modernity.

Our contemporary sense that we are living in an unprecedented age of information overload is not as new as we might think. As Ann Blair writes, "Ancient, medieval, and early modern authors ... articulated similar concerns, notably about the overabundance of books and the frailty of human resources for mastering them (such as memory and time)" (2010: 3). When printed copies of Luther's 95 theses (written in both German and Latin) began to circulate in Germany—which began a pamphlet war—it was not the first time that the new medium of print had energized a public debate, but it was a demonstration that printing and public opinion were perhaps now a force beyond the control of the Church. In the same way that twenty-first-century digital technology has given more argumentative weight to the video and sound that can now easily be reproduced in a document, the Reformation was shaped by the reproducibility of texts.

Familiar as this story is, it is worth thinking through the relationship of printing to thinking in the early Reformation years. By 1509, there were few towns of any importance in Europe which did not have at least one printing press, and the expanding culture of print provided a new arena in which to challenge Catholic orthodoxy. If you could learn how to read, it opened a new world of enlightening, but troubling knowledge. Alternatively, one must be careful not to overstate this familiar link of printing with the Reformation: paper and printing were already in place at this time and serving Catholicism. Although they were in place decades before the Reformation, the multiplication and dissemination that new printing technologies made possible are inseparable from new ways of religious thinking. Protestantism—which, in England, would require churches to buy printed Bibles—was good business for printers, and printing was good for Protestantism, as a religion of the book needs books. A standard interpretation of why the Lollards failed to gather the same kind of support that the English Reformation would is that they could not produce enough copies of their literature to distribute.

Individual parchment texts—the standard format for texts—could last for a thousand years, but, of course, once destroyed were gone forever. Although the extent to which these factors actually played out historically is debated, many scholars point to ways that the reproducibility of texts and images might change how a population thinks about concepts of the "real" and of the individual's place in society. For MacCulloch, for example:

> A culture based on manuscripts is conscious of the fragility of knowledge, and the need to preserve it… and that fosters an attitude which guards rather than spreads knowledge… A manuscript culture is going to believe very readily in decay, in knowledge as in everything else, because copying knowledge from one manuscript to another is a very literal course of corruption. This is much less obvious in the print medium: optimism may be the mood rather than pessimism.
> (2005: 74)

The new, more skeptical, more historical reading practices that emerge in the Renaissance would lead to new ways of reading the Bible and, as we have seen, heresy and changes in reading practices are inevitably linked in complicated but revealing ways. MacCulloch writes that once "printed texts were available, there was less copying to do, and so there was more time to devote to thinking for oneself" (2005: 73). From the point of view of orthodoxy, thinking for oneself or reading silently can be dangerous. Broader than just the Reformation or Europe, this overwhelming flow of information came with anxieties over authority, control, and interpretation. Lay worshipers had always learned from "sermons in stone" or paint or stained glass. Now, in addition to church approved and sponsored images, they could take home cheap woodcuts either for humorous caricatures or for devotion. One possible result of these changes was that it suddenly became a more important issue to ascertain whether a text was accurate, authentic, and orthodox. These shifts resulted in more emphasis placed on techniques of reading and determining context: date, origins, motives, and appearances. Each of these practices, although in radically different ways, is rooted in ideas and technologies of writing, transcribing, copying, and erasing words on paper. The materiality of writing is always changing, and—in the same way that Christianity was associated with the early version of the codex—each of these types of texts, and the reading experiences they provide, allows us to think about scripture in more fluid ways.

Iconoclasm: Breaking Time

In England, it was in September of 1538 that, to wipe out "that most detestable sin of idolatry," iconoclasm became an official policy of the establishment (Aston 1988: 227). Using arguments formerly associated with heresy (such as Lollardry), officers of the parish were ordered to take down images from their churches. At the same time, each parish was also ordered to purchase a complete Bible in English, further emphasizing the exchange of "books for images." In a direct attack on the importance of medieval seeing, the stated goal of Reformation iconoclasm was to rid people's minds of the old ways—"so that there remain no memory of the same" (*Injunctions of 1559* XXIII). As James Simpson writes, "the official programmes of iconoclasm between 1536 and 1550 seek to distance the past from the present as rapidly and decisively as possible either by demolishing the medieval, or, more, enduringly perhaps, by creating the very concept of the medieval as a site of ruin" (2010: 11). In the English Reformation, the experience of the Eucharist was altered in an attempt to elevate the word. Anything that produced the experience of sight, smell, touch, and sound was to be removed or destroyed. Early modern and modernist English and Irish authors—Catholic, Protestant, or heretical—who wanted to navigate issues of book, body, language, and scripture necessarily created their literary depictions of sacred space through this lens of creation and destruction.

The Reformation began with a determination to eradicate old ideas of sacred space—what Calvin regarded as Catholic superstitious fantasies of God's "local presence." This scorn for icons and images, shrines and sanctuaries, is what Christopher Haigh labels a broader Protestant attack on "Catholic symbolism and the sacralization of physical things" (qtd. in McCoy 2002: 2). Nevertheless, as Richard C. McCoy writes, "even Protestants remained reluctant to dislocate the sacred entirely from ecclesiastical and worldly institutions. Notions of a real presence proved hard to detach from a God who made himself incarnate, and traces of that belief persisted in the liturgy of the English Church" (2002: 29). Without rehearsing the whole soap-opera narrative of the English sixteenth century, it is worth reminding ourselves that just a few years later, under the Catholic Queen Mary, official iconoclastic efforts were halted and the old heresy laws were back in place, churches restocked their supply of devotional objects, and control was exerted upon the practice of reading and interpreting the Bible for oneself. And shortly thereafter, under Queen Elizabeth, it had become clear that some sort of Protestantism would be resuming. This process involved re-examining and redesigning all of the religious legislation of the previous three reigns. As Peter Marshall writes in his extensive history of the English Reformation, "England was unique in its sequence of dramatic swings of official policy, taking place over the course of a relatively short span of years" (2018: xiii).

My larger question here is to think about ways that this bewildering back and forth of change and counter-change perhaps left a permanent mark on the English literary imagination. If, from one ruler to the next, the practices surrounding the Bible, the Mass, holy relics, shrines, and pilgrimages could change so radically, then how were laypeople, clergy, artists, and writers supposed to imagine their religious role? Although there has been much speculation that these quick shifts in ideas of expressing the sacred would have been confusing to the majority of people, as Marshall argues, the opposite could have very well been true:

> A constantly changing diet of religious proclamations, injunctions, articles, catechisms, liturgies, homilies, iconoclastic spectacles and rearrangements of church interiors had the cumulative effect, to a hitherto unprecedented degree, of informing and educating English people about contested religious and doctrinal issues.
>
> (2018: xiv)

Marshall goes on to describe the English Reformation in ways that change the ground on which art and literature are created:

For the first time in securely documented history, everyone in England became acutely aware that the most important questions of human existence were capable of demanding divergent—indeed mutually incompatible—answers.

(2018: xiv)

As the role of reading the Bible, or gazing at stained glass, changed, as the source of the power was destabilized, this aesthetic ideology worked its way into poetry, music, and art. Although English writers at the time, such as Shakespeare and Spenser, did not explicitly ask these questions in their works, they were written, as Stephen Greenblatt writes, "in the shadow of these controversies" (2000: 15). When later thinkers and writers, like Joyce, look back to these literary figures, they often reframed and restated the poetics of instability and ambiguity that surrounded Reformation religion and authority.

Part VI: New World Heresy: Joseph Smith and the Book of Mormon

Post-Reformation "heresy" is harder to define. As nation-states developed and as Protestant denominations multiplied and traveled to the so-called New World, it was harder to clarify an orthodoxy from which to officially deviate. Yet debates and contradictions around ideas of the Trinity, authority and intention, biblical interpretation, and body and spirit continue to occupy Western thinkers and writers, inside and outside of confessional Christian positions. There were, however, still radical new Christian movements in England, Ireland, and the United States that were often treated as heretical, such as forms of spiritualism, Unitarianism, theosophy, and the Church of Christ Scientist. Perhaps most radical, though, and interesting is Joseph Smith, his Church of Latter-Day Saints, and the Book of Mormon—a new work of scripture that builds on ancient and early modern literature, Freemasonry, the King James Bible, fantasy fiction, and New World freedom and energy. Smith and Mormonism were not unique in their nineteenth-century American approach to creating new strands of religion. In his classic work on American Christianity, Nathan Hatch describes these new religious movements as sharing a "passion for expansion [and] a hostility to orthodox belief" (1991: 4). Like early Christians, many of these American Christians felt the Second Coming was imminent and that they needed to prepare: they were living in a final age. Coming largely from non-elite lower classes, these movements tended to downplay doctrine and formal learning.

Yet, where Smith's creation is unique is that it both fits these descriptions, but also presented a whole new set of scriptures and a new holy book.

Most non-Mormons and many Mormons do not really know the contents of the Book of Mormon, and many of Mormonism's most heretical departures from doctrine come in revelations Smith gave *after* writing the book, which creates a type of borderless scripture. Perhaps most significantly for the debates we have been tracing in this chapter is the belief that God the Father has a "body of flesh and bones as tangible as man's" (Doctrine & Covenants 130: 22), and even more radically that God "himself was once as we are now" and that "If you were to see him today, you would see him like a man in form" (King Follett Sermon). The Mormon God is not, therefore, anything close to an unchanging eternal creator, or an ineffable being-beyond-being, which disrupts the entire relationship of Father to Son, of creator to created, of the idea of the human, and of the concept of time. For Smith, matter seems to be eternal, and so creation is not the orthodox *ex nihilo*, but is more of an organization of existing material by God—order out of chaos, or, as Joyce said of his own creative process, more of a "scissors and paste job" (*L1* 297). The God of the Book of Mormon is, indeed, more like the "arranger" in *Ulysses* than the voice in Genesis.

Supposedly written and buried over 1,500 years ago, and then dug from the ground in the form of Golden Tablets, the Book of Mormon is difficult to describe in tandem with other books. Smith biographer Fawn Brodie saw the Book of Mormon as "one of the earliest examples of frontier fiction, the first long Yankee narrative that owes nothing to English literary fashions" ([1945]1995: 67). MacCulloch compares its narrative to other nineteenth-century "lost race" novels and even cites J.R.R. Tolkien's *Lord of the Rings* as a Catholic English parallel (2011: 907). The story of the Book of Mormon—like the Gnostic Nag Hammadi texts that would surface a century later—is a story of both ancient origins and modern mishaps; for example, Smith claimed his first 116 pages of transcription were lost never to be recovered, but he continued to translate the remaining plates. Eventually the book was published, and its first edition was a run of 5,000 copies, 588 pages in length, and written in a sort-of folksy King James English. The complicated stories within the book borrow from, copy, imitate, and deviate from biblical sources. It features family feuds, magic, good versus evil, and mythic migrations. Most significantly, in the end, is its importing of Judeo-Christian history to the Americas as it claims a post-resurrection Christ comes to establish his true church in the Americas. The Book of Mormon—which, depending on who you ask, can be either an ancient text or a nineteenth-century publication—provides a material and textual portal into the discussion of literature, books, and heresy that have occupied this whole chapter. Its blurred origins are both contemporary—Joseph Smith's imagination, a lost manuscript, a still-standing printing shop in upstate New York—and written into the text itself: a scripture in which characters copy, quote, plagiarize, lose, edit, and conceal stories and writings. The ambiguities of origin and authority are embedded within its very meaning. To read the Book of Mormon is to be constantly challenged in locating the source of narrators and narration. One needs to learn to separate the important *character* of Nephi, for example, from the *voice* of Nephi the narrator or memoirist. There are mid-narrative out-of-time interruptions that inform you that what you were reading was not exactly what you thought it was. And new narrators are dropped into the text without introduction or transition. Writing, remembering, storytelling, and books—written, copied, and lost—are very much a part of the fabric of the book. These modernist-sounding devices have rarely been written about in this way, but in a concluding epilogue, I will juxtapose these overlapping ideas of understanding scripture, modernism, *Finnegans Wake*, and the Book of Mormon into a conversation about the role of time, history, heresy, and our current ideas of the importance of books and reading.

* * *

Not long ago, as Bart Ehrman writes, the terms "orthodoxy" and "heresy" "were not problematic terms and the relationship between them was uncomplicated" (2003: 163). Today, however, words and concepts like heresy and orthodoxy are fluid, complex, and contested terms, and in a modern world organized through networks, and characterized by its attention to multiplicity and subjectivity, these terms are not so clearly demarcated. They are, however, still powerful ideas that matter. And as much as we try to define or domesticate these ideas—or try to confine them to the past—they continue to assert their current importance. While these are questions debated by historians and theologians, it is often within writing and literature—from Blake to Joyce, from Hegel to Derrida—where these old questions, the formative questions of early Christianity, will continue to be reopened in multiple contexts. The arguments over the nature of Christ, the Real Presence of the Host, and the idolatry of images might seem to only matter in the hallways of a theological seminary, but they resurface in the puns of James Joyce, the creative heresy of Joseph Smith, the vampires of modern literature, and the practices of scholarship, which continue to help us think through the issues of creation, life, death, and decay that define our existence.

3

Reversals of History: From Gnostic Heretics to James Joyce and Back Again

"Valentine spurning Christ's terrene body"

(*U* 1.658–9)

Part I: Shifting Sands and Sacred Time

One of the most familiar scenes in *Finnegans Wake* (1.5) describes a hen, "Belinda of the Dorans," digging up a manuscript, or a "goodish-sized sheet of letterpaper," from a pile of garbage (*FW* 111.8–9). Although, at the level of plot, the manuscript is a personal letter proclaiming the innocence of the fallen father/husband, HCE, and, more symbolically, is a synecdoche for the entire book, it is *also* described as a kind of scripture. The letter itself is referred to as a "polyhedron of scripture" (*FW* 107.8), or a sacred text with more sides than a flat sheet of parchment. The first lines of the chapter call attention to the scriptural nature of the document by opening with a prayer that blends together phrases and speech rhythms from Christian, Islamic, and Hindu traditions:

> In the name of Annah the Allmaziful, the Everliving, the Bringer of Plurabilities, haloed be her eve, her singtime sung, her rill be run, unhemmed as it is uneven
> (*FW* 104.1–3)

The letter, as a written text within a written text about written texts, is a major leitmotif throughout the whole book, with a complete version only appearing near the end of the book (*FW* 615–19). As Clive Hart points out, this final version of the letter begins with the word "Reverend," which in Irish dialect sounds almost exactly like "riverrun" (the first word of the *Wake*), and then by touching on many of the major themes of *Finnegans Wake*, the letter, "quickly comes to stand for the book itself" (1962: 200). While standing in for the book itself is the most identified characteristic of the letter, it also suggests the importance of the postal service in the novel—and therefore the plurality of traveling objects and ideas in the *Wake*. We gradually learn that it has been written by the wife Anna Livia (ALP) in defense of her accused husband (HCE), and the hen herself represents another version of Anna Livia, the dutiful wife scratching out her letter to redeem her fallen man. For Margot Norris, the retrieval of the letter to save HCE is a sacrificial and redemptive act that resonates with both Christ and Joyce's writing of the *Wake* itself (1976: 68). Yet, as she also says, like the *Wake* and like most scripture, ultimately the letter is "not a document that clarifies anything" (1976: 80).

I will revisit the significance of reading this passage *as* scripture in the Epilogue, but here I am more concerned with the effect of a sudden discovery—the intervention of one formative text onto another—and in how the materiality of the pages on which words are written can literally change narratives of history. The meaning of this specific letter in *Finnegans Wake* is confusing because it has been damaged and buried, its origins are indefinite, and, as much of the passage goes on to demonstrate, the critical questions asked of it seem to concern not the text or its meanings, but its compromised sources and material appearance. Through a quasi-lecture given by a professorial narrator, we learn about the hen that uncovered the letter, we get a description of the envelope and details—such as a tea stain upon the letter—and speculation about the conditions under which it was written. Yet, lost in these details, we barely get a sense of what the letter says. The narrator points to "scholars" of the letter who note that it has been "pierced butnot punctured (in the university sense of the term) by numerous stabs and foliated gashes made by a pronged instrument" (*FW* 124.1–3), but no one seems to actually prioritize the words on the page. As one of the first published guides to the *Wake* explains:

> The original letter proliferates into a banyan of footnotes, scholarly comments, explanations by a presumed original author, psychological analyses, Marxian commentary, and palimpsest research, until at last we have under our eye, not a scrap of letter, but a magnificent ferment of personages, places, and ideas.
>
> (Campbell and Robinson 1944: 98)

Critics often comment ironically on the text's implicit mockery of many current strands of Joyce scholarship. As we dig through Joyce's letters, notebooks, and drafts, noting the traces of pencil smudges and the color of the crayon markings, are we not the very type of critics that this section mocks? Or, conversely, is Joyce telling us that we *should* pay attention to every visual detail, that true reading means, as Joyce scholar Colleen Jaurretche writes, that "the task of the reader is to discern meaning, however obscurely, from the range of handwriting and scratches" (2015: 80–1). It does seem important to note that the hen did not just read, but "looked ad literature" (*FW* 112.27), a phrase that emphasizes the importance of the visual. Although in this chapter, I will be comparing this scene to the discovery of the Gnostic texts in the deserts of Egypt in 1945, and, in the Epilogue, to the Golden Tablets Joseph Smith claimed to have unearthed in upstate New York, Joyce's own inspiration here was the re-discovery of the Irish Book of Kells from under the sod after its theft in 1007. Throughout his description of the letter, Joyce constantly borrows from and parodies Edward Sullivan's *The Book of Kells*, a book which Joyce owned and often traveled with.

But the implied meanings go deeper than Joycean scholars' obsession over the hand-written *Wake* Notebooks or Sullivan's attention to "creeping undulations of serpentine forms" in the Book of Kells ([1920] 1993: 1). If we see the letter as a type of scripture—and, as Jaurretche notes, the very words "scribe, scripture, and scriptorium derive from the root for scratch, cut, pluck, gather, and dig" (2015: 84)—then this passage can also be seen as a comment on the whole enterprise of Christian historiography and textual exegesis, particularly around twentieth-century reconsiderations of Gnosticism and the discovery of long-lost scriptures. Joyce's implicit critique of an overemphasis on the origin of the letter echoes Karen King, a well-known scholar of early Christianity, who writes, we "have been mistakenly preoccupied with determining [Gnosticism's] origin and tracing its genealogical relation to orthodox Christianity" (2003: 52). This assumption, of being able to reconstruct origins out of what we know or what has survived, takes away the text's ability to present something new in order to change our preconceptions. What *Finnegans Wake*, and its hen, taps into are the complexities—philosophical, theological, and historical—that result from the discovery of a sacred text that forces us to reframe and re-historicize an existing sacred and scriptural tradition. The early twentieth century often saw these clashes of material evidence versus history. Even as original Gnostic documents started to emerge in the nineteenth century, Christian historians often refused to trust them because they did not seem to match the long-accepted version of history (Ehrman 2003: 121). What King and other scholars have recently reacted to is the tendency to re-bury the radically revisionist nature of historical and textual discoveries under a mound of peripheral detail.

Until the late-nineteenth and early-twentieth centuries we had very little of the actual writing of the Gnostics themselves, and our only sources of information were from the orthodox church fathers who condemned them. In addition to Irenaeus' encyclopedic work *Against Heresies* from the second century, we have writings by Tertullian and Hippolytus' lesser-known *Refutation of All Heresies* (itself just discovered in the nineteenth century), all of which summarize, paraphrase, or quote Gnostic writings. The engagement with Gnosticism in these sorts of works helped construct the basic architecture of what would become orthodox Christianity for centuries. It was Irenaeus's instructions about which writings to keep and which to destroy, and how those kept should be read, that helped lay the structure for the as-of-yet non-existent Christian Bible. The various strands of Gnosticism, as the previous chapter outlined, held multiple beliefs and myths: that matter is evil, that the Hebrew God and Hebrew scriptures are not connected to Christianity, that salvation is attained more through knowledge than faith, and that the creator of the universe was an inferior god. Joyce also often points to this flawed creator, and *Finnegans Wake* even makes the Gnostic move of locating the source of original sin in the Judeo-Christian God: "Ouhr Former who erred" (*FW* 530.36, 531.1). In Joyce's time, Gnosticism was often also strongly connected to emerging ideas of theosophy. Joyce himself seems most familiar with the Gnostic repulsion to matter and the body as indicated by his terse characterization of the most famous Gnostic heresiarch in *Ulysses*: "Valentine, spurning Christ's terrene body" (*U* 17.658–9). As the previous chapter emphasized, heresies are, in a large part, literary and textual schisms, and Gnosticism, in all its complexities and variations—with its arguments over how to read, write, interpret, and define scripture—is an obvious beginning. Thinking about Gnosticism through the lens of *Ulysses* and *Finnegans Wake* can illuminate how remnants of these early Christian theological and literary tensions still exist today, buried not only within our theologies, but within our imaginative literature and its words, genres, and interpretations.

My goal in this chapter is to demonstrate that many of the central questions of early Christian debates and their later historical accounts are the same questions with which today's Joyce readers grapple: What is a book? What is an author? What is writing? And how do we talk about the relationships between them? This linking is strengthened by recent revisionary works in religious history that have emphasized the importance of these types of questions in understanding how writing functioned in the early centuries of Christianity. Christian historian Matthew Larsen could just as well be speaking about the world of contemporary literary scholarship when he writes "in order to understand how to think about texts before the book, before authors, before publication ... we need to understand the unfinished texts, textual raw material, accidental publication, postpublication revision, multiple versions of the same work" (2018: 7). Christine van Boheemen-Saaf similarly describes current Joyce scholars who "study the text in the context of the avant-texte, the drafts, notebooks, proofs etc., not as a stable material object, but as an ideal construction of a process of creative production" (1999: 35). It is a tension in genetic criticism—of ancient and modern texts—to conduct a scientifically based analysis, but to avoid a stance of scientific positivism. As Tim Conley writes of genetic Joyce criticism, "Fixing a text—in the double sense of restoring and stabilising it—is the editorial mandate, not in and of itself the impetus for genetic research" (2018: 12). Genetic critics, like Joyce's reader of the unearthed letter, call "attention to errors, omissions, repetitions and misalignments" (*FW* 120.15–6) and are careful not to "concentrate solely on the literal sense ... to the sore neglect of the enveloping facts themselves circumstantiating it" (*FW* 109.12–4). The dissemination of history in the *Wake*—gossip, misreadings, damaged documents, and insults— echoes the historiography of Gnosticism. The Gnostic documents themselves are a study in how we are never given a complete picture, and reading them is a process of navigating gaps and fissures in ways that are similar to what modernists and their critics were exploring in the first half of the twentieth century.

Modernism, it is important to remember, is more than a movement in the arts, and to think about the "modernist imagination" is to also look to how the word was used to describe new ideas in theology as well. In ways often not discussed, these theological ideas and debates have a close relationship to movements in art and literature. Finn Fordham has shown that the so-called "modernist controversy" within the Catholic Church was anything but a marginal phenomenon in the public sphere:

> Between 1907 and 1930 there were over 350 references to the term in *The Times*: ninety per cent of these refer to the theological context of modernism; the remainder feature in articles on architecture, music, or literature. The word 'modernism' in this period could hardly be used without some echo of this other [theological] sense.
>
> (2013: 12–13)

Fordham points out that the Church's very labelling of a diverse set of intellectuals and groups as "modernist—attributing to them a 'synthesis of all heresies'"—was part of a strategy of containment (2013: 11). It is in challenging this idea of "containment" that we find overlap between Joyce's work, archeology, and new interpretations of Christian history in the early years of the twentieth century. What we understand as Gnosticism is very literally, as we shall see, a twentieth-century phenomenon, as new scholarship, philosophy, literature, and archeological discoveries in the past 100 years changed forever what we thought of the Gnostics, and the heresies and orthodoxies that surrounded them. These shifts happen on two different intellectual fronts: on the one hand, twentieth-century ideas and discoveries rewrite the history of second-century Christianity, while, on the other hand, 2,000-year-old arguments about reading and writing get reframed and reiterated in the texts and ideas of the twentieth century. In the first half of the twentieth century, poets and novelists, scholars with new tools and materials, practitioners of esoteric religions, and existential philosophers created new combinations of experimental approaches to religion and the narrative of history that shaped a modernist model of Gnosticism—a modernist model that in many ways sets the intellectual stage for understanding the paradigm shifting archeological discoveries to come later in the century.

Gnosticism therefore—that most ancient, mysterious, and misrepresented of Christian heresies—becomes a twentieth-century, post-Great War, post-Joycean meditation on history and narrative in ways that resemble and parallel experimental modernist texts such as *Ulysses* and *Finnegans Wake*. Woven in and around these works of modernist literature were the ideas of influential figures like existentialist philosopher Hans Jonas, who wrote in the 1930s that Gnosticism was a "better parallel" to the contemporary human condition than orthodox Judeo-Christian thought, or Carl Jung, who would see Gnostic thought as a representation of the other side of the mind—a model of the repressed thoughts that emerge from any enforced orthodoxy. Finally, and most fantastically, in 1945, a discovery in an Egyptian desert—and a narrative worthy of Indiana Jones, complete with blood feuds, murders, underground criminals, and shady antiquity dealers—would gradually bring many more actual Gnostic texts to scholars, and then to the general public, ultimately opening up radical new ways of reading scripture and history.

James Joyce, and the literature he created, may not have been consciously offering comment on these issues, but they were embedded in many of the same intellectual and literary trends and debates. Religion for Joyce, as Roy Gottfried writes, is "an intellectual problem, a challenge to all orders of epistemology, history, and culture" (2008: 5), and in this chapter I will take up that challenge in a series of speculative gestures combined with some closer reading of texts: Gnostic, scholarly, and Joycean. I will focus on the paradoxes of understanding the twentieth-century entrance of the Gnostic texts as simultaneously a kind of

Joycean modernist project—a meta-text in a matrix of eccentric discoveries—and a portrait of the original theological chaos of early Christianity. While a traditional history of heresy might begin in the second century of the Common Era, it also, as we shall see, begins in 1904 in Dublin, 1922 in Trieste, 1934 in Germany, and 1945 in the deserts of Egypt, where authentic Gnostic texts emerged from the sands like a letter dug from a dung heap by a hen.

Buried Scripture

The known facts of the discovery of the Gnostic writings of Nag Hammadi are that the texts were accidently dug up by Bedouin field hands in Upper Egypt in 1945. The actual details of the finding, obscured by gossip, exaggeration, contradictory versions, black market sales, and competitive collectors, and told more than thirty years later by the discoverer, Muhammad Ali, are, in some ways, more fantastic than the legend. Or perhaps, in true biblical and Joycean fashion, history and myth are inextricably blended together. The story, now told in many books, is that a fellaheen, named Muhammad Ali, and his brothers were digging in the desert and uncovered a large earthenware jar containing thirteen leather-bound papyrus books. Some time later, after their mother burned some of the books as kindling and after they avenged their father's death in a blood feud, the brothers, fearing that the forthcoming murder investigation might uncover what they suspected were valuable books, gave them to a local religious leader for safekeeping. This began a ten-year period when the books were separated, sold on the black market, survived the air raids and bombings of 1948, went through multiple court injunctions and trials, were acquired by the Egyptian government and the Coptic Museum in Cairo, smuggled out of Egypt and sold in America, and purchased by the Jung foundation in Zurich. It was not until after 1955, when a professor of religious history translated a line of one of the texts and identified it as the same as a fragment of the *Gospel of Thomas* that had been discovered in a trash dump in the 1890s, that scholars began to realize that they had a collection of Gnostic writings long-thought to have been lost forever. In other words, in the twentieth century, the heretical gospels were prevented from being read for many of the same reasons that they were initially buried, both figuratively and literally.

After Nag Hammadi, because most of what scholars knew of these early alternative forms of Christianity came from the orthodox attacks on them, not surprisingly, reading the actual words of the Gnostics themselves changed the picture considerably. As Elaine Pagels wrote in the introduction to her popular

The Gnostic Gospels, we now "recognize that early Christianity is far more diverse than nearly anyone expected before the Nag Hammadi discoveries" (1979: xxii). Although these "secret Gospels" continue to be romanticized in contemporary fiction, the texts and details of their discovery are familiar and easily available to religious scholars and to anyone interested in Christian history. Yet this persistent blend of myth, mystery, and reality that is found within the texts as well as in the story of their discovery and in their afterlives continues to suggest speculative questions: If our scripture is so formative to our imaginative literature, what happens to the literary imagination when we dig new ancient scriptures from the ground? What do these recovered lost words have to tell us about how we remember, how we read, and how written works shape our imagination? My main point is that the first half of the twentieth century—encompassing James Joyce, Catholic modernism, theosophical societies, world wars, Christian historians, and existential philosophers—helped shape our imagination to pose more radical answers to these questions that became fully possible after Nag Hammadi. Subsequently, the Nag Hammadi findings, and the new more plural ways of reading scriptural and historical texts that they encouraged, allowed us to reimagine not only the second century but the twentieth century in radically new ways. Joyce's rethinking of religion and religious history in *Ulysses* and *Finnegans Wake*—formed by these new religious ideas—finds material and philosophical justification in the later decades of the twentieth century. For Pagels, the Nag Hammadi sources "challenge us to reinterpret history—and to re-evaluate the present situation" (1979: 69). Not only do these evolving Gnostic ideas embody the romantic and appealing notion of Jung's that they represent the unconscious and repressed thoughts buried deep within orthodox belief, but they open up these repressed heterodoxies in secular forms of modern literature as well.

* * *

For all they came to represent, the actual material findings at Nag Hammadi were fading, forgotten words written on fragile decaying material that only survived to be read by twentieth-century eyes through a series of unlikely events. Once introduced to the public, this crumbling material spoke to an audience educated on modernist literature that was often self-consciously about the act of writing itself, about the material it is written on, about the idea of an archive, and—especially post-First World War—about the fragility of structures and civilizations. From the abandoned and forgotten future libraries and museums in H.G. Wells's *Time Machine*, to the letter in *Finnegans Wake*, to Proust's expansive novel of forgetting and partial memory, these works ponder a world where texts and books have decayed and no longer tell their stories.

While different kinds of actual writing are found within *Ulysses*, perhaps the most transitory is found in chapter 13 ("Nausicaa"), where Leopold Bloom is spending a late afternoon on the same beach where Stephen Dedalus has earlier in the day (chapter 3) walked and thought, written a small poem, left his snot on a rock, and mused on the lasting nature of poetry, and perhaps nasal mucus. In the first half of chapter 13, the main action is Bloom masturbating on the beach while observing a young woman. The whole scene is interspersed with descriptions of the sounds of a temperance Mass in the background and the wafting fragrance of incense in the air. While the first half is told mostly through the eyes and language of the young woman, the second half of the chapter is Bloom's long, post-orgasmic internal monologue in wandering sleepy prose that asks, among other somnolent questions, if fish ever get seasick. At the end of the chapter, Bloom's thoughts return to the young woman on the beach and he wonders if "she will come here tomorrow?" and if he should leave her a message on the beach (*U* 13.1253–4). Thinking that the words "might remain" long enough for her to read them when she returns, he writes in the sand with a stick:

I. AM. A.

He then changes his mind, thinking, "let it go," and "effaced the letters with his slow boot" (*U* 13.1258–66). While this scene of desire, writing, and erasure certainly echoes Stephen's thoughts and writing earlier in the day at the same place, it has another, more biblical echo.

The canonical New Testament offers only one scene in which Jesus seems to write his own words. In the Book of John, when Jesus is asked if a woman caught in adultery should be stoned, before answering, he bends down and "wrote upon the ground with his finger" (John 8:6). When he is questioned again, he gives his famous answer, "Let whosoever among you is without sin be the first to cast a stone." Later in the same chapter, Jesus refers to himself as "I AM," which is an echo of God's self-identifying words to Moses out of the burning bush in Exodus: "I am who I am." We don't know what Jesus actually wrote on the ground here, just like we do not know what Bloom is *going* to write. Jesus's words, like those of Bloom and Stephen (and Joyce), ultimately disappear. Despite the Joyce scholars in Dublin, London, and upstate New York poring over notebooks and drafts, or museum preservationists carefully restoring, protecting, and digitizing ancient papyrus scraps of scripture, the sands of time will literally wipe away all words,

Gnostic and modernist. Paper breaks down, libraries catch fire, and civilizations collapse.

But what happens when words and stories that we thought were lost forever are found again? Whether we are talking about the Golden Tablets of Mormonism that Joseph Smith described digging from a hill in upstate New York, or the Gnostic texts of Nag Hammadi in Egypt, these "events" are never as immediately absolute or paradigm-shifting as we might imagine them; the effects are more gradual and are buried within changing reading practices. But in each case, like the letter that the hen digs from the pile in *Finnegans Wake*, "letters have never been quite their old selves again since" (*FW* 112.24–5). The Nag Hammadi texts act as a model for how histories, texts, stories, myths, and documents are passed on, lost, found, misread, altered, misdirected, and disseminated in ways that apply to *Finnegans Wake* and *Ulysses* as much as they do to Christian apocrypha. These discoveries—Joycean, Gnostic, and Mormon—challenge our linear teleological ideas of history, scripture, books, and writing.[1] Each text in their own way turns around what we thought was the past, how we talk about it, and its relationship to the words they are written with and the materials that they are written on. These texts implicitly invite us to think about what was, what might have been, and what will be when we and they are not.

From Gnostic to "Gnawstick": Joyce and Gnosticism, 1904–39

This section will look at two of Joyce's uses of the word "Gnostic" that frame a period from 1904 to 1939, a period of time when scholarly and artistic understandings and expressions of alternative religions (new and ancient) grew enormously. Although seldom looked at together, this period saw what is generally regarded as the main "high modernist" works of Western literature and art; it was the period of "modernism" in theology; and was a period of archeological discovery about the ancient Middle East. In 1904, the year that Joyce set *Ulysses*, an archeological discovery of an ostracon (writing upon a shard of pottery) from the sixth or seventh century was published. The writing identifies Peter as one of the "Evangelists" and urges Christians to read his Gospel (Ehrman 2003: 24–5). The Gospel of Peter had been known of before,

---

1 These sorts of discoveries will, of course, continue to happen in both the worlds of Christian history and Joycean scholarship. For example, in the Introduction to *How Joyce Wrote Finnegans Wake*, the editors write "the announcement by the National Library of Ireland in March 2006 of previously unknown drafts of several sketches changes our understanding of the earliest genesis of *Finnegans Wake*" (2007: 19).

but this material evidence was only first discovered in an Egyptian tomb in 1886. This almost-forgotten piece of writing is an early account of what would be a century-long journey revealing that years after there was an established and canonical "New Testament," early Christians were still reading alternative gospels. By 1904, the material evidence for this interpretation was beginning to become too obvious to ignore; the strict canonical borders around the "Holy Bible" were beginning to loosen.

Also around 1904, Joyce first uses the word "Gnostic" in his fiction. Despite his interest in all things heretical, Joyce rarely used this term. This first example is found in a fragment of his unfinished and abandoned autobiographical novel, *Stephen Hero*. The history of *Stephen Hero* itself, written in 1903–5, partially destroyed by fire and posthumously published in 1944, is a bit like the Nag Hammadi codices dug out of the desert and then used as kindling. In practice, too, *Stephen Hero* plays the role of a Gnostic gospel: mostly unread, missing large sections of text, serving as the inferior "other" to the "canonical" *Portrait of the Artist*, and yet challenging our interpretation of the more well-known version. In *Stephen Hero*, Stephen talks with a friend about Holy Week services: "Do you know what kind of figure rises before me on Good Friday? … Something between Socrates and a Gnostic Christ" (*SH* 117). This statement seems intended to ring with youthful pretension, but it is not clear what Joyce or his readers would have understood by the phrase "Gnostic Christ." Theologically, a "Gnostic Christ" might be understood as a figure more divine than human, more spiritual than material, although Stephen also describes him as "an ugly little man who has taken into his body the sins of the world" (*SH* 116–117). The Acts of John, one of the few Gnostic texts known in Joyce's time, frames Jesus as a totally spiritual being, not human at all, never leaving footprints or blinking his eyes: "his substance was immaterial … as if he did not exist at all" (Acts of John 93). Stephen's phrasing introduces another, perhaps more radical question: What kind of Christ *rises* on Good Friday instead of Easter Sunday? The choice of the word "rising" resets the whole Easter week's crucifixion-to-empty-tomb progression and—in a very Gnostic way—blurs ideas of body and spirit, by placing a resurrection on the day of the death. Perhaps the Gnostic Christ rises while his body is still on the cross. Certainly, from most Gnostic perspectives, the body of Jesus was meaningless once dead, and many Gnostic accounts actually reverse the narrative structure of the New Testament Gospels: instead of a story from birth to death, they begin in the end, with the spiritual Christ appearing to disciples, and often do not bother with stories of the birth.

My second example of Joyce using the word gnostic occurs decades later in the "Shem the Penman" section in *Finnegans Wake*, a chapter filled with insulting allusions to heresies and heretics. The chapter is a series of mostly mocking descriptions of Shem—like Stephen, another semi-autobiographical Joyce figure—by his brother Shaun. Shaun claims that his attempt is to put "truth and untruth together" to see what "this hybrid actually was like to look at" and claims, among other things, that Shem "is a gnawstick" (*FW* 170.11). One could question whether Joyce meant to make any sort of deep philosophical point, and, as a recent book states, "the more one seeks to unravel and unpack the nuance of Shaun's bitter diatribe, the harder it becomes to understand the precise nature of Shem's alleged heresy" (Van Mierlo 2017: 55). Nonetheless, the word "gnawstick," like the word "risen" in *Stephen Hero*, is particularly suggestive, and is the kind of word that can trigger an hour-long discussion in a *Wake* reading group. A "gnawstick," while obviously meant to signify "Gnostic," could also be read as phallic, as a writing instrument, a weapon, an Islamic *miswak*, or an infant pacifier; it is heretical, sexual, religious, productive, creative, aggressive, and calming all at the same time. One reading of these two passages could see that a "Gnostic Christ" and a "gnawstick" are exact opposites; "Gnostic" suggests pure spirit or pure knowledge, and "gnawstick," just by changing the spelling, signifies materiality (literally a stick that is felt, chewed, and tasted). Between these two spellings is an opposition of mind/body and spiritual/material that the Gnostics themselves found in the figure of Jesus Christ and that framed much of the early debates over Christian orthodoxy and even between canonical Gospels (in Matthew, Jesus physically suffers; in Luke, much less). Joyce's word "gnawstick" contains, within its multiple meanings, the same tensions that the Gnostics found in Jesus Christ himself and that would occupy Christian theology (heretical and orthodox) for millennia.

It was the Gnostic emphasis on the non-material in Christ that many proto-orthodox Christians found threatening. Some Gnostics even claimed that Jesus only *appeared* to be a part of this world, only appeared to be material—"in the *likeness* of sinful flesh," as Paul says in Romans (8:3). Other Gnostics proposed other solutions, for example that "Christ" as a divine emissary of total spirit came down to "enter" the material man, Jesus. For many of these early Christians, the divine "Christ" entered the flesh and blood of the human Jesus at his baptism, stayed with him throughout his life, enabling him to perform miracles, and then ascended to heaven from the cross, essentially leaving Jesus and his body behind to die a simple human death. In *Against Heresies*, Irenaeus cites a Gnostic myth that told how once Jesus had died, the Christ returned to raise him (Jesus) from the dead (1.30.13). This idea also seems to be expressed in the Gospel of Peter, where the description of the crucifixion says that Jesus "was silent as having no pain" (Gos. Pet. v.10). At the moment of his death, his cry in the Gospel of Peter is not the famous and theologically provocative "*Eloi, Eloi, lama sabachthani?*" or "My God, my God, why hast thou forsaken me?" (Mark 15:34), but is instead "My power, O power, you have forsaken me" (Gos. Pet. v.19), which could certainly suggest a departure of a divine Christ from the human Jesus. This interpretation and this gospel were perhaps not originally as marginal as they may now seem. Bart Ehrman suggests that there is evidence, based on surviving second- and third-century texts, that the Gospel of Peter was perhaps more popular in early Christianity than the Gospel of Mark (2003: 23). These ideas were starting to emerge in the years Joyce was writing: in his personal library—now preserved at the University of Buffalo—was a 1923 edition of *New Testament Apocryphal Writings*, which included the newly discovered Gospel of Peter. Although Joyce's personal copy contains no specific evidence of his reading, and while it was probably a gift, it does demonstrate that these ideas were starting to circulate. The book's editor, James Orr, remarks upon Peter's version of the resurrections that "the Gnostic stamp of the Gospel is already apparent in such descriptions" (1923: xxi), a comment that, while it is meant to be dismissive, also demonstrates a historical awareness of non-canonical gospels that was starting to enter the public imagination.

This "gnostic stamp" and its alternative interpretations that were beginning to enter the modernist imaginations play a part in offering multiple answers to the question: "What happened on the cross?"—a theological question that echoes across heresies, and through imaginative writers from Milton to Joyce. For example, Jesus's words "why have you forsaken me?"—or, as it has been translated by Ehrman "why have you left me behind?"—can be explained as the flesh-and-blood Jesus calling out to the spiritual (Gnostic) Christ, who has abandoned him (2003: 125). Seen this way, the crucifixion then truly becomes, as Joyce puns in *Finnegans Wake*, a "cruelfiction" (*FW* 192.19). In conflating the crucifixion with a "cruelfiction," Joyce gives us a scenario in which the received narratives of the crucifixion are both false and necessary, both biblical and literary. As Stephen claims at the end of *Portrait*, it is a story not to be believed in nor disbelieved, and these are not doubts we should strive to overcome (*P* 260). These scriptural stories and images may be fiction, or symbolic, as some Gnostic Christians thought, but we are nonetheless, as Joyce suggests in *Finnegans Wake*, still bound to them. This core of this idea can also be found within Gnostic texts, as in, for example, the Gospel of Truth where the crucifixion is represented not as a sacrifice, but as a space for discovering a divine self or spark within: "He was nailed to a tree, and he became fruit of the knowledge of the Father, which ... caused those who ate of it to come into being" (18: 24–41).

By the time readers came upon the word "gnawstick" in the newly published *Finnegans Wake* in 1939, still six years and another World War before the discoveries in Nag Hammadi, Gnosticism was beginning to be understood differently. Joyce's "Gnostic Christ" of 1904 and his "gnawstick" (the word first appears in a 1925 draft) demonstrate ways in which we can use Joyce to open up larger questions about this earliest of Christian heresies and the ways in which it is part of how we understand the relationship of religion and literature, scripture and interpretation, history and belief. This Christ of pure mind and spirit has one foot in the Gnostic world of the second century and another in new ways of thinking that emerge in the late-nineteenth and early-twentieth centuries of Nietzsche, George Russell, and Joyce. This modernist Christ is unorthodox and literally heretical, occupying a space in modern branches of thought that extends from the theosophists at the turn of the twentieth century—who found a purely spiritual Christ in their search for hidden knowledge or wisdom from the ancient past—to later radical Christian theologians who find their spirituality precisely in the absence of a stable definition or a transcendent Christ.

Reading and the Book

In the years after the death of Jesus—but before such a thing as a Christian Bible, or *New Testament*, was established—the confusing array of new stories, histories, legends, texts, and scriptures floating around forced early Christians to take a position toward the earlier Hebrew scriptures. When the various strands of this new emerging sect were forced to define themselves in the context of texts and literature, and ultimately through a single coherent text, it opened up multiple questions. It was not clear whether their new Greek or Aramaic language texts (gospels, letters, revelations) could be part of the same scriptural tradition as the older Hebrew ones. Nor was it clear what authors had the right to speak God's words or had the authority to copy, quote, translate, or interpret. Were these new scriptures subject to the same kind of reading as the Jewish ones? Whose version of the Christian stories was definitive? Was it even the same God who had inspired these different sets of texts? All of these questions were formative in developing ideas of scripture and of the book. These first Christian centuries, as Grafton and Williams write, were a "crucial time of transition in the material history of texts in the West," and Christian preference for the new codex over the scroll foundationally changed what a "book" was and the mechanics of "reading" it (2009: 10). The rise of the codex "threw into question existing assumptions regarding the natural relation between the book as material object and as unit of meaning" (2009: 10). The codex could contain more and much longer text than the scroll and therefore functioned like a small library, which offered new possibilities for greater complexity and amalgamation for authors and editors.

The modern era saw changes in the long held theological assumption of the Bible as one coherent and unified book. The influential theologian Hans Frei describes this shift, saying that before the Enlightenment, the Bible was predominantly read as a full narrative that accurately told the complete story of the world from creation to the end of time. For these Christians, the Bible was *the* book, and it contained all of reality told from the point of view of God. In adopting this view, certain assumptions about books bleed into secular reading practices: the book as entire narrative, the omnipotence of the author, and the importance of written language to make sense of one's own lived experiences. By the eighteenth century however, as Frei explains, a "great reversal" had taken place. The Bible was now only one narrative, and interpretation was a "matter of fitting the biblical story into another world with another story" (1980: 99). These other "stories" came from other literature, folk traditions, songs, poetry, enlightenment science, and lived experience.

This kind of framing of a single book as inhabiting plural narratives and interpretations has a parallel existence in contemporary literary theory alongside scriptural exegesis. Since, at least, Jacques Derrida—and building on the centuries of religious debates before him—literary scholars have questioned the idea that books exist as self-enclosed systems of meaning and reference that come from a single and locatable source of authentic and unitary truth. Yet, as Gayatri Spivak writes in her introduction to Derrida's *Of Grammatology*, humankind maintains a "common desire for a stable center," and "a book, with its ponderable shape and its beginning, middle and end, stands to satisfy that desire" (1967: xi). We can see both the texts of Joyce and these new accounts of Christian history as attempts at and failures of totalization, as modernist collages of texts, and as challenges to the unified nature of a single history or a bound novel. *Ulysses* and *Finnegans Wake*, in ways that mirrored the experience of books like the Bible or the Quran, were overflowing with meaning and challenged the desire for just this sort of unified existence. Recent trends in Joyce scholarship that focus on drafts, editions, notebooks, and sources have only expanded this perception of a borderless book. These very modern-seeming definitions can be found in the second century, when debates over what we now see as Gnostic heresy and orthodoxy theology were being waged, and when the idea of a single "book" that could contain *all* the canonical scripture was still centuries away. We constantly read our own modern perceptions and definitions back onto scriptural origins and hermeneutics, so it is important to remember that there is little evidence of readers thinking of any of the orthodox gospels as a stable finished text with an attributable "author" until the end of the second century CE. Only in the third century was a "gospel" widely considered a discreet authored book (Larsen 2018: 1–2). As Matthew Larsen asks in *Gospels before the Book*: "What would it look like to construct a narrative of gospel productions that does not use ideas about stable books, author figures, or publication?" (2018: 3). Or what kind of writing, would be, as literary theorist Juliet Fleming calls it, "writing conceived without the guardrails of the book?" (2016: 2).

The Western concept of a history that is forward-looking or goal-oriented can be traced to early Christian thinkers who "in their defense of the biblical view of creation [were] obliged to take up the question of the meaning of history" (Pelikan 1971: 37). While early Christian writers were familiar with Greek theories of history that often focused on cycles and repetition, it was now necessary for them to identify historical events as unrepeatable and teleological. These early and orthodox views of history as linear and directed are represented by Eusebius and Augustine, both strong voices for Christian orthodoxy and against heresies. Eusebius and Augustine "translated apologetics into history; but the history was not merely the account of the succession of the church from the apostles, but the whole way of the divine providence" (Pelikan 1971: 41). This sense of the historically inevitable is attributed to a history guided by the Holy Spirit and will find its way into narrative structures such as the "providential plots" of eighteenth-century English novels or narrative theories like Frank Kermode's "Sense of an Ending."

According to this Christian mode of narrative, a story had a single author, a single version, and the end is predetermined from the start. These forms of reading and thinking about literature and history will become the tools for reading, writing, and understanding texts from Homer to Dante to Shakespeare, which Joyce then repurposes in *Ulysses* and *Finnegans Wake*. It is Joyce's negotiating and experimenting with the complexities between theology and literature, the mythical and the everyday, that reveal—as Stephen would say—"portals of discovery" (*U* 9.229). *Ulysses* is littered with fragments of remembered or misremembered gospel, references to formal aspects of the Catholic Mass, multiple allusions to heretics and heresies, theological positions, and Trinitarian structures. *Finnegans Wake* even more thoroughly blurs lines between the time and place of the authoritarian voices, as when, for example, versions of the four Gospel writers appear as "four old men" trying unsuccessfully to give definitive statements on various stories and events. Interpreters of Joyce as well must decide how they will read the other voices that come through the text, or the ways in which, as T.S. Eliot wrote in his 1923 essay "*Ulysses*, Order, and Myth," Joyce "manipulated a continuous parallel between contemporaneity and antiquity." Reading or studying Joyce—like reading or studying Gnosticism—is necessarily an act in which texts talk to texts and where the theory of history becomes both a strategy of reading and a result of how we read.

When Karen King reframes modern studies of Gnosticism by saying that "scholars are only gradually coming to realize the inadequacy of older models and methods, and beginning to formulate new approaches," she makes a statement that could also be made about early critics of Joyce, who had to create new models of literary analysis to explain structures and styles they had not seen before (2003: 219). On the other hand, while many recent studies of Joyce turn to hyper-specific activities, such as tracing down source texts or studying early drafts and notebooks, my approach will build on and use such methodologies while *also* looking to the ways Joyce's novels not only demonstrate but theorize the complicated paths through which language and literature create history. King could just as well be talking about the emphasis on sources and archival research in modern literary criticism, rather than studies of ancient Christianity, when she writes "in the development of modern historical scholarship the concerns of ancient discourses with origins, essence, and purity were transformed into disciplinary methodologies" (2003: 219). In each case, scholars have debated the problem of connecting textual meaning too much to authors and origins. We can find these biases toward recognizing undisputed origins in the belief that there existed an untouched Christianity that came directly from the mouth of Jesus before his message was distorted by the heretical Gnostics, but we can also find it in the intense debates over *Ulysses* and what it means to try to create a single edition that nears some imaginary "original" and "true" manuscript that Joyce magically conjured and produced in a single instant. What I am challenging here in the case of historical and textual scholarship is the assumed association between truth and origin, or, when it comes to heresy, the view that truth is always chronologically prior to error.

While these ideas are based on sweeping generalizations of how history works, we can see connections between how Gnosticism and Joyce were woven into the twentieth century. As one Joyce scholar writes, "Source hunting inevitably relies on traditional forms of historical criticism, since the critic … must deal in questions of priority and belatedness, temporal and textual cause and effect, as well as the biographical and cultural conditions that made it possible for one text to 'flow into' another in rhetorically determining ways" (Spoo 1994: 99–100). The same point is made by King, who writes "Chronology in and of itself neither guarantees nor refutes theological truth or superiority" (2003: 229), which critiques the assumption that truth (or, "orthodoxy") is characterized by unity, uniformity, and unanimity—which leads to the view that truth is pure; syncretism is contamination.

What was challenged in the twentieth century—through theology, philosophy, history, archeology, and literature—was a centuries-long way of telling the Christian story. What is important about our knowledge of Gnosticism, especially as it developed in the twentieth century, is not just its "actual" history (whatever that might mean), but that its historiography—the way its story has emerged and been told in the modern era—offers alternative heretical, views to think about how these narratives are disseminated, abused, disrupted, fragmented, and produced. This idea is my connection to Joyce and to works like *Ulysses*—an experiment in form that is most familiarly (and reductively) known as a modernized version of Homer's *Odyssey*—and *Finnegans Wake*, a novel where one time is all time, where scripture blends into the linguistic surface, and where dizzying non-linear explorations of "history" are told through puns, fragments, time travel, and the distorted words of sacred texts. This comparison opens a new model for how to read religious scriptures and literature. There is no model of history more constraining than the orthodox Christian narrative—an absolute beginning leading to a fully scripted end—and the modes of reading that come out of new theories of Gnosticism as well as the novels of Joyce point to how more plural ways of reading change the reality of history in a way that take us out of what Stephen will call a "nightmare."

Part II: A Joycean Reading of Gnosticism

In Joyce's short story "Grace," Tom Kernan falls down the stairs after drinking too much, knocking himself out and badly biting his tongue; the story literally and symbolically opens with both a sinful "fall" and a loss of language. Two days later, Kernan is visited by three friends who have conceived of a plan to help him with his drinking problem by inviting him to a Catholic retreat. Their discussion wanders, but is steered toward religion, and is full of vague claims and historical and theological errors about Church doctrine and Church history. Joyce's story, as Margot Norris writes, evokes precisely these "questions of authoritative language, the Pope's *ex cathedra* pronouncements, powerful sermons and preachings, that the story itself subverts by drawing attention to its potential for error and hypocrisy" (2004: 167). Yet, for the characters in "Grace," and for many of its readers, religious "truth," as they live it, is not defined by the Church or dogma, but by and through these very types of informal conversations. As Gottfried points out, when Joyce has his characters in "Grace" discuss the 1870 declaration of papal infallibility he

> does so not only to show their faulty memories and erroneous assumptions, but also because he saw that decision as representing the essential arbitrariness of authoritative pronouncements on dogma. Joyce surrounds this "history" with error so as to demonstrate the weakness (the fallibility) of any chronicle of ideas and events and thus slyly to undermine the very means by which orthodoxy stakes its claim.
>
> (2008: 3)

Stephen Morrison, as well, notes the importance of the "essential arbitrariness" of doctrinal statements: "The fact that almost none of the facts under discussion are correct only serves to confirm that the conversation is not about historical truth but about Catholic truth, true doctrine as identified by dogmatic utterance" (2000: 42). This blurring of historical, Catholic, and popular versions of truth becomes one of the main stylistic characteristics in *Ulysses* and *Finnegans Wake*, where often the telling becomes the story, a narrative where gossip can equal gospel.

I am not claiming any kind of specific influence, although, as we will see, ideas associated with "Gnosticism" were definitely in the air of early-twentieth-century literary culture and the Dublin intellectual elite, particularly through mystical and esoteric movements such as theosophy, but also in both popular and academic texts of Christian history.[2] The theosophical society was one of the most successful of many esoteric movements at the turn of the century. It was also the source of many later and current occult schools and organizations such as Rudolph Steiner's Anthroposophical Society. The most obvious example of theosophy in Joyce's work is in the descriptions of the wandering, shadowy

---

2 Geert Lernout questions Joyce's interest in theosophy, writing that "it is not at all clear why Joyce at times seems to have retained a measure of interest in what is now no longer taken seriously not even as an alternative to religion" (2010: 92). Yet Lernout here, as elsewhere, is—for my purposes, anyways—defining "religion" too narrowly—emphasizing belief and doctrine over practice. Theosophy, like Gnosticism is, of course, not an "alternative" to religion, it was and still is a religion.

figure of the writer and publisher George Russell (known as AE, a name based on the Gnostic term Aeon) who moves in and out of Joyce's early career and various sections of *Ulysses*, most prominently, as we will see, in the National Library scene of chapter nine. It was in 1904—the year *Ulysses* is set—that Russell reformed and became president of an influential theosophical society in Dublin. Theosophical ideas varied greatly, but in general they looked for a way to connect religions, times, and places on a spiritual realm. Their connections to the ancient Gnosticism lay in their belief in spirit over body and in the need to escape material reality by ascending to a higher reality.

Ulysses and the Nightmare of History

"History," Stephen famously says in chapter two ("Nestor") of *Ulysses*, "is a nightmare from which I am trying to awake" (*U* 2.377). The clearest reading is as an example of Stephen rebelling against the constricting national and religious traditions of Irish Catholicism. But its meaning has also been located in ways that conflate ideas of history, narrative, and writing. For Vincent Cheng, Stephen sees history "as a usurper and a destroyer of creative potential, a restrictive force that limits other, perhaps more interesting, possibilities" (2015: 142-3). For Robert Spoo, Stephen's "nightmare"—and actually the whole of *Ulysses*—can be connected to Nietzsche's "malady of history," or, in Spoo's words, a "cultural obsession with the past and with the explanatory power of historiography" (1994: 6). "Story" and "history," as Spoo writes, "are inseparable in *Ulysses*; the nightmares with which Stephen struggles are engaged by the text itself on formal and stylistic planes" (1994: 7). For both Spoo and Cheng, this early chapter breaks free from a nightmare of restricted and linear forms in order to stylistically develop into the rest of *Ulysses*. My main point here, in thinking about links between the historiography of Gnosticism with Joyce's writings—particularly *Ulysses* and *Finnegans Wake*—builds on critics like Spoo who define modernist historiography, "as the attempt to extend practices of aesthetic innovation to the representation of the past" (1994: 8), a strategy that, as we will see, radically reshapes what "Gnosticism" comes to mean in the twentieth and twenty-first centuries.

This second chapter of *Ulysses*, which takes place after Stephen has walked from the tower to a Dalkey school to teach, is constructed out of a different intellectual fabric than chapter one. Joyce himself identified the "art" of chapter one as theology and chapter two as history. But the history of chapter two is—like the theology of chapter one—complicated, subversive, and perhaps ironic. In this chapter, Stephen teaches history (among other subjects) at a private school, muses to himself on ideas of history, and talks about history with the headmaster of the school. The chapter implicitly asks if history is what is remembered, what is written down, or what actually happened. It opens with Stephen's somewhat uninspired lesson, as he asks a student for dry facts about Roman history; he then asks for names and dates at the same time that he looks down to check on them in his notes. Throughout this class, students mindlessly copy pre-given material—historical, mathematical, and literary—and are all seemingly numbed by rote repetition. Throughout this section, history is presented as monolithic, written, and unchanging.

When a student answers a question about the Greek leader Pyrrhus with the word pier, Stephen asks him what a pier is. "A kind of bridge," the student answers. "Yes," Stephen responds, "a disappointed bridge" (*U* 2.30–40). This uninspired exchange between student and teacher offers us an inspired metaphor for defining history. History is not a bridge, not a connection back to some recoverable past; it is instead a pier, a suggestion in a direction without any conclusive physical connections. Stephen's next thoughts build on this metaphor of incompleteness and ponder the "what if" questions of history:

> Had Pyrrhus not fallen by a beldam's hand in Argos or Julius Caesar not been knifed to death. They are not to be thought away... But can those have been possible seeing that they never were?
>
> (*U* 2.47–50)

In other words, "Was that only possible which came to pass?" as Stephen asks (*U* 2.52), a question that indicates all the inadequacies of assuming history as a straight line of one event after another in a never-changing and unalterable sequence of cause and effect. If history is the "art" of this chapter, then, as Edmund Epstein writes, "Joyce's concern is to make it seem a false art" and its "theme" is the "problem of the proper way to regard the stream of human history" (1977: 27). The problem of establishing a "proper theme" of history is indeed that it is an art, and, like all art, is false. Even the metaphor of a stream deceptively suggests that it is contained by banks and flows in only direction. We may like to think this is true—just like we may think biblical scriptures are clearly defined and progress from Genesis to Revelation—but both these characteristics are challenged by Gnostic versions of history and by reading *Finnegans Wake*.

Like Stephen's reading of ancient history, the study of Gnosticism, as it developed in the twentieth century, continually suggests "what if" questions. Since Gnostics tended to think the suffering of the flesh was something to be escaped, rather than addressed, how would they have dealt with issues of disease, poverty, and oppression? Or maybe their negative view of the physical would have ultimately translated into more ambitious and radical efforts to eradicate the body altogether. Although this what-if exercise obviously plays out in the realm of politics, nationalism, and religion, it can also be used as a literary thought experiment. As Hans Jonas originally wrote in the 1930s, our "art and literature and much else would be different, had the Gnostic message prevailed" (1958: xxxi). Had Gnostic Christianity become the accepted version, today's Christians would see the Old Testament only as an obscure set of Jewish myths and would not see themselves as having Jewish roots. No doubt, the history of Western literature, the genres and reading practices that we are so familiar with, would not be the same. Figurative and allegorical modes of interpretation developed by the necessity of negotiating the narrative and typological logic of Hebrew and Christian scriptures would have developed differently. As Ehrman asks:

> Who knows how the ways of reading texts that strike us as obvious and straightforward, literal readings in which we follow the words in sequence and accept their commonly accepted meanings within their own contexts—who knows how our way of reading texts would have altered if a group that insisted on figurative understandings as the primary modes of interpretation had won out and established sway in our forms of civilization?
>
> (2003: 134)

Or, what if the idea of reading, passed down through the Gnostics, was that words have secret meanings available only to a chosen few? What then would be the history of our books, our Christian epics, from *The Faerie Queene* to *Finnegans Wake*? Perhaps the arc of our reading practices would have bypassed the higher biblical criticism and the Enlightenment's path of hermeneutics, continuing instead a more esoteric strategy like earlier readers of Plato and the Kabbalah, who searched for hidden mystical meanings between the words.

Stephen ends the class session by asking a strange riddle:

> The cock crew,
> The sky was blue:
> The bells in heaven
> Were striking eleven
> 'Tis time for this poor soul
> To go to heaven. (*U* 2.102–8)

The answer? "The fox burying his grandmother under a hollybush." At first it seems that this seemingly nonsense riddle could not have any relationship to the chapter's theme of history. Unless, perhaps we read this answer as a type of Gnostic "secret." But there are several ways to interpret this riddle within the theme of interrogating history. For Spoo, the answer to the riddle "combines antihistorical forgetting with the quite different though strangely complementary notion of historical seed sowing, the planting of a riddling corpse that will rise again in the interpretations of others" (1994: 96). In other words, the answer is created *with* the riddle and is not generated *by* it. Another way of reading the riddle is to see it as offering a material answer (literally a corpse) to what are exclusively nonmaterial clues: a sound, a color, a number, a soul, and heaven—a formulation that echoes the schism between Gnostic and orthodox views toward the physical. Although Joyce scholars and students have struggled to make sense of this riddle, it is not a riddle at all, and the answer is only an answer if you already know it. Even with the solution, it still does not make any logical sense—but like history, we can only fill in the gaps after the fact, we can only interpret history when we know what happens next. In this way, the answer to the riddle suggests a form of typology. Like reading the Bible from right to left—using the "New" Testament to interpret the "Old"—orthodox Christians can know that Adam fell because Christ would come to redeem him and that Eve ate the fruit because Mary would reverse this sin. This is, importantly, the kind of biblical reading that the Gnostics resisted. As Christian historians accused them, they read the Bible from left to right instead of from right to left. Modernist authors, as well, challenged the idea of one-directional reading—perhaps most famously captured in T.S. Eliot's words that "the past should be altered by the present as much as the present is directed by the past." A literary culture that comes out of reading and interpreting works like *Finnegans Wake* and *Ulysses* teaches us to read *both* from left to right and from right to left, to see the body and text as related in complicated ways, and prepares us to see the false riddles in our own narratives.

Earlier in chapter two, the idea of a riddle crosses Stephen's mind when he is reminded of Christ's reply to the Pharisees: "To Caesar what is Caesar's, to God what is God's" (another binary framing of the separation of body and soul, material and spiritual). Stephen thinks of these enigmatic words as "a riddling sentence to be woven on the church's looms" (*U* 2.86–7), the suggestion being that it is precisely their flexible quality that allow these words to be intertwined into church history and unconsciously into the human imagination. The fact that Stephen uses a material and artistic metaphor ("woven on the church's looms") makes it an even stronger parallel to the fox riddle in negotiating the spiritual with the material and also points to how history is something that is always aesthetic and created.

Mr. Deasy, the schoolmaster, represents the false art of historical narrative in this chapter, precisely because he does not understand this more complex multi-directional model of history. Deasy represents the Victorian, teleological view of history that new versions of Christian history challenged. Later, just after Stephen has thought about escaping the nightmare of history, Deasy gives Stephen his essay on foot and mouth disease, claiming an impossible certainty in its truth: "I have put the matter into a nutshell" he says, "There can be no two opinions on the matter" (*U* 2.321–3). Deasy here makes a claim for pure linear teleology, as he then proclaims "All human history moves towards one great goal, the manifestation of God" (*U* 2.380–1), suggesting a reductive conception of narrative that reflects his views of his own writing. Stephen's immediate answer to this single god of history is to point out the window to where the students are playing and cheering (presumably for another type of goal) and say, with a dismissive shrug, "That is God ... A shout in the street" (*U* 2.386).

Single Truth or Infinite Pluralities

While Joyce's "shout in the street" is a well-known portrayal of God in *Ulysses*, his most discussed depiction of God is as author: "The artist, like the God of the creation, remains within or behind or beyond or above his handiwork, invisible, refined out of existence, indifferent, paring his fingernails" (*P* 233). This ideal artist, as completely separate from his creation, is not the only way that Joyce employs that metaphor, and the idea of the artist as the God of his creations remains a preoccupation throughout *Ulysses* and *Finnegans Wake*. If the one creator God is metaphorically linked with the idea of the author, then within literary genres it is the idea of unity, a single point of view, omniscient narration, and providential plots that point to a monotheistic aesthetic. The idea of a single text, truth, time, or historical direction, connects thematically and arguably historically to formulations of a single God, a single author, and the metaphor of God as author and the author as God. Chapter two of *Ulysses*, however, with Stephen's reference to God as a "shout in the street" complicates these themes of unification by proclaiming a God of sound instead of Word or flesh.

Stephen's alternative incarnation of sound rather than flesh participates in both a heretical and an aesthetic debate by placing God at the border of perception and existence. The shout is a representation of God that is simultaneously found, man-made, and an ineffable and transitory moment; it is a non-material Gnostic god of spirit *and* a god of lived religion created through human action. Stephen (or Joyce) is probably thinking of Proverbs 1:20 where "Wisdom crieth without; she uttereth her voice in the streets;" in locating God as a shout in the street, Stephen conflates wisdom and divinity, but also presents a non-corporeal god of pure spirit. Stephen will remember this formulation later in the novel as he begins to pontificate about Shakespeare (*U* 9.86). In *Finnegans Wake* as well, God is often equated with sound, as where the word "Lord" is also "Loud," as in "Loud, hear us!" (*FW* 258.25) or "Loud we beseech thee," or, more scatologically, when the *Pater Noster* or Lord's Prayer becomes the "farternoiser" (*FW* 530.36). We can see all the various binaries here—material versus spiritual, heaven versus earth—as part of long-running, philosophical and theological debates between unity and chaos: debates that dominated orthodox Christian resistance to what seemed like the multiple divinities of the Gnostics.

For Irenaeus and other proto-orthodox thinkers, perhaps the major complaint against the Gnostics was that they were "dualistic." Or that they believed in two Gods or "another God besides the creator," or a God who is a "complex intellect." For Irenaeus, truth must be single and unified. In describing what he thought of as the heretical beliefs of his Gnostic opponents, Irenaeus's basic strategy was to "show that in contrast to the harmony and unity of the true Church and its one rule of faith, the heretics lack any kind of social unity or doctrinal unanimity" (Pelikan 1971: 69). In contrast to much Gnosticism and in direct contradiction to the quick-to-anger God of the Hebrew Scriptures, this Christian God was unchanging. The concept of an unmoving unchangeable God existing in relation to a flawed and fluid reality is a concept that came into Christian doctrine from Greek philosophy, will be reframed in arguments about Jesus, and is a debate that still produces tension within the Western world. For example, we might even see this formative concept as partly responsible for our reluctance to accept an Einsteinian view of space that twists and bends, as opposed to a Newtonian image of a single universe or stage on which cosmic actors perform their predicted roles in linear time.

Whether we are talking about Joyce or Gnosticism (or Newton or Einstein), what these theological, historical, or literary writings share is a negotiation with two opposing perceptions of what they tend to call "God." In other words, despite their desire for unity and oneness, authors and readers of works of literature and religion often pull in opposite creative directions. The first direction is toward the fully *determinate* God, the God of positivism and certainty, and the God that makes unity possible. For Nietzsche, for theologian Thomas Altizer, and for some interpreters of Joyce, this is the God who is dead—a single authorial figure who either is or isn't. It is this God that is the author of Stephen's nightmare of history, and it is this God that has been dominant and privileged throughout much of Western literary and religious history. But this God—a totalizing force that makes meaning and closure the goal of all interpretation—is not the only way of imagining the divine. There are ways of reading God that negate this kind of conviction, a God that makes any kind of presence or certainty of object, meaning, or historical fact as impossible to locate. This God is arguably the God of heresy, of the Gnostics, of radical theology, and of *Ulysses* and *Finnegans Wake*. Mark C. Taylor could be talking about *Finnegans Wake* when he writes that God need not be the transcendental signified, but could conversely stand for the "disappearance of the transcendental signified," a void that "creates the possibility of writing" (1984: 108). In other words, both God and writing are only possible coming out of a space of nothingness. For Taylor, writing, at its most daring, stands in for God, and that "to interpret God as word is to understand the divine as scripture or writing" (1984: 104). God therefore *is* writing—the writing of literature, of scripture, and of history. This God beyond being, the God of the postmodern critic, the God who neither is nor is not, and the God of Joyce's heretical voice who cries out against the idea of the "authordux" (*FW* 425.20).

Body and Narrative

If God is always, on some level, nothing, no-thing, pure transcendence, or an ephemeral "shout in the street," then the story of the Incarnation—word made flesh, God made human, divine made material—opens up an opposing set of concerns. The body—whether body of Christ or of oneself—is often seen as a guarantee of existence, an answer to the riddle of being. God, like narrative or sound, is non-material, it moves, it changes, it threatens not to exist. The body, on the other hand, is proof of stability. When the resurrected Jesus appeared to the apostles, Thomas refuses to believe until he can see and, most importantly, *feel*, the wounds on Jesus's body: "Unless I see the mark of the nails in his hands and put my hand into his side, I will most certainly not have faith" (John 20:25). The story of "doubting Thomas," according to many scholars, was the original conclusion to the fourth Gospel and thus could have been the final word on the life of Christ.

To think about orthodox and Gnostic views of the body—and implicitly, therefore, the crucifixion and resurrection—as it plays out in twentieth-century literature is a vast subject, but one where Joyce's *Ulysses* and its reception provide an entry point. "My book is the epic of the human body," Joyce told his friend

Frank Budgen, "in my book the body lives in and moves through space and is the home of a full human personality" (1934: 21). Bodies in *Ulysses* do things that bodies had rarely done in English novels before: they fart, piss, shit, pick their nose, and masturbate. Not only do the characters do these things, but they celebrate them in joining them to sounds, smells, thoughts, and writings that make up the rich day and text that is *Ulysses*. "If they had no body they would have no mind," Joyce told Budgen. "It's all one" (1934: 21). While legal complaints over the "obscenity" of *Ulysses* argued that these words and acts had nothing to do with the "art" of the book, they are, in fact, inextricably connected to the acts of narrative, ritual, and art that create characters and ideas.

In the first chapter, Stephen's friend Buck Mulligan recites the "Ballad of Joking Jesus," introducing both his own heretical personality and the theme of bodily function as a form of creation:

—If anyone thinks that I amn't divine
He'll get no free drinks when I'm making the wine
But have to drink water and wish it were plain
That I make when the wine becomes water again.

(*U* 1.584–8)

In other words, Jesus will turn the wine back to "water" when he urinates. Urination throughout the novel will connect references to creation, to the transitory nature of writing, and to the fragility of human bonds. By putting it in the words of Jesus, in a chapter filled with references to the Catholic Mass and in the context of a type of transubstantiation (urine from wine), Joyce gives us a key to how we are to understand bodily functions in the rest of the novel. Questions about whether Jesus urinated or defecated were, in fact, serious questions for many of the early Christians, and frequent points of contention between the Gnostic and the proto-orthodox. For Valentinus, Jesus ate without excretion, and the more orthodox Clement of Alexandria agreed. Others argued that as "fully human," he would have to digest and excrete in a fully human manner. Many Gnostic doctrines deny that Jesus even had a material body or was born in the traditional, messy human way, and material creation of any kind was a questionable process. If creation was not the result of the Supreme God, but instead of a flawed Creator who was possibly even evil, then, for many of the Gnostics, there was considerable revulsion at the human processes of elimination, generation, and birth.

This repulsion to the physical brings us back to the Gnostic Christ in *Stephen Hero* and the question of what kind of Christ *rises* on Good Friday: What kind of Christ never reaches its Easter? Stephen's Christ perhaps makes the Gnostic move of dispensing with its fallen, evil human-body and becoming a savior of pure spirit—a move that renders Easter Sunday unnecessary. The depiction of the resurrection as literal and physical is not as obvious as history has made it out to seem, and it was by no means a foregone conclusion. The orthodox view is that the resurrection was a material event in history: a moment in time that changed the course of the world, a turning point that gave a new narrative direction to what had previously been a repetition of cycles of life and death. This shift in how we perceive the progression of events plays a determining role in the development of literature, and models how we write and read narratives. Forms and texts of Gnostic Christianity offer different perspectives and different models of telling the story. In the Gnostic Gospel of Mary, for instance, the resurrection is interpreted as a vision or a dream. In the Gnostic Gospel of Philip, it is written that "those who say that the master first died and then arose are wrong, for he first arose then died." Instead believers are "first resurrected" (56, 15–20), and then die, an idea that completely reverses the resurrection physically and narratologically.

Reading Joyce—like reading history, the story of Gnosticism, and both orthodox and heterodox Christian theology—is about rereading and reversal. For Derek Attridge, Joyce's writings "imply that all versions of history are made in language and are, by virtue of that fact, ideological constructions, weavings and re-weavings of old stories, fusions of stock character-types, blendings of different national languages, dialects, and registers" (2000: 80). Like themes in *Ulysses*, these ideas of history return, in fragments and phrases that are reshaped, remixed, and restructured. In chapter seven of *Ulysses*, for example, both Stephen and Bloom find themselves in the office of a Dublin newspaper. The main characteristic of the chapter is the presence of newspaper-like headlines throughout, describing, commenting on, and interrupting the narrative. The chapter features various systems of communication—printing presses, telephones, speeches, parables, riddles, and unspoken language—and the implied point is that, as Marshall McLuhan (a passionate Joyce reader) would say, the "medium is the message." An example is when Stephen hears the legendary story of a journalist who solved the Phoenix Park murders by juxtaposing a printed advertisement over the map of the park. We don't see how Stephen responds to this story, but when the journalist is credited with providing the "whole bloody history," Stephen again thinks to himself, "Nightmare from which you will never awake" (*U* 7.678). The nightmare may just be Stephen free associating, or it could be the obvious blurring of myth and fact, or cause and effect. The next words spoken are the seemingly random comment: "Madam, I'm Able. And able was I ere I saw Elba" (*U* 7.683). These two palindromes fit into a chapter that opens with a description of tram routes, coming and going, and also describes the backwards writing of a printing press, but its placement here in the discussion of history also seems to imply the way history is read from right to left as well as left to right. Language and history have to be understood both forwards and backwards.

Part III: Post-1945: Difficulty and *Finnegans Wake*

If sections of *Ulysses* can be seen as questioning the possibility of writing or representing a single history, then *Finnegans Wake* is either a massive dramatization of or rebuttal of that point. "I think I will write a history of the world," Joyce wrote in a 1922 letter, when he was just beginning to envision the book that would become *Finnegans Wake* (Ellmann 1983: 537). In realizing this project, though, he made it clear that history is far from a retelling of what happened; it is instead a chaotic, multi-vocal, narrative that breaks all the rules of storytelling. Later, Joyce also described this "history of the world" as the dream of the legendary Irish giant Finn MacCool, who lay asleep by the river Liffey as the whole history of the world flowed past. The idea of a dream is central, as the *Wake* is often described as Joyce's "night book" that follows a sort of dream logic (history as nightmare again?), but the other interesting metaphor is the idea of the *flow* of the river, which seems to imply a single direction of history and time, even if the relating, retelling, and reality of it are altered by the sleeping giant's dream logic.

If *Finnegans Wake* has a theme, it is about the falling and rising of humans throughout history—the cycle of deaths and resurrections that are both myth and fact, story and reportage. The Irish folk song "Finnegan's Wake," which inspired the title, tells of a dead man at his wake, who comes back to life when whiskey is splashed on him. In Joyce's *Finnegans Wake*, the story of the Protestant protagonist HCE (Humphrey Chimpden Earwicker, and also standing for, among other things, Here Comes Everybody and *hoc est corpus*) also involves a type of the fall (in this case, echoing Adam's) which begins on the first page with a fall of a hundred letter word which will be "retaled" (*retold*, as in restated again and again, as well as *retailed*, as in sold for a profit), "down through all christian minstrelsy" (*FW* 3.17–18). HCE's original sin may or may not have been an indiscretion of a sexual nature that he may or may not have committed in Dublin's Phoenix Park (which is also the Garden of Eden, and a reference to the mythical phoenix that rises from the ashes). What we see in the telling of HCE's sin are multiple, conflicting histories—its gossips, its books, its letters, its songs—none more definitive that the next, but all part of history, which points to an act that can never be "original."

We find glimpses of these themes in one of Joyce's many hand-written notebooks that he kept while researching and writing *Finnegans Wake*, in this case, notes he took on the book *La civilization et les grandes fleuves historiques*, an 1889 study of the influence of rivers on the development of culture. In his notebook, Joyce writes "Lower Nile made history," a comment on a section of the book describing how history would have changed if the Nile had changed courses. Below that, Joyce writes, "If Liffey had turned back" (VI. B.1 033). These words are crossed out in crayon, which means Joyce used them in a *Wake* draft, although in the final version they are morphed into a woman changing her affections:

> had faithful Fulvia, following the wiening courses of this world, turned her back on her ways to gon on uphills upon search of louvers
>
> (*FW* 546.30–2)

This great "what if?" question (what if the Liffey flowed in the opposite direction?) becomes a metaphor for the whole of the *Wake*, as it represents the flow of history, the idea of woman as water, and the fluidity and unpredictability of each—all wound up in the act of reading and writing the words in a book. Joyce both used and subverted this idea of "flow" throughout his life, writing in a youthful piece that "there is no past, no future; everything flows in an eternal present," or a "fluid succession of presents" (*CW* 211).

Edmund Epstein claims that time is almost non-existent in Book I of the *Wake*, where everything, including the river Liffey, is flowing backwards at the beginning of the novel (2009: 25). For Epstein, the whole structure of *Finnegans Wake* can be seen as time running in reverse and then shifting direction in the middle of the novel to move forward in consecutive time again. Examples of these kind of reversals are found throughout the book, often connected to religious scripture. For example, examining the *Wake* sentence, "a bockalips of finisky fore his feet. And a barrowload of guenesis hoer his head" (*FW* 6.26–7), Bill Cole Cliett writes, "only in the *Wake* with its Eve before Adam would the Apocalypse ['a bockalips'] come before Genesis" ["guenesis"] (2011: 90). The ending of the *Wake* plays with this same idea as the long, complex night turns to day, but a day first announced with the words "Pu Nuseht," or "the Sun up" spelled backwards

(*FW* 593.23). Like the "best authenticated version, the Dumlat,"—Talmud spelled backwards (*FW* 30.10)—even the movement of daybreak hints at the idea of a retrograde motion. This "reversal of history"—a sense of history in which the present influences the past, the new changes the old, or, as in *Finnegans Wake*, when all times are one—suggests, in other words, that what is interesting about Gnosticism is not just its "actual" history, whatever that might mean, but that its historiography—the way its story has emerged and been told in the modern era—offers alternative, perhaps heretical views to thinking about history, and the ways it is disseminated, abused, disrupted, fragmented, and produced. The history of Gnosticism, which emerged as a heresy in part *because* it had a different view of reading history, has now, like Joyce's Liffey, reversed directions and is being changed by the present.

Secrets, Gaps, and Aporias

During the years that stretched from the publication of *Finnegans Wake* in 1939 and Joyce's death in 1941, to the discovery of the Nag Hammadi texts in 1945, and their entrance into the academic community roughly ten years later, the scholarly world of reading changed along with the ways scholars saw the relationship between writing and religion. Movements within religious studies, literary theory, and history embraced and theorized ideas of absence, aporias, gaps, undecidability, and non-linear time: concepts, that we can now see, in retrospect, had their roots in—among other places—early-twentieth-century texts by Joyce and studies of Gnosticism, as well as world wars, genocides, and new scientific discoveries.

The tensions in *Finnegans Wake* between the specific and the universal, and the individual and society, are played out in the stories, fables, and phrases across the pages of the book. Near the beginning, in an apparent reference to the Book of Kells, the famous, early medieval illuminated Gospels, we read:

> Somewhere, parently, in the ginnandgo gap between antediluvious and annadominant the copyist must have fled with his scroll.
>
> (*FW* 14.16–18)

In this one sentence, Joyce moves between thousands of years of history and myth, and brings us back to lost texts and our imagination's role in filling in and supplementing fragments and gaps to imagine the whole. In these lines, we have three difference gaps represented. The space between "antediluvious" (antediluvian) and "annadominant" (*Anno Domini*) is the historical space between the flood and the birth of Jesus, when most of biblical history takes place. It is a time frame or the borders of historical scripture. Second, the "copyist must have fled with his scroll" refers to a vacant space on the manuscript, left when the original artist leaves the page unfinished, presumably fleeing Viking invaders. And finally, the "ginnandgo gap," while it suggests the way the endangered copyist had to quickly "get-up-and go," also points to the *Ginnungagap,* which in Norse mythology is the primordial void that precedes creation. As philosopher Philip Kitcher writes about this passage, "none of us is simply a recording device, storing up information for the future, we have to act, and action takes many other forms than writing down what we notice" (2009: 64). Joyce's sentence points to the intersecting relationship of history, texts, writing, and the spaces through which we try to read them.

I often tell my students that reading Joyce's books teaches you how to read them; that, for example, reading the first nine chapters of *Ulysses* gives you the skills and strategies necessary for reading the second nine, and the second half of *Ulysses* prepares you for reading *Finnegans Wake.* Readers of Joyce learn to read and see words in multiple ways, to distinguish the shadings of various hybrid narrators and internal and external voices, to recognize literary parodies and shifting styles, and to accept obfuscation and confusion. The experiences of readers new to Joyce also offer the opportunity to talk about the history of literary criticism—to show how interpretations of Joyce have moved from early efforts to locate single meanings, plots, and themes, to later strategies that acknowledge or embrace the uncertainty and plurality of meanings. While early critics of Joyce (such as T.S. Eliot or Stuart Gilbert) emphasized the Homeric parallels in order to convince readers of a perceptible structure amongst the verbal chaos, later critics learned to be subtler in reading the ambiguity on the level of the passage, the sentence, and the word. Similarly, while the first Joyceans to seriously address the handwritten *Finnegans Wake* Notebooks hoped to find a definitive key to understanding the work, a half-century later, we have had to admit that it is rare when an entry in a notebook provides any sort of definitive clarification. As Derek Attridge writes, studying the Notebooks only makes the texts "more complex, more fluid, more like palimpsestic cultural archives than products of a single artistic genius" (2003: 571).

To read the Hebrew or Christian or Gnostic scriptures is, as modern literary scholars discovered, also an exercise in negotiating gaps and fragments, multiple authors and points of view. When critics, shaped by Joyce, Eliot, and New Critical practices of close reading, turned to reading scripture—the phrase "Bible as Literature" is a mid-twentieth-century formulation—they celebrated elements of modernist difficulty and ambiguity. An early influential example is Eric Auerbach's classic essay "Odysseus's Scar." In comparing the Genesis story of Abraham to Homer's *Odyssey*, Auerbach finds the Bible's representation of "reality" to be full of mystery and omissions, resulting in confusion and contradictory motives. More theoretically oriented positions are found in studies such as Meir Sternberg's *The Poetics of Biblical Narrative*, which also focus on the Bible's gaps, misdirections, and ambiguities. The connections between reading the Bible and reading difficult modernist literature were noted by scholars like Herbert Schneidau, who, in his *Sacred Discontent: The Bible and Western Tradition*, argues that the books of the Bible, like modern literature, are texts of questioning and self-criticism. They are not the literal historical documents of certainty that the fundamentally religious have sought, but texts of destruction and chaos that force us to question the connection of word and event, literature and history, book and text. Although Joyce's fiction plays a small role in his book, Schneidau, a scholar of modernist literature, writes, "Joyce's work can only be understood with the Biblical concepts of historical truth behind it" (1976: 281). For Auerbach, Sternberg, and Schneidau, reading the Bible and *Ulysses* (and, more dramatically, we might add, Gnostic texts or Joyce's notebooks) are exercises in questioning our acts of writing and how we perceive the reality to which they refer. Close analyses of all of Joyce's materials, as Christine van Boheemen-Saaf writes, produce not "a stable material object," but "an ideal construction of a process of creative production" (1999: 35). We are, as she puts it, "suddenly confronted with a text which refuses to stay put in its formal boundaries" (1999: 46). These practices of reading, which subverted the idea of a single text, echoed religious scholars who found in the Nag Hammadi texts more Christian stories, legends, and beliefs than they had previously imagined. For both sets of readers, it was becoming clear that *Ulysses*, *Finnegans Wake*, and the Christian gospels (orthodox and heretical) were understood better as libraries than books, as networks rather than stand-alone texts, and as ongoing processes of understanding rather than fixed points in time.

4

Arius and the Anxiety of Vampiric Creation

Arius, warring his life long upon the consubstantiality of the Son with the Father

(*U* 1.557–8)

Part I: Arius and *Ulysses*

In the opening, theologically informed, chapter of James Joyce's *Ulysses*—which begins with a parody of the Latin Mass followed by a blasphemous "Ballad of Joking Jesus"—the Englishman Haines asks Stephen Dedalus: "You're not a believer are you? … I mean, a believer in the narrow sense of the word. Creation from nothing and miracles and a personal God." Although Stephen's answer is "there's only one sense of the word, it seems to me" (*U* 1.611–14), the rest of the novel will actually reveal multiple and opposing positions on this matter. Contrary to Stephen's evasive and reductive answer, one way of reading *Ulysses* is to see it as providing alternative readings to traditional renderings of the word and concept of "belief," as well as "God," "creation," and "nothing." Throughout the opening pages of *Ulysses*, primarily seen through Stephen—the budding poet and lapsed, Jesuit-educated Catholic—Haines's question seems to lead to musing on theology and creation, or, more specifically, thoughts of heretics and authorship. Haines's "narrow" definition of belief—"Creation from nothing and miracles and a personal God"—is not only a general description of traditional belief, but clearly suggestive of a specific Christian heresiarch. While many readers today might automatically associate this phrase "creation from nothing" with the Christian explanation of God's creation of the world *ex nihilo*, within the context of *Ulysses* and Stephen's thought, the phrase "creation from nothing" also points to the fourth-century heretic Arius, and his theory of Christology, or the nature of Christ. Arius's heresy was to claim that Christ came "out of nothing" and that "once he was not," or, in other words, the *creation* and the *non-eternity* of Christ the Son. Stephen will, in fact, just a few pages later have specific thoughts of Arius and this heretical theology of the Son. Rooted in the Arian heresy is an anxiety about artistic creation that seems to follow Stephen throughout the day: What does it mean to create? Do artists create something from nothing, or do they merely rearrange pre-existing material into a new text? By introducing Arius and his heretical Christology in the first chapter and at several other key moments in the novel, Joyce opens an alternative path—philosophically, aesthetically, and structurally—which poses multiple and subversive meanings for Stephen and for readers of *Ulysses*. The idea of "creation from nothing," as a challenge to both the origin of Christ and the origin of a work of literature, will haunt—sometimes heretically, sometimes ghostly, sometimes vampirically—the rest of *Ulysses*.

* * *

During Joyce's formative years, the idea that the first centuries of Christianity were not a period of defending an original orthodoxy but rather a search *for* orthodoxy, was slowly, and somewhat reluctantly recognized. Although this position would not be generally accepted by historians until the 1930s, such works as John Henry Newman's *Arians of the Fourth Century* and David Strauss's and Ernest Renan's "biographies" of Jesus were influential in the late-nineteenth century and offered speculative and creative ways of challenging accepted models of history. As these reassessments of Christian history slowly began to open a deeper understanding of early heresies as more than just evil, error, or a secret, magical, and forbidden knowledge, Joyce was receiving his Jesuit education and (like Stephen) reading Cardinal Newman, Strauss, and Renan.

The Europe of the eighteenth and nineteenth centuries saw a new movement in the search for the historical Jesus which consisted of academic efforts to determine what words and actions, if any, could be attributed to Jesus, and to use the findings to construct biographies of the historical Jesus. Hundreds of such biographical efforts were produced in the nineteenth century. The two most famous, Strauss's *The Life of Jesus, Critically Examined* (1835) and Renan's *Life of Jesus* (1864), were books which Joyce read with great interest (Ellmann 1983: 193); both books influentially pointed to contradictions in the biblical versions and also characterized the miraculous elements in the gospels as "historical myth" and not as actual events. Albert Schweitzer, in his 1906 *The Quest of the Historical Jesus*, wrote that there are two broad periods of academic research in the study of the historical Jesus: "that before Strauss and that after Strauss" (1910: 10). Strauss and Renan gave us a Jesus who was fully human, performs no miracles, is not the Son of God, and is not resurrected. These widely popular books appealed to a nineteenth-century readership informed by Enlightenment skepticism, and one that was beginning to read and think about history and heresy differently. Schweitzer's *Historical Jesus* also claimed that the Gospel narratives are not historically accurate, but are later accounts written by believers who wanted to convince others of the supernatural roots of Christianity. Schweitzer and others were much discussed in Joyce's time, and logically led to a re-framing of the classical idea of heresy as a deviation away from some original truth. Instead, it became clear, orthodoxy developed *after* the historical Jesus and, indeed, after the writings of the early Christian fathers.

Cardinal Newman—as both an Anglican and eventually a Catholic—was deeply orthodox, but was also a significant figure in the shifting understandings of heretical thought; in an important book, Newman portrayed Arianism as an earnest, if misguided, theological position. Newman's book came partially from a desire to explain what he saw as a threat from eighteenth-century movements such as Deism and Unitarianism—movements he thought of as forms of Arianism. Newman's research into Arianism was an attempt, as Stephen Thomas writes, to present the "definition of Christ's divinity at the Council of Nicaea (325 CE) as a 'test' in the early nineteenth-century English sense" (1991: 36). In other words, to understand modern orthodoxy through understanding an ancient heresy. Newman is an important figure to the young Stephen of *Portrait*, and also appears in *Finnegans Wake* as the "newmanmaun" who "set a marge to the merge of unnotions" (*FW* 614.17), a phrase that seems to point to heretical thought and the "new" understanding that it both exists on the margins of orthodoxy and merges with it. As Stephen Morrison writes, it is "precisely that 'marge' which the *Wake* continuously transgresses, insisting that assimilation is always a reciprocal process, implying constantly that nothing, Christian doctrine and liturgy least of all, can remain genuinely pure without the presence or an absolute authority to define its margins" (2000: 189). It is in these "mergings" and "margins" between and among religious meaning-making and unmaking (or "unnotions") that Joyce's books and language overlap with the heretical.

Heretical Creation

Heresy and related anxieties over fathers and creation occupy Stephen's thoughts throughout *Ulysses*, but the specific mention of Arius at several key moments early in the text augments and complicates these themes. In chapter one, we listened in on Stephen's mental list of famous heretics, including Arius, "warring his life long upon the consubstantiality of the Son with the Father" (*U* 1.657), and (on the other side of the debate) Sabellius, "who held that the Father was Himself His own Son" (*U* 1.660). By placing Arius, Sabellius, and other heretics and heresies in close proximity to references to poetry, Joyce emphasizes the mystery of the creative process, the imprecise ontology of a work of art, and the creator's fraught relationship to the created text. In Arius' view, to see Christ as always and eternally God denies the process through which he ascended. From the Arian position, Jesus's ascent from man to God gives humans a model for salvation. Metaphorically, this is a striving for creating meaning rather than discovering its eternal existence. The Arian Christ, in other words, represents *becoming*, rather than the absolute itself, and knowledge that is created, rather than discovered. Christ, for Arius, is not an eternal transcendental signified—or a timeless source of absolute and irreducible meaning—but is part of a process of meaning-making. Arius implicitly proposes a different way of reading that is more rooted in experience. Stephen's thoughts of a heretical theologian who posited Christ as a created (rather than eternal) being and as a sort of intermediary to the Father can be applied analogously to Stephen's troubled relationship with his father, to his reading of *Hamlet* as a tale of a playwright father grieving his son, as an answer to a question about whether he believed in "creation from nothing and miracles and a personal God," and as a comment on a poet's relationship to his poem.

Many Joyce scholars have written of Joyce's references to the Arian heresy in *Ulysses*, usually as it relates to fathers and sons. Margot Norris writes that, by invoking opposing theological interpretations of the Trinity, Stephen

> raises the logical issue of whether fathers and sons are necessary to each other in order to preserve the status of the category. "Well: if the father who has not a son be not a father can the son who has not a father be a son?" (*U* 9.864). This line of reasoning shifts the father-son relationship from the biological and genetic realm into the symbolic and aesthetically productive realm.
>
> (2011: 59)

For Stephen, Arius also seems to represent the struggle between creating art and giving it meaning. But the heresy of a created Christ complicates the creator-created relationship not only by presenting a lesser Son, but also by suggesting a more vulnerable Father. By finding it necessary to "create" Christ at a point in time, God the Father admits he needs help, that he is not enough. The opposing, also heretical, position can be found in the theologian Sabellius who posited that God and Christ were single and indivisible. This ambiguity is captured in *Ulysses* in a parody of the Sabellian position, who "held that the Father was Himself His Own Son" (*U* 9.862–5). Both sides of the debate address issues of authority, intent, and meaning through negotiating the ambiguity of language, the multiple definitions of words such as "nature" and "substance," and the difficulty (and necessity) of stepping outside of biblical language in order to comment upon it. The "solution" offered by the council of Nicaea and the half-century after—that Christ was from the *ousia* (of the Father) and *homoousios* (with the Father)—eventually became the orthodox doctrine of the church. While we will revisit the Arian heresy from multiple perspectives throughout this chapter, it is important to realize that, at this point in Christian history, the evolving doctrine of the Trinity still left one major issue unresolved: the nature of Christ himself. In other words, theological questions revolved not around the preexistent Son of God, but the incarnate one, who walked as a human.

For Arius, "God was not eternally a father. There was a time when God was all alone, and was not yet a father; only later did he become a father." Arius's claim that Christ, like humans, was also created—that he too came from nothing—forced theologians to theorize the act of creation alongside the concepts of nothing and nothingness. These two related areas of negotiation—creation and nothing—literally defining both the book and world at the beginning of Genesis, are chief areas of theological debates during the fourth century, and continue to occupy thinkers, artists, and writers today. We could point to twentieth-century philosophers such as Jean Paul Sartre or Martin Heidegger, both of whom have been influential among literary theorists. For Sartre, while "nothingness haunts being," it is also nothingness that is the defining characteristic of how human beings imagine and create themselves. For Heidegger, it is anxiety or dread that "reveals the nothing," and yet without this revelation there is "no selfhood and no freedom" (2008: 105). For both Sartre and Heidegger, humans need the nothing in order to make themselves by acting in the world: nothingness is necessary for true creativity and for self-realization. Clearly, these debates are deeply embedded in the whole of artistic, as well as divine, creation—acts that must come to terms with what exists before and the materials used during the making. Imagining oneself or a text as *being* created necessarily introduces thoughts of a previous space or time of nonexistence: a theological problem in Christology, an identity crisis within psychology, and an aesthetic problem for an author or literary critic. Planted in the early pages of *Ulysses*, the idea of nothing is explored through Stephen and Bloom, each of whom imagines the world with their eyes shut. Walking on the sand, Stephen closes his eyes, wondering if the world will still be there when he opens them (*U* 3.25). Bloom, too, ponders nothingness, and his thoughts that "no-one is anything" and "nature abhors a vacuum" lead him to question "am I now I?" (*U* 8.493, 498, 608). As created beings, Stephen and Bloom both fear and are attracted to the mystery of nothing, to a time when they did not or will not exist.

Joyce not only borrows from and uses tensions around divinity and creation, but also the complicated and problematic concept of the Trinity in which the relationship between creator and created is given a new kind of logic, more circular than linear. As Frederick Lang writes, "Joyce takes as a model for the artistic process not only god's creative activity but the Trinitarian relations" (1993: 20). Here, Lang is referring to the Stephen of *Portrait* and his idealized and artistic Trinity of truth (Father), beauty (Son), and joy (Holy Spirit). In the more complicated aesthetic of *Ulysses*, Joyce must appropriate "not only Catholic but heretical doctrine" (1993: 20). Although Joyce may have been more Sabellian in his desire to unify the relationship of poets to their works, he also seems to have found in Arius's rebellion a model for a radical rethinking of the role of the literature and its connection to how we think about concepts like divinity and the Trinity. In many ways, as Jaroslav Pelikan says, "Arianism was more aware of the nuances of the Trinitarian problem than its critics were" (1971: 200), and by using both orthodox and heretical Christian models, Joyce invited—and perhaps welcomed—all the problems that come with the assertions of Trinitarian relations. If the Son is not identical to the Father then, by analogy, the author is always separated from his text; although the author may be a God/Father figure, the resulting creation is always both part of and yet separate from its source. *Ulysses* is not created directly out of Joyce, nor *Hamlet* from Shakespeare, nor a poem from Stephen Dedalus.

The ambiguous ontologies of both Son and Father became spaces of difference and sites of emergent creativity for the next several thousand years. As competing grounds for Western epistemology, the points of view proposed by figures such as Sabellius, Arius, and their followers rise to the surface in later medieval heresies, the Reformation, anti-Trinitarian Socinianism, theosophy, Unitarianism, home-grown American Christianity, popular and folk beliefs, and in secular theoretical debate. It is these gray areas on the edges of orthodoxy that are the birth of theology, the ground of Western thought and art, and spaces that continue to be worked out in our readings of modernist literature. In this chapter, I will first outline some of the traces of Arius and his heresy in *Ulysses*, taking a perhaps unexpected detour through vampires. I will then look at *Ulysses*'s chapter nine ("Scylla and Charybdis"), which incorporates a debate between Stephen and various Dublin literati on Shakespeare and divine creation that self-consciously works through many of these Christological issues.

Part II: The Anxiety of Creation: Heretics and Vampires

After the first chapter of *Ulysses*, Stephen will specifically remember Arius by name only twice more. At the beginning of chapter three ("Proteus"), as Stephen walks along a beach lost in his own thoughts, upon sighting what he perceives as a midwife, he repeats the phrase "creation from nothing" and then returns only nine lines later to interweave thoughts of Arius and the anti-Arian Nicaean Creed with his own family:

> Wombed in sin darkness I was too, made not begotten. By them, the man with my voice and my eyes and a ghostwoman with ashes on her breath. They clasped and sundered, did the coupler's will. From before the ages he will me and now may now will me away or ever. A *lex eternal* stays about Him. Is that then the divine substance wherein Father and Son are consubstantial? Where is poor dear Arius to try conclusions? Warring his life long upon the contransmagnificandjewbangtantiality. Illstarred heresiarch! In a Greek watercloset he breathed his last: euthanasia. With beaded mitre and with crozier, stalled upon his throne, widower of a widowed see, with upstiffed *omophorion*, with clotted hinderparts.
>
> (*U* 3.45–54)

Working our way through this passage, we see Stephen confirm his association of creation from nothing with Arius in the shift from the orthodox Nicaean Creed's "begotten not made" to "made not begotten," a statement that is both an Arian reversal and a comment on the nature of creation. Like the Arian Christ, Stephen is made not begotten: in other words, an object of creation that, like art, involves a creator and a time when he was not. As Karen Lawrence writes, the "basic image of the artist fathering himself is a comfort to a young writer who scorns his natural parents and thinks of himself as 'made not begotten'" (1981: 81). The "man with my voice," is Stephen's father, and the voice here is both the singing voice and also suggests a shared essence, either consubstantial or transubstantial.

With the invented compound word "contransmagnificanjewbangtantiality" that Arius warred "his life long upon," Joyce creates a word to perform the complicated theology of Father and Son, and to represent the significance of Arius' thought. With this word, Joyce stages a theological act—constructing it to perform multiple and contradictory functions. The word suggests and collapses, among other things, anxieties about creation, fatherhood, and heresy. Framing this word are "con-," "trans-," and "-tiality" which refer to the competing theories of Father and Son: the orthodox **con**substantiality, which Arius denied, refers to being of the *same substance*, and **trans**substantiality, which Arius proposed, indicates that the essential substance changes from Father to Son. The word also contains references to the *Magnificat*, the Virgin Mary's song celebrating procreation that she sings in the Gospels. The next line ("Airs romped round him, nipping and eager airs ....") quotes *Hamlet*'s Horatio, but also suggests the presence of songs ("airs") surrounding Stephen as he ponders the ontology of voices and sons.

The last sentence of the quoted passage ("stalled upon his throne ... ") refers to a common legend that Arius died, ashamed and perhaps repentant, in a public toilet, suffering from an internal hemorrhage. We can also see the sentence as representing a form of creative failure or blockage. (In contrast, Leopold Bloom's healthy bowel movement in chapter four will be accompanied by optimistic thoughts of writing and creation.) We will revisit the legend of Arius' death in a few pages, but for now what is important is that the themes of unnatural death (Arius's) and unnatural creation (Jesus's) are introduced in the aspiring poet's (and mourning son's) mind early in the novel. The train of association that comes out of the second reference to Arius leads almost directly into Stephen's primary act of artistic creation in *Ulysses*: the one actual piece of writing that he will produce during the day, a poem he writes on the beach, shortly after his thoughts have turned to Arius and stillborn babies. The poem, which we do not get to read until later, is hastily written on a scrap of paper:

> On swift sail flaming
> From storm and south
> He comes, pale vampire
> Mouth to my mouth

(*U* 8.521–5)

Both vampires and heretics remain on the margins of Stephen's mind during the day and are related to his obsession over linked questions of artistic creation, the body, and death. As Robert Day points out, "vampires fit into the context of images in the 'corpsechewer' hallucination in 'Circe' and since these ideas figure so repetitiously in Stephen's guilt-ridden fantasies throughout the novel

Joyce must have envisaged them as obsessively present in Stephen's mind since his mother's death" (1980: 188). Stephen's fixation on heretics and vampires introduces and disrupts the reader's understandings of the concepts of death, guilt, belief, and creation.

Considering the relative lack of space that they take up in *Ulysses*, heretics and vampires have received quite a bit of critical attention, although not often together. Most of these works use heretics, and sometimes vampires, to address Joyce's relationship to religion. But "religion," in most of these cases, stands for a force of Catholic traditions, stability, and certainty. Religious thought, though, as a study of heresy shows, is deeply disruptive as well—lacking true origins and made up of competing scriptures and histories—and it is that side I want to focus on. The heretic and the vampire are suggestively linked throughout *Ulysses* in ways that point to characteristically twentieth-century anxieties that are nonetheless deeply rooted in shifting epistemologies of the nineteenth century. Although after the first chapters of *Ulysses*, specific references to heretics and vampires will somewhat recede into the background, they will continue to haunt the novel, surfacing at important moments and offering troubling and disruptive commentary on the narrative.

Like the vampiric creation of his countryman Bram Stoker, Joyce's "vampires" have the ability to change forms. Although not explicitly vampires, there is a certain undead quality that exists and lives in his 1904 Dublin: a rat in the cemetery during a funeral, a bat flying over a church, ancient mummified bodies in the crypt of St. Michan's, the imagined ghosts of Stephen's dead mother, Bloom's dead father and son, and the recently deceased Paddy Dignam, who somehow keeps being seen around town. Each of these vampiric figures "haunts" the main characters in ways that cause them to both face and question the finitude and reality of death. In similar ways, Arius, and his ideas of the non-eternal and created Christ, seems to float from the mind of Stephen to Bloom and to Stephen's blasphemous roommate Buck Mulligan, forcing them to question orthodox wisdom about creation, procreation, authority, succession, and the relationship of body to mind. Vampires and heretics are linked in various ways throughout the opening pages of the book, perhaps most obviously in Stephen associating them both with a sort of violent physical sexuality, and, therefore, also procreation and parenthood. Throughout the novel, vampires and heretics work as symbols of an alternative taxonomy, and as reminders of the threat or promise of undeserved births and unnatural deaths. Ultimately, we will see that vampire narratives, classical heresy, and *Ulysses* share a common central project: questioning and rethinking the material and spiritual act of creation.

Bram Stoker and the Heretical Vampire

The vampire entered Western Literature in the nineteenth century, most prominently through Stoker's *Dracula* (1897), but also popularized by works such as John Polidori's romantic *The Vampyre* (1819) and the Irish J. Sheridan Le Fanu's *Carmilla* (1872). In Joyce's time, references to vampires and vampirism were more commonly about their metaphorical nature than their literary importance. For example, political cartoons from the late-nineteenth century use images of a vampire to refer to Ireland, England, and the Catholic Church as evil threats.[1] Since the 1970s, however, critical writing about "vampires" often has meant, at least partly, a literal vampire: a creature of the night that exists by ingesting human blood and is neither dead nor alive. More recently, critics such as Nina Auerbach and Slavoj Žižek have addressed the figure of the vampire in their theoretical writing. For Auerbach, "what vampires are in any given generation is a part of what I am and what my times have become" (1995: 1). Many contemporary theorists have pointed out that the figure of the monster—vampires and zombies in particular—provides the modern imagination with a symbol of epistemological and ontological instability that reflects our modern concerns with porous borders between natural and unnatural, human and machine, and life and death—borders that are explicitly theological and implicitly heretical.

Dracula comes out of late-nineteenth- and early-twentieth-century concerns that were expressed through anxieties about the body: fear of the New Woman, new technology, and immigrants. As theologian Elaine Graham writes, it is the monster myths, the "stories we live by," that will be critical tools in determining what it means to be human in our new digital and biotechnological age (2002: 17), and both *Dracula* and *Ulysses* foreshadow this engagement with a strange, new world of technology. If *Frankenstein* provided the nineteenth century with a monstrous creature that reminded them of the limits of human knowledge and the line between human and divine, then *Dracula* and its many imitations are an exploration of what lies forever beyond human understanding. Whereas, in the final scene of Mary Shelley's novel, both Frankenstein and his creature—locked in an endless pursuit literally to the edge of the known world—attempt to warn a ship captain *not* to continue on his quest to explore beyond the border, Dracula

---

1 The English *Punch* published a cartoon by John Tenniel in 1885 that depicted the Irish National League as Vampire come to prey on the English ("The Irish Vampire" October 24, 1885). The *Irish Pilot* responded two weeks later with a cartoon depicting the "English Vampire" (November 7, 1885).

already comes from the beyond (the non-West, the non-living, and the unnatural) and dangerously invites us *into* such a world. In ways that we can compare to the mysterious and unexplainable divinity of Jesus, *Dracula* crosses the barriers that *Frankenstein* erects and thereby questions the gap between human and the unknown, human and other, and human and divine. Frankenstein created his monster in an attempt to play God, but Dracula—a figure of random evil and unknown origin—ambiguously relates to both the divine and the sacred.

Like early-twentieth-century England and Ireland, the first centuries of Christian history were times of political and social unrest that also manifested physically, leading to a questioning of our perceptions of the real or solid, and the very processes by which we arrive at truth claims. To connect these ideas of heretics and vampires to *Ulysses*, we can look at the critical debates over whether Stephen's vampire poem is supposed to be ironic, plagiarized, or an authentic act of creation. Although *Ulysses* seems to present the poem as original to Stephen, it is actually based on a Douglas Hyde translation of a song. Whether intentional or not, the poem also introduces questions of authenticity and origin: Does a text represent a break or continuity with its predecessors? Can one create from nothing? Is the creation part of the creator? These questions echo the debates fourth- and fifth-century Christians were having about Christ and the Bible.

In tracing connection between these stories—from the historical Jesus and the heretical Arius, to the novels of Stoker and Joyce—we find similarities by placing our focus on the *acts* of telling and writing the story, by showing just how narrative is passed on, and on how it constantly creates new histories and new realities. In the epistolary *Dracula*, Stoker intends the novel's written structure to appear realistic and feasible. Each journal entry is copied, transcribed, and re-copied from recordings and short hand notes, with an accompanying and constant tension over just who is in charge of the text. Characters are described writing, rewriting, and collating documents into what we see as the book. The documents gain in importance as the novel progresses until even Dracula seems aware of them. Immediately after the men discover Mina sucking the blood from Dracula for the first time, the count escapes and, as he dashes out, scatters manuscripts and phonograph cylinders into the fire. Although there is no explanation as to why Dracula does this—or whether it is even intentional—at this point in the text, the destruction of material records acts as an act of chaos, symbolizing the very fabric of the reality of the story. For the characters in the novel, not only is Dracula attacking their women, but, through this act, he threatens their story and thus their truth. Without written proof of their experiences, the characters are plunged once again into a gaping void of the unknown, without definitions, templates, or evidence of their sanity. The vampire here literally attacks both their sense of reality and the novel itself.

Part of the fascination with vampires, in Joyce's time and in ours, has to do with the mystery of death, afterlife, and procreation that we also find in debates over heresy. Stephen's creation of the vampire poem in chapter three seems to come out of his musings on theological creation in chapter one, a chapter which begins with a mock Mass, presents both Arian and Catholic creation, and is full of moments of transubstantiation and types of creation, from references to the creation of urine from water to "two shafts of soft daylight" creating a cloud of "coalsmoke and fumes" at the "meeting of their rays" (*U* 1.317). From the vampiric and cannibalistic suggestion of the Mass itself, to the conflation of Buck's mock-Eucharistic shaving bowl with the bowl of green bile next to Stephen's dying mother, death is strongly connected with creation—and with an unnaturalness in both religious and artistic acts of transubstantiation. On the first page of the novel, Buck Mulligan's joking "little trouble with the white corpuscles" mocks the act of creation in the Mass at the same time that it introduces the vampiric theme of blood (*U* 1.22-3). The novel begins with a Mass, but one where we are going to have to rethink the magic.

Arius in Nightown

The association of divine and vampiric creation, although surfacing at various points during the novel, is solidified at the end of chapter fifteen. The longest chapter in *Ulysses*, "Circe," is a surrealistic hallucinatory play script that reworks much of the action of the novel through literalizing the subconsciousness of the characters and the book itself. As a sort of dreamscape remix of the whole novel, the chapter is full of references to theology, paternity, and Shakespeare. The actions include dead characters coming back to life, characters switching genders, and the recently deceased Paddy Dignam appearing, rather un-vampirically, not as a wolf, but as a dog. Near the end of the chapter, as Stephen is horrified to see the ghost of his dead mother (whom he had refused to pray for as she lay on her deathbed), he smashes his walking stick into a chandelier and flees into the street where he is knocked unconscious. As Bloom, father-like, bends over him, Stephen mutters: "Black Panther. Vampire" (*U* 15.4930). The black panther—often a medieval symbol of Christ—has already been associated with a suggestion of Christological heresy when Stephen earlier thought to himself, in a particularly gothic section of chapter fourteen, "The black panther was himself the ghost of his own father" (*U* 14.1032–3). With these three terms (panther, ghost, father)—another of *Ulysses*'s many alternative trinities—we are immediately transported by association to multiple places and themes in the book: the black panther and Haines' questions about Stephen's belief in the opening chapter, the vampire poem and the live dog (which is compared to a panther) sniffing a dead dog on the beach, the birthing process described in chapter fourteen, and the whole "father and son idea" (*U* 6.578). Vincent Cheng describes this complex web as a chain of associations in which the black panther vampire is God, Father, creator, Christ, the Son, and both Simon and Stephen Dedalus (1987: 169). The black panther vampire is both a heretical and orthodox trinitarian model of the "father and son idea," as Stephen's vampire suggests a divine figure and a Christian heretic. If the vampire in the poem is father *and* son, then it leads us directly into the dialectical positions of Arius and Sabellius, the opposing heretics of the opening chapter and to the chapter nine scene in the library. These associations make an even more convincing case for the imaginative conflation of Arius and the vampire. For Cheng, "Stephen's vampire imagery in Proteus introduces sex as violent and destructive coupling, creation and art as violent destruction, and the ambiguity among God, vampire, father, creator, artist, and Stephen" (1987: 167). Within this ambiguity, and within this chain of association, lies a further sense of God and creation, and life and death, as something unnatural. As Cheng points out, Stephen spends the day "brooding about destructiveness and death (and creativity and sex) in terms of beasts and beastliness" (1987: 162). In other words, from the early stages of *Ulysses*, and embedded in the mention of the vampire and the heretic, is the concept of creators—divine or artistic—as destructive beasts, that echo not only the simultaneously murderous and life-giving vampire, but also the evil-creator God of the Gnostic Christian and the "monstrosity" of a Christ who is both, and neither, man and God.

The Death of Arius

Of the three direct mentions of Arius in *Ulysses*, two refer to the legend of his death, perhaps known to Joyce from well-known accounts like this one, dating back to late antiquity, that stressed the shame of his ignominious end:

> Arius was parading through the middle of the city … a spectacle to all …. when a fear arising from his consciousness seized Arius. With that fear followed

a loosening of the bowels... Then faintness took him, and his bottom fell through along with his excrement. The thing which doctors call the rectum immediately fell out through his bottom, with a lot of blood following, and the rest of his intestines flowed out together with his spleen and his liver, and he died immediately.

(Socrates, *Church History*, 1.38.5–10)

Other versions of his death are gradually expanded over the centuries to include more graphic details, to emphasize how the site of his death was remembered and stress his association with other heretics.[2]

Joyce's interest in this scene seems to resonate with anxieties over artistic creation—a process he often connects to bodily functions. On the beach, Stephen writes and then urinates. For Bloom, defecation is pleasurable and creative, and farting is musical: in chapter four ("Sirens"), he sits in the outhouse imagining a literary creation as he enjoys his own bowel movement, and his farts contribute to the music composing the end of the episode. Arius's moment in the lavatory means not pleasure or creation, but a horrible, guilty death, resulting directly from his "remorse of conscience" or *Agenbite of inwit*, a phrase Stephen repeats throughout *Ulysses*. In some ways, this emphasis on death is a logical legacy for Arius, whose Christology represented a turn away from eternity and whose theology represents the losing side. Yet his bloody death is almost certainly not historically true, and is likely based on the death of Judas in the Book of Acts, where he "burst asunder ... and all his bowels gushed out" (1:18). Arius's shameful death may be repeated down through Christian history, but Arius's imagined Jesus—more man than god—will never die, and instead resurfaces again and again throughout a Christian history that desires immanence as much as transcendence, flesh as much as mystery, and the story of a man who became a god. Creation—divine *and* human—as it seems to be suggested by this vortex of associations, is not pure, is not romantic, and is not true. It is never clear what is created or by whom, the created is always influencing how we understand the creator. Like paternity, creation is a mystery, and like maternity, it is bloody and dangerous. Creation is a messy business—always sacred, always heretical, always vampiric, and always misunderstood.

---

2 See Ellen Muehlberger's "The Legend of Arius' Death: Imagination, Space and Filth in Late Ancient Historiography."

Arius and the Anxiety of Vampiric Creation 101

Figure 2 Death of Arius in a public lavatory "St. Nicholas and Arius the Heretic," 1665, artist unknown, located at the Smolinsky Convent, Moscow © Prof. Michael Fuller, 2006.

Part III. Arius and Sabellius with Shakespeare in the Library

Although Christological questions of creation and creator are implicit in the theological musings of the first chapter of *Ulysses* and in the context of Stephen writing his vampire poem in the third, they are explicitly expressed in the ninth chapter. Chapter nine ("Scylla and Charybdis") stages a debate between heretical positions through the language of literary criticism. In this chapter, which takes place in the Dublin National Library, the central activity—among various interruptions, contradictory comments, and thoughts—is Stephen's "presentation" of his theory of Shakespeare's *Hamlet* to a small group of older intellectuals: the critic John Eglinton, the mystical poet AE (George Russell), the "Quaker librarian" Thomas Lyster, and the assistant head librarian Richard Best. All four were real-life figures in the Dublin literary community in the early-twentieth century, and all four inhabit complex religious identities. John Eglinton—the pen name of William Kirkpatrick Magee—was the son of a Presbyterian minister and an important figure in the Irish literary revival, who published multiple books and essays, including a biography of George Russell. Thomas Lyster—apparently not a Quaker, but a member of the Church of Ireland—was the head librarian of the National Library from 1895 to 1920, a translator of an important biography of Goethe, and—as Stephen later thinks of him—a heretical Lollard.[3] Richard Best was the assistant director of the National Library, translated a book on Irish myths, and was a reader of Walter Pater and Oscar Wilde. The most famous of the three, AE, the pseudonym of George Russell, was a painter, poet, critic, and writer mostly known as a mystical thinker and an important member and, as of 1904, president of the Dublin theosophical circle. Just from these brief biographies we see that all four—in addition to representing Dublin literary culture—fall into a space between fact and fiction where names, biographies, translations, religious affiliations, and beliefs are never definitive or stable.

The chapter takes place in the afternoon and returns to Stephen after he has walked to central Dublin from the Dalkey school where he was teaching. The previous five chapters have followed Leopold Bloom in his morning activities, ending with Bloom right in front of the library. The chapter is packed full of allusions to Shakespeare's plays, writings on Shakespeare, and theories of literary criticism, as well as fragments of poetry, theology, satire, and multiple

---

3 Gifford remarks that the real-life Lyster was often mocked for his Quaker religious beliefs, so there is ambiguity, even among educated Joyce scholars as to his actual religious affiliation.

pseudonyms and hidden frames. Joyce's own various schemas list as symbols: "Hamlet, Shakespeare, Christ, Socrates, London and Stratford, Scholasticism and Mysticism, Plato and Aristotle, Youth and Maturity." The title of the chapter, "Scylla and Charybdis" refers to the two monsters encountered by Odysseus in his wanderings as described in Homer's *Odyssey*, Book XII, where he must pass between Scylla, a supernatural female with twelve feet and six heads, and Charybdis, a monstrous personification of a deadly whirlpool. More colloquially, it means something like between a rock and a hard place, and philosophically, it means a form of dialectic. The Scylla or Charybdis dialectic has multiple echoes throughout the chapter, most notably Plato versus Aristotle, but also the competing heretical position of Christology: Christ as more man than god or Christ as more god than man. Here, it seems, Stephen's heresy of choice has shifted from Arius, and his created almost-human Christ, to Sabellius, and the opposing theory that Christ is only God, has no human body, and only *appeared* to die on the cross. It is perhaps in Sabellianism, as William Noon writes, that "Stephen finds the link for tying together the story of the murdered king of Denmark and the dialectical rationalism of a theology that makes the Son no more than a specter of the Father" (1957: 110–11). While the Christ of Arius would believably suffer on the cross and ask his superior Father if he must suffer and die, the Christ of Sabellius was too divine to actually experience any pain. This conflation of Father (author) and Son (text) underlies Stephen's interpretation of *Hamlet*, where Shakespeare's dead son Hamnet is associated with both Hamlet the character and *Hamlet* the play. Stephen's theology and literary theory suggest that the literary artist may have more than one surrogate, or "son," and that one son may also be "father" to the other.

The opening lines of the chapter describe the "quaker librarian" discussing Goethe's view of Shakespeare: "a great poet on a great brother poet" (*U* 9.3). These opening words already set up several of the themes that connect this chapter to heretical debates. Lyster's Goethe reference is taken from the novel *Wilhelm Meister*, in which the main character translates, revises, and performs *Hamlet*. The chapter, then, begins with a member of a fringe religion (Lyster) citing a fictional account (Goethe's) of a fictional revision of the play that is at the center of *Ulysses* and the center of Stephen's argument over authorship and divine creation. From the beginning of the chapter, the lines between creator and created are complicated. Translation, fiction, performance, and alternative ways of practicing religion are all introduced in the first words of the chapter—concepts that reframe the act of the poet as much as they do the death of God.

It is in this chapter, as one critic writes, that Stephen seems to have "found in the ideal of the artist as creator a substitute for the God he has rejected," and that he has "settled on the career of William Shakespeare as one which may provide a key to the understanding of his own condition" (Schutte 1971: 84–5). In Stephen's "lecture" on Shakespeare and literary criticism, he draws an obvious line between divinity and author that then connects his ideas of literature to debates over the divinity of Christ and the nature of God. It is in the slippage between author, art, and biography that we find parallels among early Christian heresies and heresiarchs. Readers of Joyce since Stuart Gilbert in the 1930s have found in this chapter a "rapprochement" that is "made throughout the episode between Shakespeare and the Creator" (Gilbert 1952: 216). Stephen's theory itself—presented in fits and starts—is both biographical and a meditation on paternity. For Karen Lawrence:

> Stephen's critical premise—that the writer reveals his psychological obsessions in disguised and multiple forms in his work—can be applied to Stephen's literary theory itself, for his elaborate reading of Shakespeare is, of course, an expression of his own feelings about paternity, betrayal, and the relationship between the artist and his work.
>
> In its broadest implications Stephen's theory represents more than a straight biographical approach to literature: it recognizes the subtle, intricate relationship between the artist's self-exposure and disguise in his work.
>
> (1981: 28)

These patterns of revealing and concealing that are woven into the chapter are simultaneously psychological, biographical, and theological. But, as his religious and literary allusions reveal, Stephen's theory is also inherently unstable. Buried within these disguises and revelations are contradictory and subversive ideas of how we define individual, author, creator, and created. Stephen's theory both depends on and questions a clear definition of each of these concepts.

Stephen is the central consciousness of the chapter—although it is narrated separately from him—and the key for first-time readers of the chapter is to distinguish between the words that Stephen speaks versus the ones that he thinks to himself. The central dramatic action of the chapter is Stephen presenting his theory of Shakespeare to these established Dublin literary figures, who each have their own point of view as to the importance of Shakespeare, the relationship of an author's life and biography to their work, and the role of literature in general. AE claims that many of "these questions are purely academic," and romantically argues that art should reveal "formless spiritual essences," "eternal wisdom," or Platonic ideas. Anything else, he claims, is the "speculation of schoolboys for schoolboys" and is no better than the "Clergymen's discussion of the historicity of Jesus" (*U* 9.46–53). In other words, he gives a Gnostic/theosophical view that art and religion exist to be discussed only in the realm of the spiritual and the immaterial, and also that discussions of the "historicity of Jesus" are rooted in a materiality that has no place in theological communication. When AE enters the debates by claiming that "the supreme question about a work of art is out of how deep a life does it spring" (*U* 9.49–50), he associates the artist and the work as one, and the soul of the work as the same as the soul of the artist. He is not that far afield from Stephen's semi-Sabellian position of the unity of Father and Son, and Creator and Created. However, Stephen laughs off AE's comments by briefly internally characterizing the theosophical thought that AE subscribed to:

> Formless spiritual. Father, Word and Holy Breath. Allfather, the heavenly man. Hiesos Kristos, magician of the beautiful, the Logos who suffers in us at every moment. The verily is that. I am the fire upon the altar. I am the sacrificial butter.
>
> (*U* 9.61–4)

Stephen's thoughts here do more than is immediately apparent: "Father, Word and Holy Breath" are the first of many alternative trinities offered in this chapter and "I am the sacrificial butter," although from the Bhagavad Gita, is a reference to the crucifixion and the Eucharist. By pointing to the "formless" and limitless God of AE's theosophy, Stephen draws a contrast to the limited and material Son ("Word" or "heavenly man") that is the Christian God's creation. Christ ("Hiesos Kristos"), as a "magician of the beautiful," links the Son to ideas of Egyptian magic that came out of theosophical fascinations with the East. And when Stephen then thinks of "The Christ with the bridesister, moisture of light, born of an ensouled virgin, repentant sophia, departed to the plane of buddhi" (*U* 9.68–9), it is again both mocking AE's theosophical beliefs and pointing to their connection to the Gnostics—in this case the Gnostic myth that "Sophia," or Wisdom, emanated from the True God, fell into our world, and was part of the creation of both Christ and the lessor God of Genesis. Although Stephen is mocking AE's theosophical bent, he is also, despite himself, setting up some of the themes of literary and divine creation the chapter will explore.

Shakespeare (and a Ghost)

"Unsheathe your dagger definitions," Stephen thinks to himself with Shakespearean flare, as he mentally "warms up" for his "lecture," trying out phrases, encouraging himself, and remembering smart things he has said before. "God: noise in the street," he approvingly remembers saying earlier in the day, "very peripatetic" (*U* 9.85–7). His theory of Shakespeare then begins with questions: "What is a ghost? … Who is the ghost from limbo patrum, returning to the world that has forgotten him? Who is King Hamlet?" (*U* 9.150–1). In this scene, Stephen implicitly points to the theological, psychological, and artistic questions that the ghost raises in *Hamlet*, and that, as Shakespeare scholar Stephen Greenblatt writes, "are ones to which Shakespeare never provides definitive answers" (2001: 146). The implicit linking of a God of sound and the ghost in Hamlet sets out the questions of being that are in the background of Stephen's reading of Shakespeare. The existence of both lies somewhere between reality, memory, and text. Like the Christ of Arius, they seem to be "created" in a manner that potentially puts them on the edge of non-existence, of nothingness.

In Stephen's reading, Hamlet in the play is replaced by Hamnet, Shakespeare's dead son, and Shakespeare the author becomes God the Father. Stephen's theory of *Hamlet* is essentially that Shakespeare is simultaneously Father (of Hamnet), Son (of his recently deceased father), and Ghost. In this way, Stephen's model of Shakespeare echoes the Trinity—the Father, Son, and Holy Ghost—and also finds parallels in Stephen himself. Stephen is the ghost who was absent from Dublin and has now returned; he is also the dispossessed son of a father he disdains, and he is a creator/Father who attempts to fulfill himself through his progeny—his as yet non-existent poetry. As support for this substitute trinity, the chapter offers multiple other alternative trinities, as well as emphasizes God *and* Father in the role of author.

Stephen continues his introduction by describing the opening of *Hamlet*: Shakespeare himself plays the ghost, and speaks to Richard Burbage's Hamlet:

Hamlet, I am thy father's spirit

"To a son he speaks," says Stephen, "the son of his soul, the prince, you Hamlet and to the son of his body, Hamnet Shakespeare, who had died in Stratford that his namesake may live for ever." "Is it possible," Stephen asks:

> that the player Shakespeare, a ghost by absence, and in the vesture of buried Denmark, a ghost by death, speaking his own words to his own son's name (had Hamnet Shakespeare lived he would have been prince Hamlet's twin) is it possible, I want to know, or probable that he did now draw or foresee the logical conclusion of those premises: you are the dispossessed son: I am the murdered father: your mother is the guilty queen, Ann Shakespeare, born Hathaway?
>
> (*U* 9.170–80)

AE predictably protests Stephen's biographical reading of the scene, complaining that Stephen is "prying into the family life of a great man" and asks "what is it to us how the poet lived?"—a question that relates to his previous dismissal of the study of the "historicity of Jesus" (*U* 9.48). Stephen's mind then drifts away, seemingly to thoughts unrelated to his theory, although still in the style of Shakespeare: "Hey now, sirrah, that pound he lent you when you were hungry?" (*U* 9.192), as he remembers that he owes AE money. Stephen's logic here is that the Stephen that borrowed the money is not the same Stephen he is now ("Molecules all change. I am other I now. Other I got pound" [*U* 9.205–6]), but he will expand this idea in his questioning of the ontology and the continuity of soul and body—questions that haunt Christological debates, as well as discussions about ghosts. The continuity of the body and personal identity are, as philosopher Derek Parfit claims, mistaken concepts based on memory, and Stephen suggests the same idea here, as well as plays on the idea of the Trinity again:

> But I, entelechy, form of forms, am I by memory because under everchanging forms.
> I that sinned and prayed and fasted.
> A child Conmee saved me from pandies.
> I, I and I. I.
>
> (*U* 9.208–13)

As Stephen asks, if I am not I, then who sinned and fasted? Readers may also wonder, is the Stephen of *Portrait* (who Father Conmee saved from being paddled) the same Stephen of *Ulysses*? Parfit continually returns to this same question throughout his career—"what makes me the same person throughout my life, and a different person from you?" For Parfit, the commonly accepted idea of personal identity as an essential fact about humans is wrong; his theory proposes a more complex and relational concept. Basically, his argument is that at one specific time and place there is a person. Then, at a later time, there is also a person. While these people may seem to be the same person–indeed, they share memories and physical and personality traits—there is no actual evidence that makes them the same person. Our whole Christian and Western theological, political, legal, and moral systems rely upon the assumption that we are the same person yesterday as we are today and will be tomorrow. The criteria for defining sin, salvation, forgiveness, confession, punishment, the soul, and afterlife all contain within them this assumption.

When Stephen begins talking again several pages later, he is still taken with these ideas, but now works them in with his theories of creation, ghosts, and voice, seeking an assurance of existence against the fragility of being:

> As we, or mother Dana, weave and unweave our bodies ... from day to day their molecules shuttled to and fro, so does the artist weave and unweave his image. And as the mole on my right breast is where it was when I was born, though all my body has been woven of new stuff time after time, so through the ghost of the unquiet father the image so the unloving son looks forth.
>
> (*U* 9.376–83)

For Maud Ellmann "Stephen is saying that despite the deconstruction of the body the mole reprints itself afresh and thus affirms the continuity of memory." She then weaves this into Stephen's theory of Hamlet: "the term 'mole' also alludes to the ghost of Hamlet's father, whose son addresses him as 'old mole'" (2004: 90). Stephen, who is haunted by the ghosts of his own past—especially his mother—and who identifies with both Shakespeare and the brooding, black-wearing Hamlet himself, believes that Shakespeare was very much like King Hamlet of Denmark, who appears as a ghost to his son. As Stephen further develops his ideas, working multiple Shakespeare references and quotes into his own language, he puts himself in the role of Hamlet's ghost, saying to himself, "They list. And in the porches of their ears I pour" (*U* 9.465). Here, Hamlet's ghost is simultaneously suggestive of a divine shout in the street, the power of fiction and language, and the holy spirit impregnating Mary through her ear. The following paragraph finds Stephen moving quickly through themes of Shakespeare, fathers, ghosts, God, and creation. He imagines Shakespeare returning home at the end of his life, "weary of the creation he has piled up to hide him from himself." No longer a writer, Shakespeare is a:

> ghost, a shadow now, the wind by Elsinore's rocks or what you will, the sea's voice, a voice heard only in the heart of him who is the substance of his shadow, the son consubstantial with the father.
>
> (*U* 9.478–81)

Just when Stephen brings all his themes together with the orthodox (consubstantial) theological explanation of the relationship between Father and Son, God and Christ, author and text, the blasphemous Buck Mulligan bursts onto the scene with an appropriate and ironic "Amen" (*U* 9.482), which also emphasizes the links between God and Shakespeare, and Christ and Hamlet. As Stephen flashes back to his list of heretical "brood of mockers" that he thought of in chapter one, Buck provides the "Entr'acte," and his first remark, "you were speaking of the gaseous vertebrate" (*U* 9.486),[4] leads to an unspoken parody of the Apostles' Creed:

> He Who Himself begot middler the Holy Ghost and Himself sent Himself … Who, put upon by His fiends, stripped and shipped, was nailed like bat to barndoor, starved on crosstree, Who let Him bury. Stood up, Harrowed hell, fared into heaven and there these nineteen hundred years sitteth on the right hand of His Own Self but yet shall come in the latter day to doom the quick and dead when all the quick shall be dead already.
>
> (*U* 9.493–9)

Stephen's internal recitation of the Apostles' Creed borrows from various heretical traditions, including Sabellius (the Father begetting himself) and the Gnostic Valentinus (body of Christ made in heaven). It also adds Christ's descent into hell onto the Nicaean creed, which "not only renders Christ's earthly mission more faithfully, but proves a fuller allusion to the actions of the novel," in which both Bloom and Stephen will endure a kind of hell. The "Apostle's Creed can so function," writes Lang, "because of the parallels between what Christ did and what both Bloom and Stephen will do on June 16, 1904" (1993: 155).

When Eglinton suggests that Shakespeare's father corresponds to the ghost of Hamlet's father, Stephen again insists that the ghost of Hamlet's father is Shakespeare himself. Lang explains Stephen's thinking as a blend of the theological with the aesthetic:

> In considering more than one kind of relation between Father and Son, theology explains how the literary artists may have more than one surrogate or "son" and how one may also be "father" to the other. Like the Father and Son as characterized by Sabellius, Joyce and Bloom are two manifestations of the same spiritual substance. Like Father and Son as Catholicism regards them, Joyce and Stephen are consubstantial separate persons sharing the same spiritual substance. Like Father and Son as characterized by Arius … Bloom and Stephen are separate persons who discover a spiritual resemblance.
>
> (1993: 20–1)

---

4 Gaseous vertebrate is an odd phrase that Gifford defines as "having a spine but without substance, a ghost; in this case, 'the son consubstantial with the father'" (2008: 224). But, as Lernout points out, in several writings at the turn of the century, the phrase simply refers to the Christian God. A 1900 book by the freethinker Ernst Haeckel refers to the "paradoxical conception of God as a *gaseous vertebrate*" (Lernout 2010: 157–8).

While Stephen is never able to frame it as succinctly as Lang, the whole of *Ulysses* combines themes of Gods, Fathers, authors, heretics, and their creations into metaphorical and linguistic patterns that never remain stable. Fathers, Stephen says—drifting away from his lecture, but not his theme—are a "mystical estate" that, like the church, are founded upon "incertitude" and "unlikelihood," a phrase that expresses doubt in every aspect of creation and meaning, literary as well as theological.

These ideas lead Stephen back to thoughts of Christology and, specifically, to Sabellius, as he seems to realize that his position is more in line with the thinking of Sabellius than Arias in his conflation of creator and created. He works Sabellius, the "subtlest heresiarch" (*U* 9.862), into the "conclusion" of his argument, although it leads him to ask the confusing question: "if the father who has not a son be not a father can the son who has not a father be a son?" (*U* 9.865). John Eglinton's proposal that the "truth is midway ... he is all in all," is a truly Nicaean compromise, especially in light of Stephen's ultimate admission that he doesn't really believe his own theory (*U* 9.1018). Stephen can be seen from a multitude of theological and critical positions, but not as truly embracing any of them. For Morrison, were Stephen to "champion any one heretical 'analogy', he would only be aping the authority he seeks to contest. What he can do is to manipulate the heretical and the orthodox to challenge the basic reasoning by which orthodox doctrine ... is enshrined" (2000: 125). By engaging with and blending the orthodox and the heretical, Joyce points to how the interplay of accepting and challenging how we process narrative, and its creation, are built into the story from the beginning.

Although Joyce himself apparently believed Stephen's Shakespeare theory (Ellmann 1983: 364), the weakness in Stephen's lecture is that his evidence is almost entirely taken from the plays themselves. There is an interesting parallel here in the assumption that many Joyce scholars have made; from Ellmann on, there has been a tendency to perhaps associate Stephen too closely with Joyce himself. Like Christian historians faced with evidence of alternative versions in the Gnostic texts, Stephen is "not interested in finding those facts which are historically accurate; he is interested in finding those facts which will bolster his preconceived notions about Shakespeare" (Schutte 1971: 54). Within the context of the Christological themes of both Joyce's chapter and mine, another parallel can be found in interpreting the Gospels as fact-based biographies of Jesus, and not the early Christian propaganda that they were. Like biographies of Joyce that rely on Stephen, like Stephen's reading of Shakespeare, like the New Testament Gospels, we often confuse the literary figure with the historical one, a fallacy that points to the necessity to separate the historical Jesus from the spiritual Christ. Ultimately, chapter nine cannot really be seen as embracing a theological, biographical, or literary critical position. Instead, it reinforces the idea that the way we read and interpret literature, think about bodies, and process history is inextricably wound up in our cultural memories of debates over heresy and orthodoxies, debates that are deeply entwined in our own biographies, critical practices, and libraries.

* * *

For Christine van Boheemen-Saaf, "Joyce's method of weaving his texts—looping, unlooping, noding, disnoding—focuses the reader's attention on an absence which defies representation and which highlights the inability to tell in one's 'own' words" (1999: 5–6). It is precisely these linguistically created absences that speak to early Christian theological debates as they are reframed in modernist literature. The Christological debates of the fifth century simmer beneath the surface of theology and literature, creating patterns of thought that continue down to present-day discussion of body, mind, soul, and creation. From the vantage point of the twenty-first century, scholars of religion such as Mark C. Taylor have drawn a line of influence from these fifth-century Christological debates through to twentieth-century Death-of-God theologians, such as Thomas Altizer and the experimental literature and theory of the twentieth century. In tracing this path, Taylor proposes that to understand our own modernity we must "rethink traditional theology," through the later intellectual and literary developments of the twentieth century, as a path to "unexpected insights" (2007: 143). It is in search of these insights that I continue to juxtapose Joyce's texts and their critics with religious studies. Modernist figures like Joyce, Borges, Woolf, Bataille, and Kafka have been important for radical theologians and scholars of religion looking to construct new ways of thinking about the relationship between religion and literature. Among these many perspectives, we might think of a figure like Altizer who, in his influential essay "William Blake and the Role of Myth in the Radical Christian Vision," points to the role of the "modern poet"—primarily Blake, but also Joyce and Kafka—as giving us a model of the "reversal of our mythical traditions"—in other words, a concept of God as loss or absence. At the same time, however, Altizer acknowledges that this poetic expression of negation is still also a "form of the mythical vision" (1966: 171). For Altizer, and for a generation of radical theologians who followed him, mythic and scriptural traditions are about the desire for or the belief in a divine figure who is also revealed to be non-existent or dead. This contradiction—literature as tearing-down, and yet also reimagining and recreating, myth, scripture, divinity, and transcendent experience—is perhaps the central and essential contradiction at the intersection of word, body and text, and of heretical and orthodox debates as staged in imaginative writing. This, too, is a theme that literature-minded radical theologians will point to in literature from Blake's "Nobodaddy" to Dostoevsky's "Grand Inquisitor" to *Ulysses* and *Finnegans Wake*. In each case, theologians find a divinity who can only "exist" by breaking away from the constrictions of traditional religion and theology, a breaking away that is often found in the difficulty of the literary text but also in the interplay between heresy, history, orthodoxy, and practice.

5

Joyce, Medieval Heresy, and the Eucharist: Fragmented Narratives of Doubt

He's weird, I tell you, and middayevil down to his vegetable soul
(FW 423.27–8)

Part I: A Modernist in Medieval York

In the summer of 2014, as the ideas for this book were beginning to take shape, I was selected to participate in a National Endowment for the Humanities (NEH) faculty seminar on devotional interaction in medieval England. I arrived in York for the NEH seminar excited, but not knowing what to expect. As a scholar of modernist literature and twentieth-century culture, I knew I would feel an outsider among medievalists and art historians. However, my emerging ideas on this book had reached a point where, in an attempt to narrow both my theme and scope, I had been trying to write closely about select places, images, and objects across Christian history. The seminar—led by Sarah Blick and Laura Gelfand—gave me the opportunity to rethink the historical and religious relationships between object and text by introducing me to new ways of understanding the performativity of space and objects, and the material nature of devotion in medieval England. I was able to focus my project to make more tangible connections to some of the literary metaphors I was analyzing in Joyce's use of Mass imagery, as well as medieval themes and language, in *Ulysses*. The idea of the Eucharist as an important symbol and structuring device in *Ulysses* is not new, but studies tend to be exclusively textual and rooted in literary criticism.¹ In this seminar, I learned to combine this type of literary analysis with visual studies: using the interior of a cathedral or a parish church to engage with the spaces and artifacts that influenced the English language and literature at the core of *Ulysses* and its readers.

York is a city famous for its medieval treasures, most prominently the towering, forever-unfinished York Minster Cathedral. Before my summer in York, like most amateur medievalists, my understanding of Gothic cathedrals was as an incoherent and overwhelming mixture of styles and periods. I did not see this mixture as an aesthetic or theological failing, and more or less agreed with Christopher Wilson who wrote that "the virtual impossibility of perceiving the interiors of the great churches as architectural entities … mirrored mankind's inability to comprehend the whole of the Creator's plan" (1990: 10). Yet I still felt compelled to look for the artistic unity, the harmonious and seamless East to West "story of salvation," as promised in the York Minster Guide Book. As a scholar of English modernist literature, who had spent limited time in England, I also imagined the medieval cathedral through descriptions like D. H. Lawrence's *The Rainbow*, when a character visits Lincoln Cathedral, which was "away from time, always outside of time!" Lawrence emphasizes neither the altar itself nor the theology, but the liminal status that the space invites—a status "between east and west, between dawn and sunset." The space—like the altar it celebrates—contains contradictions: "Birth and death, potential with all the noise and transition of life … the immortality it involves, and the death it will embrace again. Here in the church, 'before' and 'after' were folded together, all was contained in oneness" ([1915] 1995: 187). Although this chapter will engage with the conflation of time and death that fascinated Lawrence, and that also plays out in *Ulysses* and *Finnegans Wake*, it will also resist these idealized concepts of unity that modernists often ascribe to the medieval. In this chapter, I want to challenge this sense of "oneness," by looking closely at the medieval spaces that we still observe and inhabit.

In an anecdote that Richard Ellmann relates in *Ulysses on the Liffey*, Joyce tells Wyndham Lewis, as they walk near Notre Dame, that in *Ulysses* he wanted "something of the complexity sought by the makers of cathedrals" (1972: xvii). His new *Odyssey*, as Ellmann sees it, "superimposed elements of the medieval upon elements of the classical mind," but both, Ellmann adds, "are drawn into

---

1 Examples include Richard Ellmann's *Ulysses on the Liffey*, Robert Boyle's. "Miracle in Black Ink: A Glance at Joyce's Use of His Eucharistic Image," Frederick Lang's *Ulysses and the Irish God*, and Mary Lowe-Evans's *Catholic Nostalgia in Joyce and Company*.

modern experience so that they have a present rather than an atavistic past" (1984: vii). For many modernist authors, it was a common rhetorical move to compare their expansive and difficult novels to the architecture of a Gothic cathedral. Perhaps most famously, Marcel Proust thought of his 3,000-page novel of memory and art as structured like a cathedral, and even considered naming the individual sections after areas of the cathedral. He ultimately decided against this, and in the novel itself he instead chooses the metaphor of a dress. Proust scholar Margaret Topping, explains this decision by speculating that, for Proust, the metaphor of reading a cathedral depicts the reader as too "passive." She writes that "to cast his novel as a cathedral may thus have been too suggestive of monolithic conclusions, of fixed wisdom, an authoritative vision" (2013: 143). Whether or not her theory represents Proust's actual motivations, it certainly represents the type of simplification of the cathedral experience to one that is ultimately unified and "monolithic" that I wish to complicate.

While the theology of the Mass, as it developed in the Middle Ages, especially following the Fourth Lateran Council of 1215, may have suggested this "authoritative vision" and "fixed wisdom," if we look beyond Church doctrine and instead imagine the lived experience of the Mass—multiple chantries, competing elevations, partial sight lines, varying routes, incompletion, folk beliefs, and doubt—it provides a different metaphor for the experience of reading Proust or Joyce. While a reading of *Ulysses*—like the English cathedral, whose characteristically longitudinal space can seem to imply distance, but also invites a disruptive sense of movement—can include an implied journey from chapter one through eighteen, it must also allow for dark corners, forgotten passages, plural realities, nonlinear narrative, incomplete readings, confusion, and skepticism. While we could seek out Lawrence's "oneness," or follow the twentieth-century religious theorist Mircea Eliade, and discuss the cathedral, the altar, and the Eucharist as "breaks in space" that reveal an "absolute reality," or as an *axis mundi*—a symbolic "center of the world"—I am more drawn to perceptions of medieval art, architecture, and liturgy as *uncentered* spaces of misdirection and fragmentation. The churches and cathedrals of Yorkshire and East Anglia that I studied that summer show surviving visible elements of medieval Catholicism not present in either Ireland or London. For readers of modern English literature—from Shakespeare to Dickens, to D.H. Lawrence, to Hilary Mantel—the Yorkshire medieval walls, churches, and windows provide a glimpse of a partially remembered world that these authors had in mind and that they reimagined in their fiction. The multiple and fragmented theories of the medieval Mass in this chapter may seem naively anachronistic—a characteristically modern, even Joycean or Derridean viewpoint that we are imposing upon the misty past. But, as we have seen throughout this book, what seems to be modern skepticism is often an echo of past heretical positions: heresies that were never forgotten, but that continue to speak from the shadows of orthodox texts, objects, spaces, and rituals.

James Joyce, Medieval Heresy, and the Eucharist

There are many angles from which we can make these links, but here I focus on a set of issues or tensions that revolve around interpretation: modes of viewing or reading, understandings of history and narrative, the relationship of mind, body, and knowledge, and the mystery of the act of creation—divine or artistic. As I outlined in chapter two, while medieval heresies famously include Cathars, Waldensians, Hussites, the Free Spirit, and other groups, I will, for the sake of my discussion, primarily focus on arguments over the proper understanding of the Eucharist and how these debates simultaneously addressed many of the heretical arguments of the past, created new heretical movements, and foreshadowed schisms to come. While the theological questions that led to both heresy and the church councils of the fourth and fifth centuries continue to be asked into the later middle ages, we also see, in the thirteenth and fourteenth centuries, the emergence of the most influential answer to these questions in the history of Christian thought. The Eucharist was, as Miri Rubin writes, a "symbol of the utmost uniformity to accommodate a complex world" (1991: 12). This "answer"—the Eucharist Mass and the surrounding explosion of art, doctrine, ritual, and philosophy that accompanied it—was also, by its very nature, unstable and would, in part, lead to the next great heresy, the Reformation. Even more important, for my purposes, is how this complicated theological symbol and practice connects intimately to shifts in language and to explorations in literature. As Jennifer Garrison writes, "The Christian understanding of language and the Eucharist both derive from the central mystery of the Incarnation; the Word became flesh and redeemed human language, and it is through the words of the priest that the Word again becomes flesh on the altar during the mass" (2017: 7). The symbolic slippage here between Word and word—and, in the *Wake*, Joyce will add "world" and "void" to the mix—brings us back to the relationship between authors, texts, bodies, and creation that can be found within English Catholic devotional practices in ways that force us to rethink how word and image, language and ritual, and narrative and scripture interact.

The drama of the Eucharist, the interweaving of "natural and supernatural with human action," is, as Rubin writes, "the drama of human creativity and of human frailty" (1991: 1). In this chapter, rather than concentrating on a single medieval object, text, or place, I am instead seeking an altered perspective (based on a whole experience of spaces, objects, and writing) that will complicate an imagined and metaphorical modernist medievalism—much as I proposed a modernist Gnosticism in chapter three. My exploratory conclusions are drawn from my experience with learning important aspects of medieval art—the changing styles within Gothic architecture, the organization of a monastic site, the function of rood screens in a parish church, the presence of fading medieval graffiti in a cathedral—as well as my exposure to more recent trends in scholarship: the "material turn," an increased awareness of different modes of human-object interaction, the study of sight lines, and the afterlives of devotional objects. I am partially influenced here by "new materialists," such as Jane Bennett, who urge us to see material objects not as passive or inert, and not in binary opposition to the living, but to instead see them as "vibrant matter" or "vital material" that then encourages us "to theorize events … as encounters between ontologically diverse actants, some human, some not, though all thoroughly material" (2010: xiv). The material spaces and objects I was drawn to—worn surfaces in church interiors, Easter sepulchers, damaged rood screens, and modern and Victorian restorations and "reimaginings" of the medieval—pointed to rhythms of disruption, incompletion, memory, and changes over time that spoke to my interests in modernist literature and art and their challenging of narrative, space, and time.

The Eucharist—as an artistic and theological center of medieval Christianity, and as a common trope of Joyce studies and literary theory—functions as a simultaneous high point, center point, and tipping point of my research on heresy and literature. In attempting to "see" useful connections between the medieval and modern—an act that I learned to understand quite differently—I will locate my thought in the visual and the material. As Sarah Blick and Laura Gelfand write, "visual art was an intrinsic element in making the host seem more real" (2011: li). The ceremony and theology of the Eucharist, particularly the moment of the elevation of the Host, is a plural presentation that combines sight, sound, smell, taste, touch. The blood and body of Christ are created and depicted through the words of the priest, the window behind the altar, the decorated screen in front of it, and the cross shape of the church or cathedral. It is simultaneously a message of transformation and one of sacrifice, passion, incarnation, and resurrection. It takes place on a sacrificial block represented as a place of death, but of life-giving death; the altar is a liminal place of conflict that is a "richly complex symbolic network, in which narratives from the past and expectations for the future come into the immediacy of present experience" (Kieckhefer 2004: 18). As an act of viewing, imagining, touching, tasting, and digesting, the ritual is both transcendent and immanent, both magic and mundane, successfully integrating the exterior-interior of human celebrants and the public and private lives of parishioners. It is a sacrament and a social institution, a celebration of the human history of salvation, and a vision of heaven. Rubin writes that "at the centre of the whole religious system of the later Middle Ages lay a ritual which turned bread into flesh—a fragile, small, wheaten disc into God" (1991: 5). In this ritual, in this change of bread into God, we can find a complicated and contradictory theory of God, humankind, and, above all, a model for creation that—as we will see with Joyce—still occupies literary artists centuries later.

The Elevation of the Host: Sightlines and Misdirection

Our returning question—"what happened on the cross?"—is a question that echoes through centuries of heretical debates, historical, theological, philosophical, and fictional *and* is at least partially and satisfactorily answered every time the Host is raised above the altar: "the two sacrifices were one sacrifice" (Pelikan 1978: 190). This belief—connecting a daily ritual with a truly unique event—conflates the historical with the spiritual and offers a theory of the "real" based on contradictory understandings of time and space. The sacrificial understanding of the Mass became the dominant interpretation of the Eucharist so much that a theologian of the late-twelfth century said: "This sacrifice was instituted by the Lord not only to be offered, but also to be eaten" (Pelikan 1978: 188). What makes this heresy solution so powerful is that it combines the question, "what happens on the cross?" with a ritualistic answer that can be seen, performed, and experienced through creative art and action. Yet there were cracks in this presentation: the last supper happened before the crucifixion, so there is again chronological and historic ambiguity. Furthermore, Christ was sacrificed by unbelievers on the original cross, but by believers at every Mass. Therefore, while sacrifice made some sense of the Eucharist, the concept of "body" had to be further addressed. And, as Pelikan points out, this is further complicated because the phrase "body of Christ" in Scripture and in patristic usage had multiple meanings (1978: 190–1). The most important part of the debate was the gap in meaning between "body of Christ" in human form and "body of Christ" in the sacrament. This gap in understanding the body—and heretical and orthodox interpretations of it—offers insight into the "performance" of the Mass, and in how this performance is a complex metaphor for the intersection of art and theology, the medieval and the modernist.

The Mass has often been seen as a seminal act of European theater. In 1965, O.B. Hardison wrote:

> Just as the Mass is a sacred drama encompassing all history and embodying in its structure the central pattern of Christian life on which all Christian drama must draw, the celebration of the Mass contains all elements necessary to secular performances.
>
> (1965: 39–40)

But to claim that the Mass contains "all elements necessary" for *any* theatrical performance seems to leave out folk, popular, and heretical practices and rituals. In what ways does the medieval Mass help us understand the participatory, the erotic, or the heretical? A closer look reveals both the order and chaos.

The central theatrical element in the medieval Mass was the moment of the elevation of the Host. Surviving medieval baptismal fonts, windows, and

Figure 3 Elevation of the Host "Corpus Christi," early 1400s, The Ranworth Antiphoner, contributors unknown © St. Helen's Church Ranworth. Reproduced with the permission of the Broadside Benefice, Parishes of Ranworth and Panxworth, Woodbastwick, South Walsham, and Upton and Fishley.

psalters almost always depict the image of elevation to represent the Eucharist (Duffy 1992: 96). By the late-twelfth century, the elevation of the Host was becoming a widespread practice that allowed more of the faithful to actually witness the moment of transubstantiation. The *Lay Folk's Mass Book*, composed in the late-twelfth century in York and translated into English in the following century, gives instructions for the worshiper to follow when the Host is elevated. The kneeling worshipper should lift his eyes and look at God's body and blood:

> Kneland halde vp thy hands,
> And with inclinacyon
> Behalde þe Eleuacyon.
>
> (Simmons 1879: 36)

This moment—as parishioners crowded with each other to see the movement of change, and then immediately after as the priest held the now consecrated Host over his head—was simultaneously dramatic, social, historical, individual, spiritual, and theological, but it was also an artistic moment, when the church architecture, the biblical language, the stained glass, and the painted rood screen, all became more "real" at the hands of a divinely inspired artist.

Even though the elevation seemed to be intended to allow as many worshippers as possible to see the Host, here too, we find obstructions and complications that are most materially evident in the construction of elaborate screens: "in many parts of northern Europe, and nowhere more conspicuously than England, the late Middle Ages saw the construction of ever more formidable screens," which are often interpreted as functioning to obstruct the view (Brooke 1971: 164–6). I will talk more about screens later in this chapter, but it is important to note that, in recent decades, scholars have argued that the isolating and dividing function of screens has perhaps been exaggerated. Duffy claims, for example, that late medieval screens in English parish churches were porous, allowing much more lay access to the Mass than was previously asserted (1992: 157). Screens also enhanced drama and preaching, and scholars point out that lay people actually moved in and out of the choir and could also often see the high altar from the sanctuary (suggesting, then, that the screen is not really a barrier, but a symbolic frame or marker). A screen is sometimes an open metal frame that barely impedes visibility; however, the rood screens in medieval English parish churches were most often a wooden partition with windows, partially restricting vision, but also serving to frame and enhance the sight of the Host (Duffy 1992: 485).[2] So while often read as an ocular impediment, the rood screen could also be seen as emphasizing and, artistically, augmenting the elevated status of the priest and the exalted nature of the Mass. It is in this paradox, of concealing and revealing, where we find our literary parallels and metaphors.

Modernist Nostalgia for Presence

As I mentioned earlier, whether coming from a position of belief or unbelief, scholars writing about literary relationships between the modernist and the medieval tend to contrast the doubt and ambiguity of the modern with a more solid and secure medieval epistemology. This can manifest as either nostalgia for a purer presence or a rejection of that nostalgia. But both of these positions reductively frame the medieval aesthetic as a less complex, less plural, and less fragmented experience than the modern, the modernist, and the postmodern. We can find this nostalgia for presence—for a metaphysics of presence—in literary critics, in modernist authors, and in contemporary philosophy. In recent theory, as Carolyn Dinshaw critiques it, "the Middle Ages is still made the dense, unvarying, and eminently obvious monolith against which modernity and postmodernity groovily emerge" (1999: 16). And yet, as our study of heresy has shown, all readings of historical religious events contain the core of subversion within them. In looking more closely at how we read the material culture of the medieval, we can find that the same structures that elevate the spirit—the cathedrals, screens, porches, and doors—also chip away at belief and offer their own forms of instability and doubt. While in York, I focused especially on literal and metaphorical readings of obscured sight lines, obstructions, and incompletion as expressions of a desire for absolute presence but also as dramatic demonstrations of its difficulty. Instead of just the cathedrals, stained glass, and altars that harmoniously accompany and amplify the elevation of the Host, I discovered—through graffiti, iconoclasm, and incompletion—a fragmented experience that is enlightening when placed in the context of Joyce's Mass-like language and structure in *Ulysses* and *Finnegans Wake*.

One way to organize this narrative of twentieth-century literature's relationship with medieval religious practice is to find literary critics or modernist authors either imagining a pure relationship to faith, images, and the word or, alternatively, dismissing such direct and "pure" encounters as coming from a

---

2 This sort of discussion of sight and screens extends beyond the rood and beyond England. See, for example, Jaqueline Jung, *The Gothic Screen: Space, Sculpture, and Community in the Cathedrals of France and Germany, ca. 1200–1400*, and Sharon Gerstel, ed. *Thresholds of the Sacred: Architectural, Art Historical, Liturgical, and Theological Perspectives on Religious Screens, East and West*.

naïve, superstitious, or primitive mind set. Although it is not hard to find evidence for these opposing positions, it is also not hard to find evidence for an awareness of a more complicated narrative. However, these nostalgic positions persist, even within theoretical discourse, and some aspects of the recent "turn to religion" in theory and literary criticism demonstrate that these ideas are still very much on our intellectual landscape. The theoretical movement known as "radical orthodoxy" (a relatively conservative movement not to be confused with the "radical theology" to which I often refer in this book) is driven, at least partly by the awareness of "a richer and more coherent Christianity which was gradually lost sight of after the late Middle Ages" (Milbank, Ward, Pickstock 1998: 2). Although most radical orthodox thinkers will claim more of a medieval presence in language than I am asserting, these theoretical approaches have significant parallels in thinking about the idea of the Mass in Joyce and its link to the tension in religious language. Radical orthodoxy "posits the centrality of the medieval in the ongoing encounter between contemporary theology and the theoretical discourse of poststructuralism and postmodernism" (Holsinger 2004: 120), but ultimately it points back toward a desire for stable meaning and presence. Theologian Catherine Pickstock's reading of Derrida demonstrates this desire, as her appeal to restoring meaning to language through the Eucharist is both medieval and Joycean, just as it opens itself up for multiple interpretations in much the same way as *Ulysses* or the elevation of the Host. For Pickstock, in the Eucharist "where death is not held as over against life, it is possible to restore meaning to language ... [through] the integration of word and action in the event of the Eucharist." The Eucharist is a "theological sign" which "reveals the nature" of "divine mystery" (1998: 252). In other words, her sense of the Eucharist as a sort of super language that communicates beyond any one-to-one signification is in some ways similar to Joyce's restoration of the word in *Ulysses* and *Finnegans Wake*. What is significantly different from Joyce or Derrida, though, is that her "restoration" is linked to a desire to look back to a purer presence that we have lost, rather than using the loss of presence itself as a space to create new, multilayered meanings.

My main idea in presenting these details of the history and aesthetic of the English medieval Mass is to show how it comes out of and leads to debate over heresy and orthodoxy and how we can read the whole narrative—from 800 years of history to the single raising of the Host in a York parish church—as a theory of reading and as a model of literary criticism. Each process is a dramatization of the relationship of language (broadly defined as spoken, written, imagined, or the metaphorical Word of God) to a transcendent, and yet paradoxically material and bodily, experience. The ritual of the Eucharist stages an "event"—an unrepeatable moment—that is yet repeated regularly. It is theological, it is an act of lived religion, but it is also a statement of art's ability to move beyond representation—beyond mimesis—as the architecture, stained glass, and rood screens become part of a higher reality exemplified by the Host as the body of Christ (or Word of God).

But what happens when we move to the "Mass" that is *Ulysses*? Does Joyce elevate an absent Host? George Orwell famously remarked of *Ulysses*, "What Joyce is saying is 'Here is life without God. Just look at it!'" While, as we have seen, some Joyce readers find God and others find only his absence, my point is that the history of Christianity itself echoes this dialectic. The history of Christianity, its practices, its creeds, its schisms, and its sacred texts and theological writings are not about an unmovable transcendent God, not about the security or certainty of the divine. To imagine a "life without God" can still be a practice of atheism or a practice of Christianity. This imagining of the "without God" is the yearly or daily imagining of the crucifixion; it is the imagination of Easter Saturday. It is part of a centuries-long struggle of Christians to define what they mean by God and to decide what to do if he is unfair, dead, nonmaterial, or nonexistent.

Part II: *Ulysses* and the Mass

In a letter to his brother Stanislaus, Joyce asked "don't you think there is a certain resemblance between the mystery of the Mass and what I am trying to do?" (S. Joyce 1958: 116) For a Catholic author like Joyce, writing in the tradition of English literature, what the church says God does in the consecration of the Mass, the literary artist does through his imagination, and—like Christ in the Host—enters the world in another form, as a book. Throughout his career, Joyce plays with this balance of sacred and secular creation. In his early short story, "The Sisters," he symbolically subverts and reverses the action of the elevation of the Host by having a feeble old priest drop the chalice which "contained nothing" (*D* 17). *A Portrait of the Artist as a Young Man* describes the Eucharist in terms that emphasize the similarity to artistic creation: "The great God of Heaven [comes] down upon the altar and takes the form of bread and wine" (*P* 171). When Stephen attempts to explain his new artistic sensibility in *Stephen Hero*, he uses the same metaphor:

> Phrases came to him asking to have themselves explained. He said to himself: I must wait for the Eucharist to come to me ... He spent days and nights

hammering noisily as he built a house of silence for himself wherein he might await his Eucharist. (*SH* 30)

But by the time Joyce writes *Ulysses*, his Eucharistic references have become more complicated. The mature Joyce would likely have agreed with Miri Rubin that the drama of the Eucharist is the drama of human creativity, whether or not he believed in any kind of literal transubstantiation.

As we saw in chapter one, *Ulysses* opens early in the morning on the roof of a tower where Stephen Dedalus is living. The first words of the novel are spoken by medical student Buck Mulligan, who will play the role of a comic blasphemer throughout the novel. He carries a bowl of lather out onto the roof, raises it aloft, and intones the traditional call to God's altar and the opening of the Mass: *Introibo ad Altare Dei*. The bowl of lather here clearly represents a chalice—which will be echoed by different types of chalice substitutes throughout the novel—and the call to the Mass seems to announce the creation of the novel itself. Where interpreters differ, though, is in determining whether this opening is ironic, subversive, blasphemous, confessional, or all of the above. The round gunrest on the tower to which Mulligan calls to Stephen—"Come up, you fearful Jesuit!"—represents the altar of the Mass and, after Stephen emerges, Mulligan makes "rapid crosses in the air" and announces that this is the "genuine christine: body and soul and blood and ouns." But although he builds up the drama ("Slow music, please"), he jokes that the moment of transubstantiation of blood into wine proves resistant: "A little trouble about those white corpuscles" (*U* 1.1–23). At the same time—which we discover in the fourth chapter—our other main character, Leopold Bloom, is enacting a more everyday type of Eucharistic activity in his actions: the first words he thinks to himself as he prepares a tray and tea kettle for his wife are "another slice of bread and butter" (*U* 4.11).

As Frederick Lang points out, Stephen and Bloom will "proceed through the day from one 'altar' to another," and Lang's book even includes a chart that identifies parallels between each part of the Mass and passages in the novel (1993: 109; 113). Bloom and Stephen will separately and then together participate in different sorts Eucharistic activities (literal and symbolic) throughout the day, finally sitting down together at a table in Bloom's home. Although Lang sees all these as part of Joyce's efforts to "undermine Catholicism" (1993: 114), the function of the Eucharist in the novel also has as a positive and creative role. For example, as we have seen, after the opening "failed" transubstantiation, the complex issues of creation are expressed in various ways in this first chapter of *Ulysses* by featuring multiple moments and types of transformation or creation.

One traditional way to understand this comparison is to see the medieval and the modernist as two opposing points on a continuum representing a gradual decline in the performativity of language and the stability of its meaning that it accompanies, moving steadily from magic to doubt. This view would find in Joyce's metaphorical and failed Masses a characteristically modernist dramatization of the disintegration of a transcendental signifier. Richard Santana, for example, opens his book *Language and the Decline of Magic* by claiming "once, language had the power to change the forms of the physical world; now its power is limited to describing it" (2005: 5). Santana traces a centuries-long "epistemological shift" from the Corpus Christi plays in York to James Joyce's *Ulysses* in which language loses its power and becomes "more symbolic than real" (2005: 5). Umberto Eco, like Santana, sees the language of the medieval Mass and the language of *Ulysses* in binary opposition, and writes that Joyce finds a "radical opposition between the medieval man, nostalgic for an ordered world of clear signs" and "the modern man, seeking a new habitat but unable to find the elusive rules" (1989: 3). Both Santana and Eco would agree with Cordell Yee that, while the medieval language of the Church and the mystery play had unquestioned meaning and power, "instead of stabilizing language, Joyce destabilizes it. His purpose is to show how the idea that language expresses particular fixed significations is illusory" (1997: 47). But the study of heresy reveals that rules and signs have always been elusive, playful, and malleable and, while I think that there is value in these formulations, I find that the extent to which this sense of modernist language as positioned as *opposite* to the medieval has been overstated. While some scholars, like Yee, argue for a more conservative view of Joyce's language, I am instead positing a more experimental and experiential view of the medieval—a medieval experience seen through the eyes of a Joyce reader, but also through the recent scholarship on medieval Europe.[3]

Santana writes, in a perhaps contradiction to his earlier point, that Joyce's use of the structure of the Mass "recuperates the performative power of language of medieval England" (2005: 9). Lucia Boldrini also paints a somewhat different version of Joyce's medievalism as she writes that Joyce's works start:

> from a position of (idealized) medievalism that seeks to find in the Middle Ages a transcendent formal language and a poetic direction while knowing that this

---

3 See, for example, Sarah Blick and Laura Gelfand, eds. *Push Me, Pull You: Imaginative, Emotional, Physical, and Spatial Interaction in Late Medieval and Renaissance Art, Volumes 1–2*, or Janet T. Marquardt and Alyce A. Jordan, eds. *Medieval Art and Architecture after the Middle Ages*.

cannot be integral to the modern world; but ... he arrives at a deeper and more pervasive sense of the medieval.

(2002: 13)

It is this "deeper and more pervasive sense of the medieval" that I find not only through Joyce, or through language, but through medieval spaces and objects as well. It seems clear from what we know about the experiences of the medieval Mass that the experience of medieval humans was not really only that of seeking an ordered world of clear signs. And does not Joyce's *Ulysses*, despite all of its celebrated difficulty, also demand that readers create order? What we have here is not really a "radical opposition" after all. While Joyce presents a type of a failed Mass in almost every chapter, there are also spaces in which language—often religious language—creates something new or material in a way that could be identified as a more medieval than a modernist conception of language. We can use these much-discussed aspects of *Ulysses* in dialogue with medieval physical spaces to add to and complicate metaphors of words and sacrament, literature and creation, and comparisons of the medieval and the modernist. By expanding the complexity and multimedial nature of the Mass, we expand the metaphor of the Mass-as-creation in a way that gives a thicker reading of modernist/medieval comparison to issues of language, doubt, and artistic creation. In bringing the medieval to *Ulysses*, the ideas of the image and word, form and content, and body and mind as expressed through medieval interaction with art and the Mass become theories of unity and fragmentation that are central to Joyce's aesthetic and the modernist experience of reading.

Although the Eucharistic language in the opening scene of *Ulysses* seems to be presented as blasphemous and ironic, if we accept the proposal that the novel is as much structured by this very ceremony as by the more familiar Homeric model, the roles of the Mass and the Eucharist become less ironic. The transubstantiation on the first page of *Ulysses*—echoed throughout the chapter—is a performative model of the novel itself: a text made of words, and the Word, that is in constant tension with the idea of a single body and text. Ruth Walsh offers a refutation of locating a Mass structure in *Ulysses* by claiming that to do so is to commit an "aesthetic fallacy by ignoring differences between creative art (Homer's *Odyssey*) and religious ritual (the Catholic Mass)" (1969: 321). But whatever else it might have been, by the thirteenth century, the climactic moment in a Mass had evolved into a powerful and spectacular ritual that was effective on multiple fronts, including the aesthetic, the dramatic, and the creative. The priest, in elaborate ceremonial garb, his back to the congregation and partly concealed by a rood screen, lifts the consecrated wafer. As kneeling parishioners look up, the wafer is highlighted against the backdrop of stained glass—perhaps a huge east window of Creation to Revelation, as in York Minster, or a Corpus Christi window, as is still extant in York's Holy Trinity Goodramgate parish church. This means that the wafer, now as "Body of Christ," is at the center of a building representing the body of Christ, and framed by the backdrop of a window portraying the "Body of Christ." At this dramatic and magical moment, a bell rings and all around look up to see, and perhaps crowd and push each other for a better viewing angle. This very moment—the vision of the Host, the scent of incense, the pain of kneeling on stone, the sound of the bell, the body of your neighbor, to perhaps be followed by the taste of bread—is an intensely plural, erotic, and sensual one that must be read in multiple ways—it is created art and religious ritual, theater and sacrament.

A Jew in the Cathedral

While my reading of Umberto Eco and twentieth-century religious studies scholars like Mircea Eliade point me toward exploring the moment of elevation and the space of the altar as a centralized and ideal model of artistic creation, studying the cathedrals and parish churches of Northern England provided another narrative beyond the unifying power of altars and east windows. Influenced by medieval art historians and theories of lived religion, my inquiries turned to the multiple perspectives and experiences of human bodies. The medieval Mass is not just a more plural and simultaneous experience of theological language and space organized around an uncontested center or issue; it is also movement: the movement of bodies through—often incomplete or disrupted—spaces and the movement of texts and objects through time. As Sarah Blick and Laura Gelfand write:

> Late medieval and Renaissance art [and] architecture demanded that people move through certain passages; its sculptures played elaborate games alternating between concealment and revelation; and its paintings charged viewers with moving visually through two dimensions, recreating long and imaginative journeys. Viewers of this period were meant to push back, interacting with artwork in a performative manner in order to gain insight into religious belief and their own reactions to these demanding works of art.
>
> (2011: xxxix)

The Dublin of *Ulysses* is also full of bodies moving through spaces, both sacred and secular, from churches and cemeteries to pubs and libraries. The most direct engagement with a physical space of Catholic worship happens through the eyes of the Jewish everyman Leopold Bloom, whose morning Dublin wanderings take him into a Roman Catholic Church where Mass is being performed. This scene has a distinct medieval echo. It was a common strategy in medieval exempla to introduce the mystery of the Eucharist to non-Christians, usually Jewish men, often in violent and horrific ways.[4] Joyce, characteristically, creates an everyday version of this trope in chapter five of *Ulysses* when, after pausing at the door where the "cold smell of sacred stone called him," Bloom enters the church and watches a celebration of the Eucharist:

> The priest went along by them, murmuring, holding the thing in his hands… The priest bent down to put it into her mouth, murmuring all the time. Latin. The next one. Shut your eyes and open your mouth. What? Corpus: body. Corpse. Good idea the Latin. Stupefies them first. Hospice for the dying. They don't seem to chew it: only swallow it down. Rum idea: eating bits of a corpse. Why the cannibals cotton to it.
>
> (*U* 5.347–52)

In this deeply meta-textual passage, Joyce is simultaneously commenting on the Catholic Mass, on the construction of his whole project as a redefinition of the Mass, and on the performativity of the Christian word. Bloom's naïve (yet perceptive) observation of the ritual combines text, taste, death, and bodies in ways that echo the opening Mass imagery from the first chapter and that will continue to be developed throughout the novel. Bloom may not understand Eucharistic theology, but he does know that there is a "big idea behind" it, and assumes that it produces a "kind of kingdom of God is within you feel" (*U* 5.361–2).

By retelling the Mass through the eyes of a Jewish character, Joyce offers us a mode of discourse that oscillates between medieval and modern models. From their early and contradictory attempts to define themselves, Christians have struggled with their position on Judaism and Jews, and this tension was often represented in art through an emphasis on physical difference. For the first two generations of Christians, the essential question—and the debate that led to the first articulations of heresy—was whether they were still Jewish or not. For the next 1,800 years of Christian history, the Jew represented both the archetypal Other and the repressed core of the Christian origin narrative. By the time of medieval Christianity, when theological questions had been dramatized into the

---

4 See, for example, Miri Rubin's *Gentile Tales: The Narrative Assault on Late-Medieval Jews.*

rituals of the Mass and the Eucharist, the figure of the Jew continued to play an important role for Western Christian self-identification, and "unbelieving" Jews regularly featured in Eucharistic miracle stories. An example of one of these narratives taken from the late medieval Vernon Manuscript tells of a Jew who follows a Christian friend into a church and sees the priest, and every member of the congregation, devouring a child. His friend explains that his vision is a sign of God's wrath against the Jews for killing his Son, and a Christian would only have seen the Host. As Duffy glosses it, "what is torn and bleeding flesh to the Jew, in other words, is the bread of Heaven to believers" (1992: 105). The Jew immediately wants to be baptized so as to never see such a vision again. In the fifteenth-century *Croxton Play of the Sacrament*, a group of Jews bribe a Christian man to steal a consecrated Host for them. To prove the falseness of Christian belief, the Jews stab the Host and "crucify" it by nailing it to a cross. The Host bleeds and is then followed by scenes of farce where a Jew's hand comes off and, still clinging to the Host, it is flung into a cauldron of boiling oil that then (like a Lollard priest's chalice) overflows with blood. When the hand and Host are then placed in an oven, the oven (tomb) bursts open and Christ appears displaying his wound and reproaching the Jews for again crucifying him. The Jews, of course, repent, believe, and dutifully go to Christian baptism.

But it is also possible to see another side of the story, a side of Christianity that recognizes how Eucharistic practices dramatize unstable gaps in understanding: gaps between priest and congregants, nave and chancel, author and text, body and mind, reality and imagination.[5] As far back as the fourth century, the theologian Ambrose of Milan felt that the Real Presence of Christ in the Host was something from which the faithful needed to be protected. The Ambrosian position won out in the Middle Ages, although thinkers like Thomas Aquinas did not emphasize the graphic physical nature of the act, focusing instead on the mysterious presence of Christ in the Eucharist in ways that are "real," but can only be perceived through faith and intellect, not through sight and taste. Ultimately these are debates over perception, over interpreting an act that is a kind of reading—something that a modern writer like Joyce understood. There is, in Western literature, a sense of the physical in our perception of words, a danger of the graphic lying behind our understanding of the real, and a way in

---

5 These gaps and doubts were not always so repressed. A young Martin Luther recalled monks in Rome laughing about how they sometimes blasphemously changed the Latin words at Mass to "bread thou art and bread shalt thou remain, wine thou art and wine shalt thou remain" (Oberman 1989: 149).

which the medieval tensions between the more figurative approach and literal readings continue to play out in an imaginative sense.

Part III: Medieval Re-Joycing

Thinking about this space between the image and word is one of the ideas that emerged from my studies in York, a summer spent looking at medieval art and talking with medieval art historians, but also reading and writing about Joyce. York Minster Cathedral is typical among English cathedrals in that it was largely built in the thirteenth and fourteenth centuries, exhibits multiple architectural styles, has suffered much damage from weather and fires, has been regularly restored, and is itself unfinished. Characteristically, for English cathedrals, the Minster is long, and, at 264 feet, the nave is one of the longest in England. Official guidebooks to York Minster, past and present, follow the standard cathedral metaphor in announcing the building's "great journey" to the altar. The great journey of salvation, from the Great West Doors along the nave to an altar lit by the east window, is a "way lined with the stories of the Bible, the lives of the saints, and the deeds of faithful Christian people." The path leads to a choir and altar, "the very gateway of Heaven where Christ himself feeds and prepares us" and the Great East Window, shining above the whole scene with its depictions of Genesis to Apocalypse, with God the Father at the top, is both "origin and goal" (York Guidebook 2014: 6). But, as Richard Kieckhefer writes in his book *Theology in Stone*, "people seldom leave longitudinal space alone" (2004: 30), and to think about how bodies actually moved through this space is to tell a different story. The actual experience was—and is—more indirect and disrupted. The recent (2008–20) restoration of the East Window was only the latest disruption of the imaginative experience of a pure theological journey from nave to altar.

While we might be tempted to imagine cathedrals as embodying a grand narrative of teleological west to east movement, the actual lived practice in medieval English churches was one where the customary entrance was through a south porch, and the west door was reserved for ceremonial entries; the processional character of the interior was therefore most fully realized only on special occasions (Brown 2003: 36). To enter York Minster through the south door not only changes the route and the symbolism, but offers the grisaille and geometric Five Sisters Window as a backdrop rather than biblical narrative of the Great East Window. Finally, English cathedrals like York Minster typically have a longer structure, and also tend to demonstrate many marked divisions along this space—and the fact that chantry chapels and side aisles were common to English cathedrals further complicates the ideal of a unidirectional flow of worshippers and sight lines from west door to altar and the east window. By the late Middle Ages, according to Kieckhefer, processions in a major church often recognized the "church as a whole" rather than just the altar, and the "interrelatedness of its parts" became more important (2004: 28). Instead of a single altar or a linear structure, we have—architecturally and imaginatively—more of a network. This network further increases the tension between a "pure" experience of the Host and a complicated, nonlinear reading involving multiple Masses, multiple Hosts, and a movement of bodies not just west to east, but in more chaotic patterns. These nonlinear patters are a way of studying lived religion, but are equally related to how we think about narrative—and while part of this process is theological, it can also be linked with artistic responses to the Eucharist. If the cathedral is a guide to reading the Eucharist—and the Eucharist is a key to understanding medieval aesthetics, theology, and narrative—then by noticing different entry points into cathedrals, by noting the complicated sight lines, spatial divisions, multiple experiences, ways of expressing doubt, and the impossibility of locating text or objects at a single time, we complicate the analogy to the modernist novel.

The point here is that Joyce's "Mass," as realized in *Ulysses*, is not a modernist reversal of medieval unity, but is a similarly complicated and spectacular structure with multiple entrances, alternative histories, contradictory images, and patterns of presence and absence, complexity and simplicity, and construction and decay. Chapter fifteen of *Ulysses* is an example of this kind of structure. The hallucinogenic dream vision of "Circe"—written in the form of a surrealistic play in the "night town" section of Dublin—is, as I tell my students, a "trippy remix" of the whole novel, and is a magical event made out of the mundane daily bread of the rest of the novel. All the events, characters, objects, and themes of the novel—including the religious imagery—are rendered in reverse, perverse, or distorted forms. Like the novel itself, and many of the other chapters, "Circe" has an identifiably Eucharistic structure. It opens with the entrance to a brothel and with Stephen Dedalus chanting the *introit* to the Mass, just as Mulligan did on the first page. Stephen and his friend Lynch continue to chant from the Mass while they metaphorically characterize sex workers as baptismal waters. The later climax of the chapter is a type of Black Mass complete with imagery of the crucifixion, last judgment, and resurrection. In keeping with existing Black Mass descriptions, as well as the sexualization and gender reversals of this episode, the "altar" for this Mass is the pregnant Mrs. Mina Purefoy, a "goddess of unreason" who lies "naked, fettered, a chalice resting on her swollen belly" (*U* 15.4690–3). In an echo of chapter one, Father Malachi O'Flynn opens this Mass: "*Introibo ad altare diaboli,*" or, "I will go to the altar of the devil" (*U* 15.4700). The priest then takes from the "chalice" and elevates a "blooddripping host," proclaiming "*corpus meum*" (*U* 15.4703). The chapter moves swiftly from this point to its more realistic ending, with Stephen and Leopold Bloom alone together for the first time. It is almost as if the novel itself has now achieved its own transubstantiation: a moment where its narrative, characters, and plot lines come together to create something new—the confluence the novel seems to have been preparing us for. Of course, this transubstantiation can be seen as leading to another failed Mass, as, in the next chapter, Bloom and Stephen retire to a cabman's shelter where they attempt, mostly unsuccessfully, to bond over multiple topics—including an almost incoherent discussion about the incorruptibility of substance and proofs of the existence of God—while snacking on ironically Eucharistic stale rolls and bad coffee.

Seeing Is Not Believing: Squints and Screens

Although he left the Church as a young man, Joyce remained drawn to religious spaces and rituals. Maintaining a distance that was part Bloom and part Stephen, Joyce would attend services but off in a corner, leaving quietly after the Mass, presumably observing, but with an intentionally compromised sight line (Ellmann 1983: 309–10). Joyce also used to attend Greek Orthodox rituals (*L2*: 89), and expressed a particular interest in the "image-screen" or *iconostasis* used as a divider between the altar and parishioners. "The altar is not visible," Joyce relates to his brother (*L2*: 86), in which his surprise or fascination at a non-visible altar points to the important role of seeing and sight lines in the Mass, and the tension with the modernist position that seeing was no longer believing.

But, as I have been claiming, this mediation is not just a modern experience. As Jennifer Garrison writes, "despite the various physical and conceptual boundaries between the believer and the Eucharist—from altar screens to infrequent Eucharist reception to a doctrine of transubstantiation that defied human logic—the desire for direct contract with Christ's body in the host became increasingly fervent in the later Middle Age" (2017: 2). Yet worshippers were also encouraged to take in the Host with their eyes, and for many that was often as close as they got. For most practitioners, the Host was something to be seen and rarely physically consumed. But seeing the Host was not always such an easy or simple matter. The chantries, side entrances, and screens compromised the pure experience of viewing and experiencing the Host, and dramatized the tension between seeking a pure experience and mediating that same experience. As rood screens grew more common, those closed off from the ritual strove to make certain of their ability to witness the elevation of the Host. Kate Giles observes that this urge "was facilitated through a range of strategies, including the piercing and creation of peepholes in screens and 'squints' through side walls to provide the laity with views of the High, or other subsidiary, altars" (2007: 115). These squints, generally completely unadorned, proved an interesting contrast and point of view to the beautiful but partially obfuscating screens. This contrast is striking in medieval parish churches across England where there can be a stunningly beautiful screen and an unadorned squint just feet away.

A strict definition of the squint is difficult to articulate; they are generally an aperture, usually oblique, providing a view of an altar. According to Simon Roffey, squints were commonly small, internal windows, or view-holes, that were inserted within the fabric of aisles, chapels, and arcades to afford a line of sight between particular areas of the church, where such a view would otherwise be obstructed. Most importantly, the squint would have facilitated clear lines of sight within the increasingly busy and complex topography of the parish church

Figure 4 Squint at Church of St. Thomas of Becket.

(Roffey 2006: 128). Squints—perhaps because of their unadorned nature—have not been researched or written about as much as most medieval church architectural details, and the descriptions and even the identified purposes vary from scholar to scholar. Whether the person looking through the squint was an anchoress, a dignitary, or perhaps someone separated because of illness, what is particularly interesting to me is the contrast between viewing the elevation of the Host through a squint and looking through a rood screen. We can read this in multiple ways: in one sense the view from in front of the screen is disrupted and partial, while the view through the squint is direct and framed. On the other hand, the view through the screen is elaborately adorned and, as the Host is raised, not only does one look through the decorated screen, but the east window in the background gives an appropriate theological and ritual frame.

This contrast escapes a narrow desire for pure presence, and instead also sees medieval spaces as sites of misdirection and fragmentation. Rood screens, doors, windows, and rough cruciform squints give us material objects to build literal and metaphorical readings of sight lines, obstructions, destructions, and incompletions in ways that express a desire for absolute presence, but also doubts in its possibility. The answers to questions such as whether screens obstruct or enhance the view of the Host are less important than the constant interplay between the two options. It is this tension—between part and whole, between fragmentation and unity—that is explored in Joyce, and screens and squints act as useful metaphors for the process of reading *Ulysses*. The fact that screens and squints *both* obstruct and enhance—depending on one's point of view, depending on definitions of sight and interpretive agency—echoes the metaphorical Mass that we can see in *Ulysses*. The *Ulysses* Mass suggests fragmented glimpses of the "real presence" seen through the blasphemy of Mulligan, the heresy of Stephen, and the Jewishness of Bloom, each offering their own incomplete versions of Catholic transubstantiation as an artistic experience.

Concluding with Joyce

In returning to teaching and writing about Joyce and religion after my summer in York, I found that I brought a fresh sense of the medieval with which to work. This new way of thinking about spaces and sight lines offered me a corrective to influential twentieth-century definitions of religion as a force for order. While there have been multiple studies of Joyce and the language of the Mass, studying medieval devotional art in York gave me the opportunity to redefine these ideas in the context of the sights, sounds, and spaces of cathedrals, churches, and ruins. My essential argument is that a close engagement with medieval spaces and objects complicates the claims of many commentators on Joyce, who offer conceptions of the Eucharist as representing a direct and more unified language in contrast to Joyce's literature of suggestion, ambiguity, and deconstruction. Ultimately, I want to complicate both sides of this story: to see Joyce's relationship to the medieval Mass as central to modernist creativity, and to also show ways in which the medieval Mass is more plural, more "modernist," or even more "Joycean" than most literary theorists communicate.

These shifts in emphasis—from a single altar to multiple points of interest, from priests and bishops to parishioners, from the language of the missal to the physical barrier of the rood screen—allow us to see Joyce's metaphorical Mass differently. It is neither a nostalgic nod to a pure language of creation, nor a cynical and fragmented representation of Catholic superstition, but is, instead, another complex narrative of creation that is both medieval and modern in the same way that any existing thirteenth-century object viewed in the twenty-first is both medieval and modern. Studying the interaction of medieval art, *Ulysses*, and Christian scripture allows us a view of each of the texts outside of linear historical narratives—to see each of them as a type of time machine. The elevated, medieval Host is therefore not only viewed indirectly but across multiple moments in time. Ultimately, we can continue to point to passages and themes in *Ulysses* that directly engage with Eucharistic themes, but that also function as rood screens, squints, side chantries, and south doors: readers of *Ulysses* must work their way through riddles, puns, allusions, slang, archaic language, and nonlinear and truncated narratives before they can get a glimpse of the larger meanings. These physical and metaphorical passages allow a view—indirect, disrupted, and incomplete—of the shadows in language, text, and object that connect the medieval and the modern.

Joyce's works anticipate recent trends in medieval studies by revealing the flaw of imagining a simple opposition between the medieval and the modernist; the distinctions do not hold nearly as much meaning as modern critics have presumed. Boldrini writes that Joyce uses the "aesthetic foundations" of medieval models, by "transposing" them (2002: 13). It is in this "transposing" of the medieval into the modern world to challenge the history of the present where we find a deeper connection between *Ulysses* and Christian history, and where traditional distinctions between medieval and modernist are blurred or erased. When Stephen's musings on creation and Christological heresies in chapter one lead him to invent the word, "contransmagnificanjewbangtantiality" in chapter three (*U* 3.51), it is, as we saw in the previous chapter, a word that is both creative and deconstructive, and that performs competing and complicated theologies of creation. Joyce's use of language is both medieval and modern, and it is important to see his words as historical documents, and as containing a medieval etymological sense of essence: his words function as both postmodern signifiers of absence and suggestions of a Real Presence.

Probably the most important lesson I learned in York about viewing medieval art and objects is not to try to see the object as it existed in the thirteenth or fourteenth century, but to instead look at a six- or seven-hundred-year conversation about our relationship to and definition of the medieval. The obvious—but often neglected—point is that "how we understand and appreciate medieval art has been filtered through the lens of time" (Marquardt 2011: 1). What interests me in the context of this chapter is not trying to make this lens as clean as possible—like some direct squint looking back into the "Real Presence" of the thirteenth century—but to analyze the lens itself and then, in turn, the viewer. Seeing is always interpreting; as Joyce writes as a footnote in *Finnegans Wake*, you must "Wipe your glosses with what you know" (*FW* 304, ftn.3). The turn toward this kind of study by medieval art historians has not only "revealed the extent to which we have hung our notions of history upon object" (Marquardt 2011: 1), but also changes how we see our modern selves.

* * *

In the final chapter of *Ulysses* ("Penelope"), where Molly Bloom gets the final remix by giving her own version of the day and of her history with Leopold Bloom, she summarizes an explanation her husband had given her earlier in the day as "some jawbreakers about the incarnation he never can explain a thing simply the way a body can understand" (*U* 18.566–7). Molly, in her characteristic way, has put her finger on the complex Eucharistic structure of the novel. Readers of *Ulysses* will remember that it was not actually the "incarnation" that Bloom had tried to explain to her, but the word "metempsychosis." Molly's one sentence, then, joins the ancient Greek and medieval Christian roots of the whole book, and then asks us to understand it physically, as a body, a *corpus*. Molly's concluding monologue—which is filled with references to bodies, and bodily functions—narrates, one more time, many of the same events we have already read, but now reframed as physical. If the "Circe" chapter reimagines the events of the day as a surrealistic dream, Molly's chapter makes words into flesh, makes the text material. The ending of the 35-page, run-on, punctuation-less monologue is, appropriately, a memory of Bloom proposing to her that flows from the unanswerable question of the creation of man to a Eucharistic private sharing of a piece of cake:

> who was the first person in the universe before there was anybody that made it all who ah that they don't know neither do I so there you are they might as well try to stop the sun from rising tomorrow the sun shines for you he said the day we were lying among the rhododendrons on Howth head in the grey tweed suit and his straw hat the day I got him to propose to me yes first I gave him the bit of seedcake out of my mouth.
>
> <div align="right">(<i>U</i> 18.1569–75)</div>

The novel—which began with a failed Mass and takes us on a journey of misdirection, ambiguity, obfuscation, and blasphemy—in the end gives us the creation of the world in a piece of cake.

6

Alternative Reformations: Iconoclasm and *Finnegans Wake*

> "But the world, mind, is, was and will be writing its own wrunes for ever"
> (*FW* 19.35–6)

Part I: Art Under Attack

I began writing this final chapter originally with one basic idea: that the literature of Joyce, particularly *Finnegans Wake*, could be usefully seen to borrow, break apart, reshape, and reimagine religious scripture and devotional objects in ways that we understand differently and are retroactively transformed because of how we think about the Reformation. The way that this one idea, which occurred to me gradually as I worked on the other chapters, developed into the various sections of this chapter is, as we will see, a literal journey—the result of years of thinking and traveling. The story begins with a Joyce seminar in Dublin and moves to a small English church, then to a museum exhibition in London, and from a rainy day in Kilkenny, Ireland to the Joyce archives at the snowy University of Buffalo. Each of these places and experiences helped me see that the narratives and histories that Joyce builds in *Finnegans Wake* allow his shifting language to show the passage of time, and reveal a past and a present shaped through the creation and destruction of the Reformation.

The Irish and English literary traditions that deeply influenced Joyce are unthinkable outside of Reformation history and theology. Joyce, of course, and other authors important to this book—Shakespeare, Stoker, Chesterton, and Spenser—were inspired and fascinated by medieval England, but living in a post-Reformation England or Ireland, they would have been surrounded by damaged, vandalized, and abandoned objects of medieval art, architecture, or devotion. These broken and defaced images are more than just a record of what was. Iconoclastic images become a visible theory of history and the sacred: a blend of the glory, magic, and superstition of the past with the excitement of violence, and the beauty of the fragment. These images embody the tension between three types of time: the gradual changes over the centuries of an object's existence, the brief moment in which it was dramatically altered, and then, finally, in many cases, a Victorian or modernist idea of "authentic" restoration. While the deliberate and ideological destruction of religious images was not new, what *was* novel, according to Margaret Aston, was the "attempt to make of destruction a systematic process of elimination, to alter minds as well as change the face of buildings" (1988: 2). These altered minds—minds that learned to see destruction and historical alteration as part of their religious narrative—are what I am interested in, particularly in their place in a twentieth-century imagination that grew out of the destruction of two major world wars.

During the English Reformation, the plural and complicated experiences of the Mass that we saw in the previous chapter were questioned, subverted, and reversed in an attempt to elevate the "pure" word itself over the material and sensory experience. In Reformation England there was, in the words of Stacy Boldrick, a "breaking of the bodily experience of belief" (2013: 21), or, in other words, a separation of the material and the spiritual, the physical and the verbal. For many reformers, anything in the church that produced the experience of sight, smell, touch, and sound—anything, in other words, that communicated a sensorial blend of faith and doubt—was to be removed or destroyed. These acts of religious iconoclasm create and destroy in ways that thread into past and future. Iconoclasm paradoxically "attempts to reinstate true history by an act of violence that is always anti-historical; by that anti-historical act it activates a new historical tradition" (Simpson 2010: 15). In this way, an act of iconoclasm paradoxically resembles the act of the Catholic Mass or a passage in *Finnegans Wake*. They all flatten out history in an attempt to reshape it as non-linear—reading both from left to right and from right to left; in the Mass, Christ's sacrifice is in the present: all history exists at the same time, on the same page. In the *Wake*, the protagonist HCE is always both a modern Dublin pub owner and a fallen Adam, expelled from the Garden—a Garden that is also Dublin's Phoenix Park. If, as authors such as Ernest Gilman have claimed, the "phenomenon of iconoclasm itself and the body of controversy it provoked are sharply etched in the literature of the period" (1986: 1), then it makes sense that Joyce, whose works are written with, through, and against so much of English literature, would inherit elements of these tensions. My reading, through thinkers like Joyce and their complex use of Mass and scriptural language and imagery, is that the unity and the fissures—the presence *and* the instability—come from the same artistic, intellectual, and theological spaces, words, images, and stories, the same heretical and iconoclastic motivations.

Stepping on Jesus

In a controversial incident in 2013, a professor from Florida asked students to write the name "Jesus" on a piece of paper and then step on it. The negative outrage that followed the event tended to reiterate the familiar narrative of college students being taught to scorn traditional religious values by elite, atheist faculty. The actual story was more complicated. The instructor was a self-identified Christian who took the exercise from a Catholic teaching manual, and the point was, the instructor explained, to get students to think about the power of cultural symbols. "This exercise is a bit sensitive," the manual says, "but really drives home the point that even though symbols are arbitrary, they take on very strong and emotional meanings." Most students, he said, "hesitate" to step on the paper, and many declined. "In fact," the professor added, "the point is knowing that they won't do it. I accept that and then ask them 'Why won't you do this?' Then they reaffirm their faith" (Bennett 2013). What is interesting here is that students seemed to think they had created something with their own hand that could then be blasphemed against, something that was in some way sacred. This event is a contemporary dramatization of the centuries-old discussion of images, words, writing, iconoclasm, and divine identity. It is the kind of newspaper story you can imagine Joyce jotting down fragments of in one of his *Wake* notebooks, as a combination of language, popular culture, and myth (what kind of monstrous creature, after all, gets to "stomp on Jesus"?). But the implied questions here go straight to the core of religion and literature: In what ways does a handwritten piece of paper with five letters on it—letters that you yourself have written—represent anything "real" or sacred? And would it have been different if they had drawn a picture of what they thought Jesus looked like and then torn it up?

When students find it disturbing to write the word "Jesus" on a piece of paper and then step on it, they are making a culturally conditioned statement about the sacredness of image and text. For Jews, Christians, and Muslims, the sacred text is often assumed to be a perfect copy of a heavenly original. But, as scholars of the book know, texts are always in flux, both in their content and in how they are read. Books of scripture are always copies of copies, with multiple variants and without a clear original. When religious texts moved from scroll to the book or codex, it changed practices of reading and interpretation; readers could flip back and forth between pages, finding connections and repetitions not possible before. Reading practices, of course, continue to change in our own time. On both my phone and Kindle, I have multiple translations and editions of the full text of the Hebrew and Christian Bible, the Quran, the *Book of Mormon*, *Ulysses*, and *Finnegans Wake*—all almost instantly available and open to word and phrase searches. They are manipulable searchable, and malleable in ways not previously imagined. Digital texts and reading devices give us more flexible scripture, and, as Rachel Wagner writes "our fascination with fluidity results in a transformation from stories as fixed texts to stories as fictional worlds" (2011: 17). These shifts in meaning and perception of what a "book" is are inevitably woven into the mental material that connects scripture and literature. When *Finnegans Wake* and *Ulysses* were digitized and searchable, or when the drafts and notebooks became available online to scholars, the interpretation of the texts—in fact, the definition of the texts—expanded: the act of meaning-making itself shifted.

As we have seen in previous chapters, questions of literary interpretation, authority, and representation have divided the borders of orthodoxy and heresy since the second century. If the Reformation was a heretical movement that "succeeded," it was because of a complex web of political/technological/historical/theological factors. What the Reformation *did* do, however, that is useful for us, is to provide artistic and literary models of thinking about questions that also define twentieth-century literature and theory. While some historians resist these large narratives, and big histories, Reformation historian Brad Gregory writes, "we *cannot* understand the character of contemporary realities until and unless we see how they have been *and are still being shaped* by the distant past" (2012: 15, emphasis his). Gregory's main point in his book, *The Unintended Reformation*, is that:

> The Western World today is an extraordinarily complex, tangled product of rejections, retentions, and transformation of medieval Western Christianity, in which the Reformation era constitutes the critical watershed.
>
> (2012: 2)

These tensions, between medieval and then Reformation sites, enact the unifying ideology of the medieval Eucharist that we looked at in the previous chapter, as well as the cracks in this unity that opened it up to the iconoclasm of the Reformation. In response, I propose a big working theoretical question: What is the relationship between an image, its description, its title, and its "real" presence or origin? Thinking about texts historically allows us to put these actions into conversion with that of a sixteenth-century Englishman, who could bash in the sculptured head of the baby Jesus while singing a psalm, and with a twentieth-century Irish novelist, writing both within and against a Catholic tradition.

* * *

In 2013, I attended a show at the London Tate Museum that linked the ideas of British iconoclasm past and present in an exhibition titled "Art under Attack." In the introduction to the exhibition catalogue, Penelope Curtis points out that iconoclasm can be creative as well as destructive, writing that it "is as much about changing the meaning of an image as about destroying it completely" (2013: 6). The first part of the show focused on religious iconoclasm in the English Reformation, and presented close-up versions of the art of medieval parish churches and monastic ruins. It featured scratched-out faces of saints, smashed-in baby Jesuses and Virgins, and literal God-shaped holes in stained glass and manuscripts where the figure of God the Father had been removed. A centerpiece of the exhibit, from Binham Priory in Norfolk, England, was a section of a painted medieval rood screen showing Christ as the Man of Sorrows.[1] The image, like rood screens and wall paintings all across England, had been whitewashed and painted over with biblical text during the sixteenth century. Since unmediated access to God was believed to come through reading, replacing the potentially idolatrous image of Christ with biblical text was a theologically appropriate solution, and, for years, this painting of Christ was invisible (perhaps forgotten) beneath words from Cranmer's 1539 Bible. This image, however, like all images and texts, has changed over time, so that now, as the whitewash wears away, the late medieval Christ has re-emerged and coexists with the text. To look at this painting—a conversation over time of competing theologies and theories of art—is to see a new image, neither Catholic nor Protestant, and one that flattens the difference between image and word. This palimpsest of image and text seems to show simultaneously a coexistence of word and image, as well as a representation of a history of their conflict.

For modernist authors like Joyce, who celebrated multiple and contradictory meanings, seeing such palimpsestic images could have presented more artistic

---

[1] The image is also well known as the cover art of Eamon Duffy's *The Stripping of the Altars*.

Figure 5 Medieval Man of Sorrows painting with Reformation era text "Christ the Man of Sorrows," undated, text added 1539, 1525, 1535, contributors unknown © St. Mary and the Holy Cross Binham. Reproduced with the permission of the Rector and the Church Council of St. Mary and the Holy Cross Binham.

possibilities than images or text alone. *Finnegans Wake*—filled with literary representations of religious figures from one time period peeking through texts of another—can be seen as an analogous example of the tensions between diachronic and synchronic history, image and text, and creation and destruction. Among many examples, we might think here of the opening to Book IV, a chapter that will announce the beginning of a new day, a new era, and another cycle of death, birth, and resurrection. The first words of the chapter—"Sandhyas! Sandhyas! Sandhyas!" (*FW* 593.1)—contain within them the Hindu goddess Sandya, the word Sunday, the thrice repeated *Sanctus* of the Mass, and the last words of Eliot's *Waste Land* ("Shantih, shantih, shantih").[2] These three words offer a multiplicity of religious texts and modern literature woven into each other, both concealing and revealing shades of meaning, each peering through another.

Reading Joyce in the context of the Reformation demonstrates that acts of religious iconoclasm are never just in the past. Even after the iconoclasm of the sixteenth and seventeenth centuries, damaged or, in some cases, entirely absent figures and images retained devotional importance (Duffy 1992: 4). These conflicting concepts of devotional art, and the blurred lines between absence and presence, memory and reality, are deeply woven in the post-Reformation Christian imagination. As Jaroslav Pelikan reminds us, "the presentation of Jesus in the New Testament is itself a representation, resembling a set of paintings more than a photograph" (1978: 9). If restaging or re-experiencing Christ's sacrifice and re-imaging the crucifixion is at least partly about understanding the absence of the divine as well, then the encounter with Reformation iconoclasm also has an element of the fragility of divine presence. Iconoclastic images become a visible theory of time, aesthetics, and the sacred. While *Finnegans Wake* is perhaps not usefully categorized as Protestant, it does represent a radical Catholicism that has been through a Reformation and has experienced iconoclasm as creative events. Stories, scripture, and literature are retold again and again only to fall—without beginning or end, forever damaged and incomplete, yet open to change and full of possibility.

Questions that were debated in the sixteenth century included whether idolatry was in the object itself or in the eye of the beholder—the same debate about images and the Host found in medieval texts. Some argued for the role of

---

2 In the *Wake*, Eliot's poem of death, religion, and thunder is referred to as the "wastobe land" (*FW* 62.11)—a land that was-to-be but is not yet—which gives the sense of looking forward as well as back that is woven into the final pages of the *Wake*.

context and claimed that secular surroundings could make the experience of an image safe (Barber 2013: 24). There was no doubting, however, the slippery slope that many found in the experience of art itself, as one could first admire and then, perhaps, idolatrously worship a piece of wood or paint on canvas. Second, as we think about the relationship between Reformation ideologies and the development of the modern and modernist literary imagination, it is instructive to think about the aesthetics of fragmentation and incompletion central to both that developed in the presence of partially damaged Christian art.

Reformation and Reading

While the Reformation is an impossibly large topic to summarize, I will outline a few themes that are most applicable to the literary project we are embarking on. In that context, I will focus on ways that the Reformation continues to shape how we think of writing, the distribution of information, the act of creation, and the destruction of art, ideas, and narratives. There were multiple forces and multiple Reformations, and scholars are still sorting out the details and the legacies. But whatever else they were, the various movements of the Protestant Reformation and Catholic Counter-Reformation certainly were debates over theories of reading, language, words, and books. No religious movement—or "heresy"— has been more associated with the acts of reading and the material aspects of writing and books than the Reformation. Among other developments, the steady rise in literacy rates and the 1476 arrival of the printing press in England, as Peter Marshall writes, "slowly began to transform the possibilities for religious practice" (2018: 22). In choosing to look at religious objects and iconoclasm, I am particularly interested in how we, as observers, see across time: imagining the past (the object as it was), the act of violence and damage, and the present; each becomes a moment of meaning and of creation, and none are stable, as our perceptions flicker between these states. One person's transcendence is another's blasphemy, and the effectiveness of theological concepts lies partly in this ambiguity.

A fundamental tension in Western literature and theology is found in the idea that God's word (by orthodox definition, perfect) must somehow be transmitted and translated into human (and therefore imperfect) words. This gap between the absolute real and the flawed and imagined is a fertile space for literary, artistic, theological innovations and ideas that are created to connect the divine to the human, the transcendent to the immanent. As we have seen in previous chapters, Christ's ontological status as a God/man was one solution to this problem, the elevation and consumption of the Host in the Mass was another, and gazing at devotional iconic images was yet another; each example presents a paradoxical and fragile relationship between divine/human and word/image, and each example is surrounded by multiple debates over heresy and orthodoxy. This variability is also at the core of the Reformation which, in the words of Brian Cummings, was characterized by the paradoxical poles of an "appeal towards certainty" and its "conflicts over interpretations … poised between the clarity of faith and the melancholy of skepticism" (2002a: 5). The tension between these paradoxical poles of positivism and doubt, certainty and impossibility, is exactly what modernist poets, writers, and artists were employing in their aesthetic experimentation. If the modern literary experience can be traced back to various negotiations of the gap between human and divine creation, then Reformation debates over words and images provide a useful example of the power of art and poetry to negotiate and dramatize religious conflict.

To demonstrate these abstract ideas in a text, we can look to the works of Protestant poet Edmund Spenser where, as literary critic Kenneth Gross writes, "to break an image is not necessarily to break away from images. Hence a complete grammar of iconoclasm would also teach us to look closely at the partial survivals of and substitution for images, at the forms or fragments left behind and at what was raised up in their place" (1985: 11). Often what was raised up in their place was a new way of writing. For Anglophone literature and its authors—from Spenser to Joyce—these damaged medieval spaces were not just metaphorically fragmented and incomplete, they were literally so. It is with these very spaces where we can begin our discussion of the Reformation. It was on a medieval church's south porch after all—a complex space of border, threshold, and liminality—where Martin Luther supposedly posted his ninety-five theses, in what would become the symbolic beginning of the Reformation. The fact that this seminal event is now assumed by historians to be fiction is a perfect representation of how much of the theological and artistic tensions surrounding the Reformation are about absent spaces, memories, and imaginative writings.

Historians placing the Reformation within the history of theological debate either claim it is a period after which there is no single "Church" from which to measure theological deviation, or they argue it is the (often inevitable) and culminating moment to all previous heretical attempts to chip away at a monolithic and deeply flawed Catholicism. The Reformation, according to the second tale, was "the place where heresy finally triumphed" (Wright 2011: 161). Although scholars have been challenging the idea for several decades now, the received knowledge is still often, as William S. Scott writes at the beginning of his *Sources of Protestant Theology*, that "the religious situation in Western Christendom had been moving toward crisis for several hundred years" and that the late-medieval church was "crying for reform." Despite continuing differences among historians, what is generally agreed upon now is that the "notion of Europe being instantly and irrevocably divided between Protestantism and Catholicism does a huge disservice to the lived reality of the Reformation era" (Wright 2011: 171). England, in particular, "was unique in its sequence of dramatic swings of official policy, taking place over the course of a relatively short span of years" (Marshall 2018: xiii). These dramatic swings—no doubt confusing experiences for many people living during the Reformation—are helpful in thinking about other moments of heresy in a more nuanced manner, and perhaps "offer a glimpse of how a heresy actually unfolds" (Wright 2011: 172). What seems especially important for English literature is that for the first time in history, as Peter Marshall writes, "everyone in England became acutely aware that the most important questions of human existence were capable of demanding divergent— indeed, mutually incompatible—answers" (2017: xx). In other words, the history of how the Reformation played out—textually, artistically, and in the lived experience of everyday people—allows us to trace the intersections between an emerging modernity and the resulting shifts in belief and scriptural practices.

During the Reformation, England experienced a state-sponsored and wide-ranging campaign focused on the destruction of religious devotional images. As Peter Marshall writes, "there is no simple explanation for why in the sixteenth century growing numbers of English Christians came to believe that true discipleship of Jesus meant demanding that the sacred figure of the rood be pulled down from its lofty perch, broken into pieces and burned to ashes" (5). But although the motivations are much debated, one cause was the general Protestant belief that the devotion of people toward images meant that they were worshiping the wood or the paint themselves and not the divine figures suggested by them. Many reformers considered idolatry the deadliest sin of all. A 1530 Reformation treatise on the destruction of images by the German Martin Bucer declared that images should be destroyed, without sympathy, for what they might represent: "breke them ... all to powder that they might never be made whole agaiyne" (qtd. in Boldrick 2013: 20). Other iconoclastic acts acknowledged that the represented figures themselves might have evil power: these acts included scratching out the eyes or faces of figures to avoid direct communication, a practice that is very evident in surviving rood screens across England. As James Simpson writes, "the official programmes of iconoclasm between 1536 and 1550 seek to distance the past from the present as rapidly and decisively as possible either by demolishing the medieval, or more enduringly perhaps, by creating the very concept of the medieval as a site of ruin" (2010: 11). On the other hand, it is clear that Thomas Cranmer, Spenser, and other reformers did not expect worshipers to just cut themselves off from the past; in fact, they often emphasized England's heroic deep past (Celtic and Arthurian), which they understood as corrupted by the arrival of false Roman religion, an attitude which is refashioned in Joyce's use and parody of Irish Literary Revival tropes.

One way of describing the Reformation is that words replaced images and pulpits replaced altars. When reformers claimed that "popish" images needed to be torn down to be replaced with only the word of God as understood through the Bible, they were making a statement about language: the assumption was that biblical language represented the true and *unmediated* Word of God, and was a pure form of communication. As MacCulloch writes, "Reformation disputes were passionate about words because words were myriad refractions for a God one of whose names was Word: A God encountered in a library of books itself simply called 'Book'—the Bible" (2005: xx). But while it is tempting to see the Reformation as representing the triumph of the word over the picture, more recent scholars such as Cummings have emphasized the "conflict evolved in the very attempt to construct a division between these phenomenological fields" (2002b).

My main idea is to use ideas of iconoclasm as they existed in early modern England, and as they have been understood in the twentieth and twenty-first centuries, as metaphorical tools of reading. The twentieth-century emergence of a medieval religious painting from behind a layer of whitewash in Yorkshire, the medieval face of Jesus peeking out through Reformation words, and the discovery of a sculpted image of the Trinity hidden in the walls of a medieval church in Ireland are all modern moments that reveal ways that religious meanings are created, hidden, and partially and gradually emerge to us from the shadows of the sixteenth century. *Finnegans Wake,* in some sense, elevates the idea of the word over the image, but it also demonstrates how understanding words depends on visual, material, and communal contexts. Recent Joyce critics have more often emphasized the visual, and Colleen Jaurretche goes so far as to say that the "essential aesthetic premise of *Finnegans Wake* is that representation does not distinguish between logos and image" (2020: 27). Understanding the *Wake* in the context of thinking about the Reformation—and through material culture and images as well as scripture—allows us to construct a model of religious interaction that builds on an acknowledgment of the role of difficulty, fragments, destruction, misunderstandings, textual violence, and the relationship of word to image as they apply to theological interactions and reading practices.

The relationship between Reformation ideologies and the development of a modernist or Joycean literary imagination is found in the aesthetics of fragmentation and incompletion that emerge in the presence of partially damaged art that has gradually regained its importance and presence. Joyce's iconoclasm, while often blasphemous, may appear more ironic, humorous, and scatological, than it does violent. But as *Wake* scholar Finn Fordham writes, the "power of laughter does not necessarily undo power itself, but it reminds us of the vulnerability and mortality of all forms that are made to embody power" (2007: 5). Reading Joyce teaches us that literature can be constructed out of the idea that we see the past incompletely, and in ways totally colored by our own context and our own biases. We find these ideas on every page and even in single words of the *Wake*. The word "goddinpotty" (*FW* 59.12), for example, suggests both a "garden party" (in a posh English accent) and, with it, a sense of growth and renewal, as well as a conflation of urine and Eucharistis wine. As Vincent Cheng memorably writes, "there is God not only in the flowerpot but in the potty" (1992: 91). To fully appreciate just this one word, we must think of the medieval Mass, the Reformation, Victorian gardens, and modern toilet humor.

When modern authors borrowed words, stories, and images from medieval literature and history, they were necessarily imagining the object from both before and after the violence of the Reformation—already thinking of whole and part; unity and fragment; time and decay. In Leonard Barkan's *Unearthing the Past*, he writes that the fragment "has been robbed of its completeness by time" and that even complete works "become fragments if they brandish an identity without fully revealing it" (1999: 119, 124). Throughout all those images and ideas—which can also be applied to a damaged rood screen or crumbling ivy-covered monastery—the fragmented nature of borrowing and quotation is a sort of re-creation, or, even more radically, a denial of an original that can be perceived, created, or presented outside of its fragments. Iconoclasm is particularly significant in thinking through the relationship between heresy and modernism because understanding the violence towards art, and the resulting absences within art (missing figures, partial images, ruins), became part of the English literary imagination that Joyce and his literary fathers (Milton, Shakespeare, Spenser) take up—very literally reconstructing religious images and narratives and then breaking them down again—in their own work. *Finnegans Wake* both universalizes and tears down scriptural and sacramental language, and—like a religious object existing in time—it constructs layers of meaning through a dialectic of accretion *and* destruction. Joyce's attempt in *Finnegans Wake* to "contain within itself all the sacred books which had ever been written" is only possible through his strategy of "selecting fragments from all he could find and distributing the fragments in his own pages" (Atherton 1959: 169). Joyce's language in *Finnegans Wake* challenges the relationships between text and reality, word and image, creator and text, and fragment and whole in ways that reshape the reading of scripture and that are in dialogue with the iconoclastic ideas and legacies of the Reformation.

Part II: Scripture, Radical Theology, and the Pun

Joyce's favorite heretics and theologians, as we find throughout *Portrait* and *Ulysses*, are pre-Reformation: Arius, Aquinas, Valentinus, Photius, and Sabellius. In *A Portrait of the Artist,* Stephen's oft-quoted claim is that he prefers Catholicism as "an absurdity which is logical and coherent" over a Protestantism which is neither (*P* 265). Yet this rejection does not rule out the presence of Reformation and Protestant tensions and themes within the works, especially in *Finnegans Wake*, which at times seems to embody all ideas, scriptures, and theologies on the same page. The *Wake* acts as a sacred text in two different ways: as fragments or echoes of sacred relics, and as a repository of various relics in the form of a novel. For Joyce scholar James Atherton, "what Joyce is attempting in *Finnegans Wake* is nothing less than to create a third scripture (after the universe and the Holy Bible)" (1959: 28). Creating new scripture out of old is a scriptural characteristic in itself. Like the Christian Bible, the Quran, and the Book of Mormon, Joyce borrows and adapts stories and passages from earlier scripture to create a new version. Of all these sacred texts, the Bible is the most important book woven into the pages of the *Wake*, and Atherton suggests that Joyce replaces the Old Testament with *Finnegans Wake* and "[substitutes] his theology for the religion of the Bible" (1959: 179). To see *Finnegans Wake* as a type of scripture, however, is to read a self-conscious rendering of scripture that is always more about modes of telling than truth claims—a telling that is about plural meanings and voices, changes over time, and the indeterminacy of language. What Joyce develops in *Finnegans Wake*—through fragments, puns, and multiple histories—recreates a theological vocabulary that, like images damaged during the Reformation, grows in meaning rather than diminishes; words and phrases contain the original meaning as well as the alteration and violence done to them. The physical damage to religious objects functions as a metaphor for the layers of meaning given to scriptural texts as they are radically re-written in *Finnegans Wake*—a practice of "sacreligion" (*FW* 365.3–4) that becomes scripture. Joyce, like reformers and heretics before him, insisted that new ideas required new ways of reading, and that new ways of reading engendered new ideas.

If *Ulysses* stages the constructive and destructive potential of the Mass itself, then *Finnegans Wake* invents new languages and a new theoretical and textual home for scripture. In *Finnegans Wake*, Joyce's use of scriptural words takes on a different role than in his earlier works: more creative and yet subversive at the same time, they challenge us to re-engage with historical and scriptural ideas from the past to develop new meanings. Joyce uses the technique of punning to build an entire structure, ideology, and (perhaps) a theology. As he famously said, "The Holy Roman Catholic Apostolic Church was built on a pun. It ought to be good enough for me" (Ellmann [1959] 1983: 546). The pun Joyce refers to—"you are Peter (*Petros*) and upon this rock (*petras*) I will build my Church"—is from Matthew 16:18, and plays upon the Greek word for Peter and for rock. Many of the great puns in *Finnegans Wake*—"cruelfiction," "schisthematic," "Eatster," "hellmuirries," "fincarnate"—provide opportunities for reflection upon the complexities of religious meaning and language. They offer concepts, images, and events seen over time—gaining meaning through accretion, disputation, destruction, and restoration. We see this in Joyce's continual restaging of the fall as a creative—rather than a tragic—event, which is built through the structure of puns. For example, Augustine's "O felix culpa" becomes (among many other renditions) "O Phoenix Culprit"—a reference to a crime in Dublin's Phoenix Park, but also to the original Garden, the original sin, and to the phoenix myth of resurrection.

We might see this process of reading, as described within the *Wake*, as "our tour of bibel" (*FW* 523.32), which is a *tour* of the *Bible*, a tour of babel, and the destroyed *Tower* of *Babel*—a survey of, a building up, and a tearing down of epic language captured in the same phrase. Within the *Wake*, the Tower of Babel represents a type of the fall—an event echoed from Adam, to Humpty Dumpty, to Wall Street—but also as a creative event that resulted in all the multiple languages that will supply the many shades of meaning reflected in the pages of the *Wake*. Joyce's strategy of quotation, imitation, neologisms, and puns is essentially iconoclastic in that it both destroys and creates, and offers a dialectic of past and future. The Joycean pun, like radical religious language, "shows that meaning transcends and spills over the signifier and is not confined to the straightjacket of the official version" (Boheeman-Saaf 1999: 118–19). A simple phrase like "our tour of bibel" suggests that the book we are reading is canonical scripture and the breakdown of communication at the same time. *Finnegans Wake* is Reformation, Counter-Reformation, and an act of iconoclasm, all in literary form.

Although, like Shakespeare, Joyce grew up in a culture torn between Protestant and Catholic forces, unlike Shakespeare, there is little argument over whether Joyce leaned Protestant or Catholic, or if he had a secret confessional affiliation. Joyce, like Shakespeare, lived and wrote in a world of what Stephen Greenblatt has called "damaged ritual." Greenblatt suggests that Shakespeare, like many of his countrymen, would have found himself "still grappling with longing and fears that the old resources of the Catholic Church had served to address" (2001: 321). Joyce—as deeply Shakespearean, but with a complicated and contradictory position toward Catholicism and the English language—produced in *Finnegans Wake*, a new kind of damaged scripture that embodies all of these anxieties and contradictions. We can perhaps see Joyce as making a move to redeem this ritual through a new kind of writing. This type of damaged scripture is akin to the literary experience expressed in certain schools of radical theology that look for the meaning of Christianity and Christian scripture in the absence of a transcendent God and a savior. This absence, however, is one that needs to be experienced through the texts, history, and rites related to the religious experience—what theologian Thomas Carlson identifies as "the experience of 'unknowing' in all of its various forms" (2001: 142). The radical theologian Thomas Altizer, author of *Christian Atheism* and one of the founders of the "Death of God" theology, who was fascinated with Joyce his whole writing life, writes, "scripture is more fully and more universally present in *Finnegans Wake* than it is in any other text" (1985: 237). For Altizer, this "presence" is not one of immanence and certainty, but is instead found in fragility, fragments, and incompleteness. In other words, we need the Christian myth, but partly to establish its own impossibility or fictionality. Both Altizer and Carlson find in *Finnegans Wake* a version of a "writing and a voice that may indeed be seen and heard as revelation after the death of God" (Carlson 2001: 155). For Carlson, *Finnegans Wake* offers a "strikingly medieval vision" that yet, paradoxically, provides a "self-expression of an absent subject" that is "not quite human, not quite divine, and incomprehensible to itself" (2001: 149). Or, as Joyce might say, "seemself" (*FW* 143.26), or "humself" (*FW* 3.20)—two Wakean neologisms that question the essential self, capturing instead what seems like a self, or an absent song that is wordlessly and internally hummed.

Finnegan Begin Again: Words, Word, and the Word

Finnegans Wake famously opens with—not a Mass or a parody of the creation, as we might expect—but with a lowercase letter:

> riverrun, past Eve and Adam's, from swerve of shore to bend of bay, brings us by a commodius vicus of recirculation back to Howth Castle and Environs.
>
> (*FW* 3.1–3)

After first noting the lowercase letter, my students notice the theme of time, rivers, and cycles. Looking closer, we find that the river (in Dublin, the river Liffey or "life") flows "past Eve and Adam's," or in other words, the mythical start of human history. But there is also an actual nineteenth-century Catholic church on the Liffey known as Adam and Eve's, located on the former site of a pub (in contrast, the central home and drinking establishment in *Finnegans Wake* is located on the former site of a church). This first page of *Finnegans Wake* continues with references to Genesis and the Fall of man (and the fall of Rome and Humpty Dumpty) mixed with Irish legends, medieval knights, Dublin geography, and the song "Finnegan's Wake."

A few lines down from the opening sentence, the book introduces the theme of the pun on Peter's name along with the voice of God—a voice that spoke (and wrote) itself and the world into being: "avoice from afire bellowsed mishe mishe to tauftauf thuartpeatrick" (*FW* 3.9–10). This more or less translates to: A voice from a fire (and afar) bellowed "Moses, Moses" to baptize (*taufen* in German) "thou art Peter (or Patrick)." Of course, there are more embedded meanings and readings, including a playful "mishe mishe to tauftauf," which sounds like an address on an early radio. The beginning of the sentence—"Avoice from afire"—has echoes of God speaking from the burning bush, but also of John the Baptist and his voice "crying in the wilderness" (Matthew 3:3). The next word, "bellowsed," suggests an act of shouting and the bellows used to stoke a fire, which maintains the double sense of voice and fire. "Mishe" is at once Moses (Moishe) and also "me me" in Irish (*mise*), which then echoes back to the voice from the bush proclaiming "I am who I am" (Exodus 3:14). But it is the last word, "thuartpeatrick," that is the most important. "Thuartpeatrick" brings us back to Jesus' pun on Peter, which is made more obvious by all the other scriptural references on the first page: Adam and Eve, Isaac ("bland old isaac"), Noah, Moses, and the multiple falls. Standing for both "thou art Peter" and "thou art Patrick" (patron saint of Ireland), the passage simultaneously suggests God speaking to Moses, Jesus to Peter, and the dream voice calling

Patrick back to Christianize Ireland. It also may be "pea trick," a reference to the familiar con-game of peas and shells, which dates back to ancient Greece. Building on the Christian pun of Peter and rock, we can also see "peatrick" as peat—the dark, decomposed, damp vegetable matter that is literally the foundation that much of Ireland is built upon (Joyce will also use the word "bog" in place of god). Furthermore, since the novel's title and the first page also reference the resurrection of old Tim Finnegan from whiskey in the song "Finnegan's Wake," we can also see peat as the ingredient used to give Irish whiskey (or "water of life") its smoky taste, in which case it is the foundation of a resurrection of sorts,[3] or, as we read in the *Wake*, "peats be with them" (*FW* 202.30).

The Joycean pun breaks down borders in that it both expands the meaning-making potential of language at the same time that it subverts it. On the one hand, it dramatizes the power of a word to simultaneously or alternately inhabit different meanings. On the other hand, it demonstrates the essential instability of language—the one-to-one correspondence between word and meaning that we often assume in communication. This dialectic resonates with the tension between the Christian (and Jewish) view of God as transcendent and not fixable in words or ideas, even though he has revealed himself in and through words and a sacred text. Debates over heresy, from the Gnostic to the Mormon, continually come back to this question of a God of language who is yet ineffable, a being who makes all things possible, but who is impossible. Joyce's wordplay in the *Wake* is taken as much *from* Christian reading practices as it is a challenge to them. Christianity and the Christian practices of reading the Bible rely on an understanding of double meaning that resembles the action of a pun. Orthodox Christians choose to believe that the "king" in Isaiah also refers to the not yet born Jesus, or that the unidentified snake in Genesis is also Satan in disguise. Whether these relationships are literal, allegorical, typological, or symbolic has been material for Christian debate from the Gnostics to Dante to Luther to Bultmann. In adopting, editing, and collating the Hebrew texts with the new texts into the Bible as *their* book, Christians made the decision to give words and passages double meaning. The Christian pun begins with Paul and the Pauline tradition that insists that the Hebrew Bible is really a Christian book, and later Christian Fathers and Christian writers worked out even more elaborate

---

3 I initially resisted this interpretation, as most Irish whiskey (at least until very recently), as opposed to much Scotch whisky actually is not peated. However, I have now been informed that Irish whiskey in the nineteenth and early-twentieth centuries would have used peat in the distilling process and therefore would have been peated.

types and antitypes than are in the Bible. Think, for example, of the use of the word or image "tree" in Christian thought and art and how, from Augustine to Milton, it always represents a complex relationship between the death-giving tree in the Garden of Eden (which yet bears fruit) and the life-giving tree of the cross of Jesus (which yet also brings death), as well as the Tree of Jesse from Isaiah.[4] The idea of the "tree" is even further complicated in an almost Joycean manner by early Christian thinker, Clement of Alexandria, who read the mast to which Odysseus ties himself as foreshadowing the tree to which Jesus was bound. Across the history of Christian writing, phrases and images—tree, body, word, book—gain meaning, building a complex network of discourse, a process that Joyce uses across all of *Finnegans Wake*. Not surprisingly, trees are also an important religious motif in *Finnegans Wake*. One example is in a description of a garden and a tree (an "ashtray") by which the "illassorted first couple," HCE and ALP (or Adam and Eve), first met (*FW* 503.7–9).[5]

Perhaps the central pun in Christian theology is "word" as it was used to translate "*logos*" in the Gospel of John's "in the beginning was the word." Since the actual speaking or word of God is only one possible translation, what readers and translators of the Gospel of John do is to use the rhythm of language and a pun to connect the "logos," or word, in the Gospel to Genesis' "And God said." (Like *Finnegans Wake*, whose last sentence connects back to the first, it links the end to the beginning). Novelists and poets have, not surprisingly, been drawn to this conflation of divinity with language. In Goethe's *Faust*, for example, the "philosopher" tries out different translations for *Logos*: In the beginning was the word ... the mind ... the power ... the deed. While the number of references to the word or Word in the *Wake* is too numerous to mention, we can again point to one formulation of creation borrowed from John: "in the buginning is the woid" (*FW* 378.29). In Joyce's version, "word" (with an old-school Brooklyn accent) and "void" are combined. This conflation suggests the cyclical relationship between Genesis and the Christian Gospel and also places an absent void on top of the most enriched signifier in the Christian narrative. Joyce's version gives us creation from nothing and a *void* where there should literally be the eternal Christ or Word (also, within the *Wake*, the word "bug" is often a replacement for "god"). Throughout the *Wake*, like Goethe's philosopher, Joyce expands the meaning of this passage, in various offerings:

---

4 For one example, see the early medieval poem "The Dream of the Rood."
5 See, for example, Atherton, *The Books at the Wake*, pp. 112, 185, and Martin Brick, "Joyce's Overlisting Eshtree: A Genetic Approach to Sacred Trees in *Finnegans Wake*," *Genetic Joyce Studies*, 12, Spring 2012.

"In the beginning was the gest" (*FW* 468.5)
"In the becoming was the weared" (*FW* 487.20–1)
"The war is in words and the wood is the world" (*FW* 98.34–5)

Added to "void," then, are suggestions of gesture, guest, guess, jest, and spirit (*geist*), weariness, weirdness, erections and trees (wood), and a war of words (or *War of the Worlds*). Like any good pun or metaphor, the meaning is unstable, vacillating between one meaning and another, and finally creating something new: a God or Author-figure who is material and spirit, present and absent, permanent and finite, deeply strange, virile, and perhaps alien. A figure that is radically Christian, heretical, and blasphemous at the same time.

In many ways, heresy functions as a theological pun. It gives multiple meanings to the same word ("substance," "begot," "spirit") and is creative and destructive, producing new more plural or different meanings, and muddling what might have been thought to be the original meaning. Potential for creativity is generated through the instability that results from the desire for a word or image to be permanent and unchanging, and the inevitable changes and decay over time. The process is what Joyce might call "overlisting" (*FW* 503.30)—a combination of everlasting, obsessive note taking, and tipping over. Both puns and heresy challenge the idea of origin and any kind of "everlasting"—or "evernasty" (*FW* 503.7)—meaning at all; to "exist" is to be written down (to be "listed"), but also ultimately to fall (to "list"). We might also think of "listen," as when the ghost begs Hamlet to "List! List! O list!" (1.5). Thinking through and with puns and with acts and objects of iconoclasm—like thinking through heresy—involves a cognitive act of imagination and plurality; to think about each is to ponder intellectual, artistic, and theological possibilities and paths not taken.

The Possibility of the (W)hole

With the twin brothers, the orthodox Shaun and the heretical Shem, *Finnegans Wake* builds on the familiar biblical trope of two antagonistic brothers—"I cain but are you able?" (*FW* 287.11–2)—to represent conflict and paradox in negotiating word and image. One iconic example is in the clash between Moses's orthodox, but ineffable God and Aaron's heretical, but material, golden calf. Although the dialectic of body and text is found throughout the *Wake*, it is most graphically presented in Book I.7, in a passage where Shaun depicts Shem—a writer figure and a scatological alter ego for Joyce—as creating ink out of his own excrement and urine, and writing on his body (*FW* 185.27–186.18). As we discussed in the previous chapter, Joycean scenes of writing will often conflate themes of the body and Eucharist with artistic creation. Furthermore, the theological resonances of Father/Son so central to *Ulysses* are here broken into father and sons, matter and spirit, body and text. This description, by Shaun, is written in a typically Joyce fashion: it begins in a fragmented, but ecclesiastical Latin amidst references to the Roman satiric tradition, blending the scatological with the theological and the classical or "highly prosy, crap" (*FW* 185.17). While Shaun's destruction of Latin could be seen as a type of Protestant iconoclasm, it is also a passage "echoing faintly," as Robert Boyle writes, "the instructions for the preparation of the host" (1972: 56). The paragraph, however, is more graphically about a priest figure defecating into his hand and then placing it, into a vessel into which he then urinates happily while singing a song (*FW* 185.14–26).[6]

In this scene, Shem the "penman," or, here, the "last alshemist," is described as using this solution to write "over every square inch of the only foolscap available, his own body" (*FW* 185.35–6). The passage seems to point toward disgust of both the body and writing, but it also acknowledges the power of each. The writing slowly unfolds into a text that is a "marryvoising moodmoulded cyclewheeling history," that is "transaccidentated through the slow fires of consciousness into a dividual chaos" (*FW* 186.1–5). The word "dividual" suggests both individual and divided—both unified and plural—which is the paradox that I have been locating in damaged devotional art. The word "dividual" has also been used since Joyce by anthropologists such as McKim Marriott to critique Western-centric models of the self; "dividuality" for Marriott, as opposed to individuality, takes form through comparisons not just between the West and non-West, but also between two or more non-Western areas. This model results in a less egocentric sense of the self. *Finnegans Wake*, as well, suggests a view of the human that is best thought of primarily as multiple rather than singular—more of a network of relationships than a centered grid; more dividual than individual.

A theological reading would see the bodily ink and paper as a way of theorizing the relationship between author and text, Father and Son, and God and Word in a process where they are "transaccidentated." Joyce's creation of the "transaccidentated" here, clearly meant to evoke theological debate over transubstantiation, is reversed so the appearance or "accidents" change but not the essence or substance—the opposite of the orthodox Aquinas explanation.

---

6 See Robert Boyle's 1966 article "*Finnegans Wake*, Page 185: An Explication." *James Joyce Quarterly* 4, no. 1: 3–16.

This passage also folds in a reference to alchemy, a practice that blends religion, science, and magic; it also indicates the shifting of the physical body of the writer into the words of his works, or as Robert Boyle suggests "containing in himself all humanity, as the particular contains the universal." The word "transaccidentated" is "Joyce's ... most revealing Eucharistic coinage." For Boyle, a Joyce scholar and a Catholic priest, the word changes the focus from the bread to a Christ who has not changed or moved, but becomes present through "transaccidation" (1972: 53).

But we can turn Boyle's interpretation around; the passage also suggests—since the implication is that the author dies leaving only his body as text—a type of death-of-God or radical Protestant theology in which we are left with holy scripture but no actual divine presence to root our beliefs in. Although we may read the *Wake* as a kind of scripture, it is a scripture where, as Fordham writes, "the idea that it will somehow explain the structure of history, of hatred, of human division, and somehow provide solutions to the problems inherent in those structures is exploded" (2007: 5). Like radical readings of the crucifixion, it is a kind of scripture whose profundity exists in proclaiming the impossibility or absence of a transcendent god or text, and yet insists on the sacredness of the desire for one. Any text—Shem's text, the *Wake*, the Bible—open and living as they are, is no longer connected to the body and mind of a creator. They are scripture without a present divine author. As interpreters, it is up to us. The *word* is truly a *void*.

* * *

Reading the words and narratives of *Finnegans Wake*, like viewing a painted, damaged, and restored rood screen in a parish church, we must necessarily read outside of linear time: looking not from beginning to end, Genesis to Revelation, creation to decay, but to instead see all times at once. The study of Joyce's manuscripts, notebooks, drafts, and proofs, or the "genetic" criticism of *Finnegans Wake* offers another interpretive approach to narrative and time, as not only does it provide insight into Joyce's creative process, but, as critics demonstrate, it offers a very literal demonstration of multiple coexisting times, texts, and meanings. Looking at the early drafts of the *Wake*, Fordham writes, "we actually get to see most of the material in the final text" (2007: 2). In every "instant of making," he continues, the *Wake* "became something new," yet does not lose the memory of what it was (2007: 3). Fordham's book—*Lots of Fun at Finnegans Wake*—has a full chapter on *Wake* I.7—called "Shem's 'Cyclewheeling History'"—which gives a detailed account of the sections as they progress through various revisions. Fordham's focus on the changes, development, and gradual obfuscations of words aimed at certainty and truth—"universal," "human," "author," "body," "history," and "self"—suggests a metaphor for how the process of the writing itself offers a dialogue between existing pages, erasures, memories, absent or partially deconstructed texts, and theological concepts rendered more fragmented and contradictory.

Fordham devotes a section of his chapter to various versions of the description of Shem using his "dye" of excrement and urine to write upon his body. The description, as was characteristic of Joyce's writing of the *Wake*, becomes more obscure and longer as it moves through the various drafts—from 41 words to 177. The word "human"—Shem is writing a history as "one *human* integument" (or a single human skin)—left essentially unproblematized in an early version, later becomes "*one continuous present tense* integument" (*FW* 185.26–186.1, emphasis mine). If belief in a single, autonomous self would suggest a single, unquestioned history, this augmented version suggests a history that is "continuous, still living, and blending all time as if all is present" (Fordham 2007: 55). Like the medieval spaces and objects in the previous chapter, this kind of reading also indicates an alternative way of seeing images or texts: across time, rather than at a single moment. For example, the beautifully complicated phrase "marryvoising moodmoulded cyclewheeling history" was, in an earlier version, only "universal history" (*FW* 186.1–2). The difference between the two could hardly be more dramatic: a universal history—one version and applicable to all—could only come from sacred scripture produced by a divine voice, whereas a history influenced and molded by cycles, moods, and many voices will constantly wheel out from any single reality or truth (in other words, *Finnegans Wake* or perhaps the Bible, itself). The difference here is the structuring dialectic of "certainty" versus "conflict of interpretation," which Brian Cummings assigned to the Reformation (2002a: 5), a movement that, for many, left Christianity forever fragmented.

While the "numerous levels of revision in *Finnegans Wake* finally produce pages that resemble the convoluted pre-Gutenberg manuscripts rather than anything printed" (Fordham 2007: 35), we can also make an analogy to damaged post-Reformation religious art. If the book's matriarchal character, ALP, is not a "mythic Earth Mother but a greatly abused figure" (Fordham 2007: 36), we can also see her as an image of Mary or a female saint who has been created, worshipped, painted, vandalized, forgotten, restored, and remembered—and who now embodies all of those stages at the same time. Joyce's writing process, his puns, and his portmanteau words, in the context of his scripture-loaded prose, function in that heretically sensitive space between the medieval Mass and a Reformation object of iconoclasm. The making of meaning in religious art reflects levels of building, decay, destruction, and restoration. *Finnegans Wake*—as we focus on how it was made and the layers of subsequent interpretation—mimics this process.

Part III: Traces of the Future

One weekend during the 2007 *Ulysses* seminar, I took a day trip away from Dublin and its fading Joycean echoes to go to Kilkenny, a nearby Irish town often described as "medieval." Although much of the day was spent enduring pouring rain and then drying out by a pub fireplace with a steaming bowl of Guinness stew, there was one location and experience that has stayed with me as this book developed. After visiting St. Canice's Cathedral, a gothic structure built on sixth-century foundations with medieval architectural elements such as the classic Irish round tower and an eleventh-century bishop's chair, I followed the signs to the nearby Black Abbey, another medieval building and now a parish church. The church was empty except for the elderly man who let me in, and I was soon drawn to a glass-encased object next to the altar: a striking white alabaster figure of the Trinity, representing God the Father, with God the Son on the cross between his knees, and the Holy Spirit above him, between the Father's uplifted hands.

The figure caught my attention, partly because of its placement, partly because of its beauty, and partly because—in my Joyce-influenced mind—I could see an interpretation wherein the Son seemed to be replacing the Father's erect penis, which points upward to the Holy Spirit. Dated by scholars to the fifteenth century, the structure's base displays the written date 1264, which is thought to have been added in the eighteenth century. Sometime after that, the piece was buried or hidden within the wall, then lost and forgotten until sometime in the late-nineteenth century, when it was discovered during restoration. The combination of perceptions intrigued me: the piece was simultaneously high art, orthodox theology, Papist idolatry, a vulgar visual joke, a historical lie, a tourist attraction, and an object of worship with ambiguous origins and a history woven into the Catholic/Protestant debate over images and divine presence. It was a visual and theological pun in the most complex way, exactly what I was starting to look for in the language of *Ulysses* and *Finnegans Wake*. Before I left the church, I took some time to look at the stained glass, some of which supposedly

Figure 6 Recovered sculpture of the Trinity in Kilkenny parish church.

dated to the fourteenth century. I asked the older gentleman, whom I assumed was the sexton, if a particular set of windows was medieval in origin. He was silent for a moment and his face narrowed in anger. His answer finally was just two words: "Fucking Cromwell … "

I often tell this story to my American students on our trips to Dublin to demonstrate the nearness of the Irish past—to show the level of resentment many Irish still have toward the English and the violence and destruction committed in the seventeenth century by, in this case, Oliver Cromwell, who was greatly admired by Milton and is still considered a hero to many British. The nearness of the past and the history of the present read through the complicated multiplicity of Joyce gave me a new way to think about the history of Christianity and its heresies. Furthermore, it encouraged me to look not only at literature and language, but at objects—objects that have been lost, damaged, restored, forgotten, and found.

* * *

Twelve years of teaching, writing, and reading later, I received a 2019 grant from the Poetry Collection at the University of Buffalo to spend several weeks researching in their James Joyce Archives, which house a significant collection of Joyce's notebooks, drafts, sketches, and miscellaneous papers. The archival and genetic studies "turn" in literature and in Joyce studies is familiar to scholars and has been much discussed, but has rarely been a major part of my own methodology. While most scholarly work on the collection still emphasizes looking at Joyce's notebooks in a continual practice of dating material, identifying source texts, or pointing to their uses by Joyce, my archival research was not as quantifiable. Although the increased attention to and study of Joyce's drafts and notes has tended toward questions of intense specificity, my questions about the notebooks were on a more speculative level.

I had several ideas going in: I wanted to look at the *Finnegans Wake* Notebooks to think about Joyce's shifting relationship to religion, particularly his reading on Christian history, heresy, and early-twentieth-century studies in Christology. I wanted to see his actual reading notes on, for example, the medieval Albigensian heresy and the ancient Pelagian heresy, his thoughts on a biography of St. Patrick, and on the filioque. My second idea was to expand my reading of *Ulysses* and the *Wake* within the context of "scripture" by adapting some of the practices of recent scholars of the Bible and the Quran, which emphasize ambiguity, gaps, erasures, and changes over time. By looking closely at notebooks, manuscripts, and other material in the collections, I hoped to dramatize this kind of model of knowledge and scriptural production. I wanted to place this whole endeavor—my book, my research, and my life as a professor—into a model of lived religion and material culture which lives on the fringes of much of this book. Finally, since so much debate over the Reformation and Reformation-era literature is about the concept of the "real" and of decay and destruction of material, I was particularly interested in the physical ontology of the notebooks. I wanted to think about models of studying objects and images and alternative ways to incorporate them into reading and lived religious practices. This kind of work has encouraged me to pay more attention to the visual and the material: handwriting, book covers, erasures, and accidents both old and new, work which can only be done by looking at and handling materials in person.

While I did spend time with the physical *Wake* Notebooks, most of my work involved looking at scans of them on the collection's "Joyce computer." Although it might seem strange to travel hundreds of miles—and walk daily through snow and freezing rain—to look at digital scans, as of now, this is still the only place in the world that most of these pages can be seen in full detail and color. The Notebooks contain Joyce's reading and thinking over the years (1923–38) that he worked on *Finnegans Wake*. They are filled with short phrases and single words, often almost unreadable, written in pencil with various phrases crossed out with colored crayon, mostly red, some blue, and some green. As several generations of scholars have confirmed, the crossed-out passages were ones that Joyce entered into a manuscript, and the colors have no apparent pattern—just whatever Joyce happened to have close at hand. We also know from painstaking scholarly work that many of the crossed-out phrases are not identifiable in any manuscript and others are altered so drastically by the time they get to the *Wake* that the meaning or context is lost. As many Joyceans can attest, any thought that these Notebooks might more clearly elucidate the published texts are swiftly defeated.

In general, I did not find much that I had hoped for, or at least much that I had not already found in other scholar's work—scholars who are much more skilled at archival research than I am.[7] But I was by no means disappointed: what I *did* find was a new way of seeing and reading. Like my reading of Joyce in general, I am most interested in what these texts help us to do, rather than what they might tell us about the works or the author. What do we do with the notes *not* crossed out, which means they supposedly were *not* used? Are

---

7 I have especially benefited from the genetic work of Finn Fordham, Chrissie Van Mierlo, Wim Van Mierlo, and Geert Lernout.

these phrases somehow less important? What do we do with the Notebooks themselves as literary creations? To engage with the Notebooks is a process of reading both forward and backward in time, through the meaning-making process of imagined reader and author. Writing about Joyce criticism, Dirk van Hulle suggests that genetic criticism is always "bidirectional," working backwards, to find the sources of particular passages, and forwards, to follow these passages through Notebooks and drafts to the final text (2009: 120). Although most scholars would claim to be interested in pursuing Joyce's writing process, the whole thing is, in many ways, more about how *we* create and make meaning from our own different processes of reading—processes that blur the definitions of author and work.

Thinking about iconoclasm and material culture at some imagined intersection of the Reformation and Joyce involves speculation and thought experiments outside of literary criticism. While most of this chapter's main ideas lay in large speculative statements and comparisons, in this section I will look to find the local within this global, through specific objects and images, and by paying close attention to handwriting, book covers, and doodles, and, by extension, the visual impact of Joyce's handwritten Notebooks and *Finnegans Wake* itself. The first step of my thought experiment starts with an idea I introduced earlier: in *Finnegans Wake* itself, Joyce is recreating a type of "scripture" that, like reading the Bible, the Book of Common Prayer, or a medieval wall painting, forces us to see a text as a multi-directional discourse across history and through destruction and reconstruction rather than as a synchronic or teleological text. Although the text of *Finnegans Wake*, with its shifting sense of time, captures a sense of this kind of motion, to truly study the *Wake* means to look at drafts, erasures, corrections, reading notes, publishing history, and reception in ways that take us into the archives and Notebooks, and beyond the published versions.

The *Wake* Notebooks "exist" in neat little boxes in the University of Buffalo Poetry Collection, to be selectively brought out and carefully paged through by a curator. While scholars are still, upon specific request, able to see and touch some of the Notebooks, others are too fragile to be brought out for viewing and will soon be put into "dead storage." The Joyce computer, a single monitor against a wall in the Special Collections reading room, is where, in a sense, the Notebooks also "exist." While current copyright restrictions prohibit the viewing of these scans outside of this specific reading room, many of the Notebooks also exist in published transcriptions, facsimiles, and in copied notes. The "meaning" of the notes comes from being framed by three flexible contexts. The first is the identification and then study of the source texts, or the books or journals

Joyce was taking notes from. The second contextual frame is to trace these words and phrases through alterations, drafts, and editions to the published version of *Finnegans Wake*. The third frame points to the biographical details of what Joyce was doing or experiencing during the exact time he was keeping a specific notebook. Of course, it is easy to problematize any of these frames: we are still discovering what Joyce's sources were, he often used little known texts, and some have been lost, destroyed, or forgotten. The published versions of *Finnegans Wake*, as many scholars today are exploring, are versions of a book that developed across multiple revisions and drafts over seventeen years; the idea of a "final" or "definitive" version is, for many, not only impossible or unimaginable, but undesirable. And trying to point to the entirety of what Joyce was doing and thinking during a specific, say, three-month period in 1924 is, naturally, also impossible.

Yet, as Derek Attridge writes, "the notebooks are fascinating documents *in themselves.*" In his review of a series of published transcriptions and commentary on the Notebooks he writes that while,

> these volumes provide no key to the mysteries of *Finnegans Wake*, reading through them conveys a vivid sense of the kind of book the *Wake* is… an intricate weave of verbal and cultural materials… so numerous and so various that detective work, however assiduous and penetrating, is baffled … Though readers who are not Joyce manuscript scholars may only dip in here and there, it makes a great difference that what they are getting wet in is not a pond, but a sea.
> (2003: 573)

But what if we accept the accidents and the effects of time and instead study the Notebooks as visual art or poetry? What if we use the Notebooks to think about the role of texts in shaping ideas about time, history, scripture, iconoclasm, and the history of heresy? In some ways, this means reading the Notebooks as art works, like Rosmarie Waldrop's "overprinted poems," street Graffiti turned high art, or a poem by Susan Howe. But the difference in looking at the Notebooks is the indefinable and often untraceable connection to the *Wake*—whatever we think the *Wake* ontologically "is"—and the connection and presence that are always there; the shadow or ghost of a source or of origin that always haunts our reading. This kind of reading mirrors the way we read the *Wake* itself, where one word or one passage moves out through one interpretation to comment on all possible others, or on the book itself. This "scriptural" move of reading, studying, and interpretation is my focus here: looking at the Notebooks as art or poetry. As decaying objects. As scripture.

The Wake Notebooks and Tipsy Scripture

An example of how one place in the Notebooks might be seen to offer this experience is the appearance of the single word "Gutenberg," crossed out in red in Notebook number seven (VI. B. 7 70 b). Unlike a lot of the words in the Notebooks, the word Gutenberg is actually legible. The James Joyce Digital Archive connects this word to page 20 in the *Wake*, where we find the phrase: "and Gutenmorg with his cromagnom charter, tintingfast and great primer" (*FW* 20.7–8). This passage is found in a section about printing, reading, drinking, and writing religious texts, with additional references to paper ("papyr"), punctuation ("Fillstup"), and the Quran ("alcohoran"). The word "Gutenmorg," in addition to the printing press and the Bible, echoes both death (morgue) and morning (*Guten Morgen*), and was actually just the word "day" in an earlier draft. What is important for my purposes is the suggestion that printing and history are connected to both beginnings and endings (morning and death), and that Gutenberg and the printing press are associated with the Protestant Reformation, the history of materiality, and the book. A central word in this section is "alcohoran," an Arabic sounding name (al-coharan), which combines alcohol and the Quran. ("Horan" is also an Irish surname.) In writing the sentence "For that … is what papyr is meed of, made of, hides and hints and misses in prints" (*FW* 20.10–1), Joyce in later drafts changed the word *paper* to *papyr* and adds *meed* to *made*, therefore introducing suggestions of papyrus and alcohol to his tale of the Quran and the Gutenberg Bible. Scripture here—as is my point throughout this book—is never stable but is instead always full of misprints ("misses in prints"), hidden ("hides") meanings, drunken mistakes, and murky origins. Again, we find scripture not as a definitive word, but as a wandering, unframed, and unraveling text.

We can see *Finnegans Wake*, and the slowly decaying *Wake* Notebooks in Buffalo, as participating in this process of appearing and disappearing, through destruction and reconstruction, through competing interpretations of history and time, and through visual meaning (often coded "Catholic") competing with verbal meanings ("Protestant"). We continue to construct meaning in this way, whether it is in looking at monastic ruins, or rubbed-out faces on a rood screen, and damaged devotional objects, all of which are still easily found across England and Ireland. In each case, Reformation art and Reformation literature work out—in the same ways as *Finnegans Wake* and the Notebooks do—themes of meaning deferred, delayed, and outside of time and history. Thinking about the *Wake* in this way is both a different way of reading and of understanding the relationship of text to time. Again, the process of multiple contextual meanings framing a hard-to-read text is similar to the practices of reading *Finnegans Wake*. It teaches us to see text and its structures across time; to see them in the act of becoming, in the now, and after they cease to exist. All of these reading and viewing practices echo how the *Wake* comments on how we "read" the history of orthodoxy and heresy, and the ways that it, in turn, maps the confusion back onto and into our own texts and reading strategies. It is, as Kenneth Gross writes of Edmund Spenser's *Faerie Queene*, like a "church in which the idols were made and broken at the same instant" (1985: 12).

Spenser's Faerie Queene: Blasphemy and Iconoclasm

Oliver Cromwell is not the only sixteenth-century Englishman who can prompt curses from today's Irish. In "*The Faerie Queene* at *Finnegans Wake*," Brad Tuggle writes of a time when "in a pub in Youghal, County Cork, the mere mention of Spenser's name elicited curse words from a gentleman patron with whom I was engaged in conversation on a Sunday afternoon" (2016: ftn. 4). The hatred of Spenser in Ireland stems in large part for his infamous pamphlet, "A View of the Present State of Ireland," in which he claimed that Ireland was a diseased part of the State, greatly in need of moral and religious reform. When Kenneth Gross writes that "Spenser sees the Irish as a people enchanted by the false authority of custom, folklore, and superstition, by the false magic of ancestral names, tribal allegiances, even of their native language" (1985: 81), it sounds a lot like Joyce's dismissal of Irish Renaissance figures like Yeats and AE, and his labeling of the Irish Celtic Twilight as the "cultic twalette" (*FW* 344.12). On the other hand, both Spenser and Joyce created enchanted worlds in their writings that seem to borrow from (and sometimes even to celebrate) such "superstitions," even as they tear them down.

Despite Spenser's role in the English subjugation of the Irish, if there is a Reformation Protestant text that seems Joycean or Wakean, it might be Spenser's *Faerie Queene* (1590–6), a massive epic poem that seemingly combines all previous myth and story, biblical or classical, into an endlessly complex and often self-conscious and philosophically contradictory narrative, full of word play and retold stories. Like Joyce scholars, Spenser critics place his text at different places on the religious continuum, ranging from radical Protestantism to Scholastic or even Catholic. Gross writes that the poem, if not the poet, "holds in suspension and sometimes sets in subtle conflict both Catholic and Protestant attitudes toward the image" (1985: 31). While Joyce's specific references to Spenser or *The*

Faerie Queene were few ("our fiery quean" [*FW* 328.31]), his connection to the Christian epic as developed by Dante, Milton, and Spenser is significant, and scholars like Altizer see Joyce's works as part of that Christian lineage. Both *The Faerie Queene* and *Finnegans Wake*, if looked at broadly enough, complicate the whole idea of religious literature or scripture, particularly through the lens of iconoclasm.

Throughout *The Faerie Queene*, Spenser painstakingly builds spaces of luxury, art, and magic out of shards of older (often pagan or Catholic) literature; he then has one of his heroic knights destroy these evidently idolatrous images, often in just a few lines. The poem creates extravagant worlds out of a poetry that is connected to centuries of other poems, myths, paintings, and tapestries, and then seems to deem them dangerous or unfit to exist on either page, in memory, or as material objects. As Gross writes, "many of the poem's heroes quest for an idol to destroy rather than for a prize to recover or redeem" (1985: 18). The most significant example of this is the Bower of Bliss in Book Two, a luxurious, artistic, and erotic paradise into which Spenser lures his reader and then has the knight Guyon destroy. There is, as Greenblatt writes, a "taint of the graven image" in this scene (1980: 188), and the point of the poem is that apparently this space of bliss is "false." Yet this reading then suggests that the opulent poetry that created it is also false. In other words, Spenser's poem *seems* (often an important word in the poem itself) to be a Reformation poem aware of its Catholic and Classical aesthetic; not only that, but the poem itself is at least structured around that awareness in that it "announces its status as art object at every turn" (Greenblatt 1980: 190.) Yet, the nature of a poem, and of a book, as opposed to material art objects, is that these destroyed worlds continue to exist, and we can turn back to them anytime we want. Like our revealed painting of the Man of Sorrows or the Kilkenny Trinity emerging from behind a wall, the medieval is always peeking through and around the Reformation's iconoclastic tendencies.

In the final book of *The Faerie Queene*, the last canto ends with the "Blatant Beast," a dog-like creature with multiple heads and poisonous tongues, often allegorically associated with slander. In the final cantos, however, the beast grows in power, breaks free of its allegory, and seems to randomly attack knights and ladies, across the faerie and pastoral world. Near the end of the book, the Beast is associated with blasphemy (often connected to a sin of tongues) and, as a figure of iconoclasm, takes its final path through monasteries (seemingly still functioning in a pre-dissolution world) before being captured and chained. At the very end of the poem, the Beast again escapes to apparently bite the poem itself, casting doubt upon just where the blasphemous and iconoclastic forces are. The Beast, "broke his yron chaine,/And got into the world at liberty againe" (Spenser [1590;1596]1978: 38.8–9). The Beast can be seen to represent the magical and Catholic worlds of art, poetry, and ritual that the poem has presented and then often destroyed. The chains could then represent a type of Reformation iconoclasm that contains this power even further. Building on this reading, then the Beast's escape echoes the memories and images that persist in the minds of practitioners and that peek through the whitewash, the scratching, and the ruins. Using a familiar Joycean pun, Gross writes that the "Beast is not only loose in the world, it is loose in the word" (1985: 229). If so, has Spenser's Protestant poem failed? Are the blasphemous forces that he dangerously played with free to roam in the literary imagination of the world?

These are common questions throughout Spenser criticism, but when we see them in the context of *Finnegans Wake* they take on another layer. As Gross writes, "just as he evades any final image of truth, so the poet will not claim any pure power of demystification, nor any mode of iconoclasm free from the possibility of error. By the end of the poem, in fact, iconoclasm itself becomes just as much of a threat as idolatry" (1985: 18). Like Joyce, Spenser is "a skeptical visionary, a demythologizing mythmaker, and iconoclastic iconographer" (Gross 1985: 16). The fact that Joyce comes from a Catholic tradition and Spenser from a Protestant one almost seems to strengthen this comparison of their paradoxical making and breaking, and their use of wordplay, ambiguity, and contradiction as performative acts of iconoclasm. On the one hand, *The Faerie Queene* seems to be almost the opposite of *Finnegans Wake*, as it is written by Protestant poet and is therefore often seen as invested in attacking Catholic superstition and glorifying the Church of England. Joyce, on the other hand, as religious, heretical, or blasphemous as you want to paint him, is deeply Catholic in his frame of references and his education. But the ways that they employ, alter, reframe, and remix older literary and religious traditions follow similar paths.

From Spenser to Joyce, words about images have been written with the understanding that images disappear, fade, and are destroyed, but so too do books and words. And while the idea of iconoclasm and of the finitude of images and words are implied themes in the *Faerie Queene* and in *Finnegans Wake*, these themes are more drastically enacted in surrounding material documents, in the illegibility and erasure that are limiting and inevitable, but also poetic. In the opening of his book, *Iconology: Image, Text, Ideology*, W.J.T. Mitchell asks "What is the difference between images and words?" In order to address this question, he frames his work as "a book about vision written as if by a blind author for a blind reader" (1986: 1). In the reading the *Wake* Notebooks, we can find this thought experiment woven in with what seem to be Joyce's personal comments about his own often near blindness.

In Notebook VI. B. 14 at the very top of page 22 is written: "Vision always disappearing"—where the word "disappearing" is somewhat hauntingly, partially rubbed out. Then, in the lines beneath that, is written: "not enough imagination/ to imagine a furnished/room empty"—with the word "imagination" almost unreadable. Although the rubbed-out word—which will no doubt disappear years before the rest of the page fades—and the unreadable handwriting are accidents of history, they offer their own commentary on how we can use the rubbed out, erased, and illegible to theorize the gradual disappearing of all texts and all things over time. As Craig Dworkin writes in *Reading the Illegible*, these "garbled and damaged messages" should perhaps be "read less as regrettable losses and more as exciting, poetic possibilities" (2003: xxiii). Certainly, there is something about this Notebook entry that reminds us of the act—known from Heidegger and Derrida—of crossing out a word so as to let both deletion and word stand. The act of placing a word "*sous rature*" ("under erasure") points to an inarticulable or absent presence within the word; it is, as Spivak explains, the "lack at the origin that is the condition of thought and experience" (1976: xvii). We must, as Derrida seems to suggest, "learn to use and erase our language at the same time" (1976: xviii), a practice similar to that proposed in the Gnostic Gospel of Philip where we read that names "are utterly deceptive, for they turn the heart from what is real to what is unreal" and that "whoever hears the word 'god' thinks not of what is accurate, but rather of what is unreal" (Meyer 2007: 162). Joyce's disappearing notebook entry unintentionally points to how this same process works within *Finnegans Wake* and across Christian theology.

Later in the same notebook, also at the very top of the page, the phrase "sounds when blind" seems to refer to the intensity of sound when sight fails. Here the word "blind"—which might also be read as "blur"—is followed by illegible writing of lines written on top of each other. Is there a productive way to talk about what these "mean" outside of biography and intent? If we read it *like* we read the *Wake*, these parallel phrases, indecipherable handwriting, and multiple meanings seem to offer a way to "see" Joyce's notes on the misty Irish legends and folk tales that echo in the phrases in the surrounding pages of this same notebook. These are tales passed on in ways where the visual, the audible, the mistaken, and the invisible literally blur into each other as ways of remembering and of telling the story.

Monastic ruins, whitewashed medieval paintings, vandalized rood screens, and the *Finnegans Wake* Notebooks—like *Finnegans Wake* itself, and like Christian heresies—are stories of decay, damage, and rediscovery. Iconoclasm, especially in reference to medieval and Reformation England, is part of the interactive history. But much like the lost, faded, illegible, and decomposing *Finnegans Wake* Notebooks, instead of just viewing it as a tragic absence, these broken structures go on to tell and develop their own narratives. Iconoclasm paradoxically "wants to reinstate true history by subtracting; it attempts to reinstate true history by an act of violence that is always anti-historical; by that anti-historical act it activates a new historical tradition" (Simpson 2010: 15). Like the Notebooks, the images and architectures resulting from religious iconoclasm create and destroy in ways that thread into both past and future.

The idea of *Finnegans Wake* as a kind of apocalyptic symbol of the end of scripture is something that the infamous death-of-God theologian Thomas Altizer was fascinated with his whole life. While Altizer's point rests fully within his brand of heretical and radical theology, the same ideas can be applied to literature. As Samuel Beckett wrote in a letter, "more and more my own language appears to me like a veil that must be torn apart in order to get at things (or the Nothingness) behind … Is there any reason why that terrible materiality of the word surface should not be capable of being dissolved?" (2009: 171–2). Beckett's use of the word "terrible" here is what interests me—he finds the implied permanence of writing to be its danger. But words—whether they are written in sand, printed on paper, or are commandments divinely etched in stone by the finger of God—eventually all decay. Like destroyed, but remembered devotional art, buried and rediscovered codices and plates, and fading, decaying but temporarily digitally preserved notebooks, the truth is always disappearing and fading away—but for thinkers like Altizer (and perhaps Beckett) this is what makes it sacred. Thinking about the *Wake* and the Notebooks in this way is perhaps both a different way of reading *and* of understanding the relationship of texts to time. It teaches us to see texts and structures across time; to imagine them in the act of becoming, in the now, and after they cease to exist; to know that all of these are contained in our understanding of any image, text, person, or idea. There is never a primary source, a final edition, or a definitive version—there is only copy after copy and then decay … and then nothing.

Epilogue: Heretical and Sacred Reading Strategies: The Book of Mormon and *Finnegans Wake*

The earliest heresies remembered by the Christian Church revolved around issues of whether or not they were Jewish, whether they worshiped the same God, and whether they should accept the Hebrew scriptures. Following generations of heresies came out of debates over just what kind of "being" Christ was, or if he was a "being" at all. Where these debates, heresies, and unstable theological positions intersect with our reading of Joyce is found in homologous relationships between God and author and between scripture and book. To say that *Finnegans Wake* provides a new way of not only thinking about these questions, but enacting them is, in a sense, to claim the *Wake* as a type of scripture—a scripture like all scripture, in that, despite our desires and efforts, it is unstable, misread, and without pure origin. To fully claim the *Wake* as scripture, however, invites questions and skepticism. There is, though, a work of modern literature that *is* a work of scripture, that lives both on the edges of the idea of heresy, and also provides a *Wake*-like counter-narrative to the Bible: The Book of Mormon.

The Book of Mormon and *Finnegans Wake* both simultaneously rewrite history, give a modern conflation of Hebrew and Christian scripture, and yet also implicitly acknowledge a deep theological irresolvability, beginning with how we understand the God of Genesis—the contradictory "jewgreek" God, created out of Jewish legend and Greek philosophy. This God paradoxically has a personal relationship with individual human beings and is also beyond all naming and all characterization—both immanent and transcendent. The orthodox Christian concepts of an unchanging god, creation from nothing, original sin, and a Satan of pure evil were not in the Hebrew Bible and were not agreed upon in the early church. And, as we have seen, groups later labeled heretical and Gnostic held multiple views on these issues. *Finnegans Wake* and the Book of Mormon revive several Gnostic and heretical readings of the book of Genesis. Both the Book of Mormon and *Finnegans Wake* have heretical views of the concept of divine creation and original sin. In the Book of Mormon's Gnostic-like reframing of the Christian Bible's most foundational myth, the Fall is a necessary and righteous path to humanity's eternal salvation. As we read in the Book of Mormon, "Adam fell that men might be; and men are, that they might have joy" (2 Nephi 2:25). Likewise, the attribution of original sin to God is one of the central heresies of *Finnegans Wake*, where the "continually repeated fall" points to a cyclic placing of the original sin on God (Atherton 1959: 143). Like Gnostic writings that elevate the snake in the garden or hail Judas as heroic, in the Book of Mormon, Eve becomes the "bold heroine, rather than the weak vessel, of the race's founding story" (Givens 2009: 77). If we start with Joyce's familiar analogy of author and God, then the very style of both works suggests instead an "arranger" in the *Ulysses* sense. Understanding the Mormon God as an organizer, not a creator, narrows the gap between the human and the divine— indeed in Mormon theology, both God and Christ are men of flesh and bone, and humans can one day ascend to divinity. While officially heretical for a Catholic or mainstream Protestant, none of these viewpoints are new to Christianity.

To compare *Finnegans Wake* and the Book of Mormon as "scripture," though, involves some preliminary explanation. Clearly both draw on, borrow from, quote, and parody canonical scriptures. To begin reading either one is to instantly recognize that you are in a world heavily influenced by the Hebrew and Christian Bibles. Part of the value of both *Finnegans Wake* and the Book of Mormon is that they force us to rethink our assumptions. Mormon scholar Terryl Givens cites Miriam Levering's definition of sacred scripture that defines it *not* by divine origin or truth claims, but by the "multidimensional ways in which scripture can be experienced by a community." For her, "scripture emerges out of a set of reading practices and from the sacred purposes a text serves for a community." She suggests that we examine:

> all the ways in which individuals and communities receive these words and texts, the ways people respond to the texts, the uses they make of them, the contexts in which they turn to them, their understandings of what it is to read them or to understand them, and the roles they find such words and texts can have in their religious projects.
>
> (qtd. in Givens 2002: 176)

In other words, reading practices do not just develop because of the sacred nature of a text, rather they also help create it. While this may remind us of the hundreds of *Finnegans Wake* reading groups across the world, this definition of scripture also leads to a more ambiguous reading of the Book of Mormon. In *The Book of Mormon: A Very Short Introduction*, Givens offers, from the point of view of a believer, a more fluid reading of Mormon scripture. For him, the Book of Mormon's "complex, multilayered, at times Chinese-box structure evinces important principles of how scripture is constituted" (2009: 35). It is, like *Finnegans Wake*, a kind of bricolage, or an assemblage of already existing pieces into a new mosaic. For these modern works to say something about scripture, and for us to consider them *as* scripture, they must acknowledge older religious texts *and* more contemporary ideas of god, history, writing, and the book, which have emerged over time (yet owe their origins, in large part, to those very works that preceded them).

Although non-Mormon scholarly interest in the Book of Mormon has grown in recent years, the book has yet to fully experience the type of critical attention European scholars gave to the Bible in the eighteenth and nineteenth centuries. This criticism interrogated questions of authorship, historicity, and dissemination, and in the process complicated binary claims of true and false. This kind of interpretation naturally challenges traditional practices of scriptural reading. While scholars like Givens and Grant Hardy have been expanding interest in the Book of Mormon as literature, in many ways, readers of the Book of Mormon still tend to side with early Mormon leader Orson Pratt who famously said, "The book must be either true or false. If true, it is one of the most important messages ever sent from God to man … If false, it is one of the most cunning, wicked, bold, deep laid impositions ever palmed upon the world, calculated to deceive and ruin millions who will receive it as the word of God" (1991: chapter 7). While some more modern studies of the Book of Mormon have moved beyond debates of true or false, prophecy or fraud, they are still unsure about where to credit authorship and the time and place of origin. They often invent new formulations that offer close readings informed by recent scholarly movements, and yet continue to equivocate about origins. For Grant Hardy, almost all approaches to the Book of Mormon "have in common the urge to start with something outside the book—Joseph Smith, Jacksonian America, Mesoamerican archeology, ancient Near Eastern culture, Mormon theology, or a personal spiritual quest" (2010: xiii). The broadness of these approaches might remind us of *Finnegans Wake* studies—which move from the specificity of Joyce's handwriting to the vastness of the Kaballah. Hardy's question about the Book of Mormon can also be applied to the *Wake* (and to my own methodology): "What is one to do with such a text other than scan it for phrases and incidents that might have some bearing on a particular thesis?" (2010: xiv). But recent claims by Hardy and others to instead focus on the "book itself" or the "book between the covers" seem theoretically limiting as well. The Book of Mormon, like *Finnegans Wake*, reaches out into the world in so many ways—to revert to a pseudo-New Critical stance seems to already make arbitrary statements about where meaning lies and how it is created. To read *Finnegans Wake*, *Ulysses*, or the Book of Mormon is to think about notes, drafts, history, plagiarism, forgery, quotations, interpretations, paraphrases, and reading practices. When we think of the Book of Mormon outside of faith and truth claims, and instead place it within the context of heretical thought and *Finnegans Wake*, we can demonstrate how the theological is also aesthetic, and show that both texts *use* alternate theologies to challenge "secular" concepts of history, book, body, and subject.

If the Book of Mormon and *Finnegans Wake* function as scripture in their incorporation of earlier texts—religious texts are never created from nothing—since they are both written in the age of the printing press, books, newspapers, and media, they also have no choice but to let this world seep into the porous borders of the texts as they are written. The Book of Mormon, although it claims to date back to 600 BCE, seems to present modern concepts of a book, of history, and the role of a God. For example, while the Bible almost never mentions writing, the act of writing is a constant theme in the sealed tablets, abridgements, and lost translations of the Book of Mormon. To read even just a few pages of the Book of Mormon is to read a book that is obviously *written*. "Everything is mediated by the narrators," writes Grant Hardy, (2010: xix), narrators who even worry about their "weakness in writing" (Ether 12). Unlike the New Testament—where Christ speaks just to his immediate followers—when the Book of Mormon narrators use the word "you," they seem to specifically mean a modern-day reader holding a modern book. Like the recurring letter in *Finnegans Wake*, the process and materiality of writing are important to reading these texts. We can also see this in the current interest in textual scholarship: theories of origins, drafts, errors, and corrections. Scholars of the *Book of Mormon* as well look at various drafts and edits by Joseph Smith and its complicated publishing history. Even though the opening of the Book of Mormon, "I, Nephi," seems to be a simple journal entry in which Nephi will "make a record" of his "proceedings," we soon learn that he is writing based on an abridgement of his father's writing, and that what we are reading is actually a second version of an earlier, more detailed family history. Although the Book of Mormon presents a narrative thread that claims to reach back unbroken through the centuries to its origins, it is also a story that is written in both 1830 and the sixth century BCE. One must imaginatively read it as both pre- and post-King James Bible, pre- and post-colonial America.

Finnegans Wake, as well, forces one outside of linear history, as past and present influence each other. In the *Wake*, this can be seen in the way that the early histories of our protagonist HCE, for example, are layered across time. They are told within sacred and classical texts, through street gossip, and electronic media, from voices influenced by Dublin slang to the four old men—or "MaMaLuJo," signifying **Ma**tthew, **Ma**rk, **Lu**ke, and **Jo**hn—who represent academic and orthodox ecclesiastical history, but are also just four gossipy Dublin men or "our four avunculusts" (*FW* 367.14). Another comparison finds both *Finnegans Wake* and the Book of Mormon as family dramas—feuds between brothers, sons usurping fathers, sons punished for their sins against their fathers—and as essentially stories of clans made universal. As Ellmann writes, "for Joyce no individual is so unusual and no situation so distinct as not to echo other individuals and situations" (1983: 550)—a form of modernist typology in which Anna Livia is also Eve and Mary. Like the Book of Mormon, *Finnegans Wake* seems concerned with family, family betrayal, sin, and with falling. It offers, as the *Wake* says, a "series of prearranged disappointments down the long lane of … generations, more generations and still more generations" (*FW* 107.33–5), which might remind us that the Book of Mormon is also essentially a tragedy traced through multiple family histories.

The Book of Mormon, too, is the story of a family, in which each individual is read as a universal. In the Book of Mormon, while God leads three groups to the Americas, each migration ends in disaster. In the main narrative, the chosen family of Lehi travels from the Old World to the New, survives a thousand years, but ultimately is wiped out as well. Like a classic sci-fi plot (the original *Planet of the Apes*, perhaps), the audience that Nephi seems to address in the opening books is shockingly extinct by the end, no longer able to read his words. For Givens, the Book of Mormon "incorporate[s] familiar elements of biblical Christianity into new patterns of meaning" (2009: 47), a phrase that also describes *Finnegans Wake*. In both works, God, Father, author, king, and everyman blur together in a theory of constructed meaning and writing that is both like and unlike the sacred texts they borrow from.

Looking at *Finnegans Wake* and the Book of Mormon together—even with, and perhaps because of, their opposing claim toward truth and origin—allow us to develop a new "heretical" view toward the theological ground of the idea of the book. Contemporary theorists, building on works like Derrida's *Of*

Grammatology in the 1970s, have critiqued the idea of books as self-enclosed systems of meaning and references that can be traced back to some original and unifying source. When we read and discuss the *Wake* and the Book of Mormon, in each analysis of a phrase or word they already include assumptions about the entirety of the work itself. This includes not only what decisions are made by or for us as readers, but how these decisions are echoed within the texts. We shift between understanding characters as autonomous individuals, as spun out of the material of a central dreaming consciousness (be it HCE or Joseph Smith), and as a bricolage of a cultural and historical imagination and memory.

Like the Book of Mormon, *Finnegans Wake* often reads like an assemblage of already existing parts of scripture. As difficult as reading it can be, one of the *Wake's* most obvious characteristics is the references to the Bible, the Quran, and other sacred texts on almost every page—and we can read the *Wake* as a sacred relic of as a repository of various relics in the form of a novel-as-reliquary. As we have seen, Christian theologian Thomas Altizer finds *Finnegans Wake* as a form a radical scripture (1985: 237), and by this he seems to mean the *Wake's* construction and deconstruction of literary and divine presence in the same gestures. Altizer finds this heretical character across the history of the Christian epic, ending in the *Wake*, and uses it to point to the absolute necessity of Christianity as ground not only for the epic but for the whole modern world as represented in books like *Finnegans Wake*. In Joyce's epic-like novels, history and myth are conflated and not only does myth pass into our time, but "our time and history thereby realize a full ritual and mythical identity" (Altizer 1985: 212). What makes *Finnegans Wake* a religious or scriptural text is precisely this tension between ancient and postmodern conceptions of narrative and history. *Finnegans Wake* invents a new type of scriptural writing that is anti-presence—a writing where words, books, documents, stories, and characters are never stable, never ontologically identifiable, and are deeply rooted in biblical language.

It is one thing to posit *Finnegans Wake* as a type of decentered, nomadic text that denies pure origin or linear development, and in the process creates a type of postmodern scripture. Obviously, it is a different claim to make the same assertion about the Book of Mormon. But even though the Book of Mormon appears didactic, literal, and free from the sorts of ambiguities that define the Bible, there are other ways in which it also emphasizes the very gaps and indeterminacies that make up the type of scripture suggested by *Finnegans Wake*. Whereas the *Wake* expresses scripture through biblical quotations and allusions that are "invariably inversions or reversals of the gospel text" (Altizer 1985: 238), the Book of Mormon presents quotations and allusions as truth claims which are often subverted through their inability to signify just one true and absolute meaning. Because it cannot escape the indeterminacy of modern writing, the Book of Mormon—like *Finnegans Wake*—also becomes a way of calling into question this notion of truth that lies at the heart of the Western tradition formed out of the sacred texts that the Book of Mormon mimics, paraphrases, and copies. Philosophers of religion have often associated monotheism with the idea of a single capital "T" truth. This characterization seems to define the Book of Mormon, which is often described as an attempt to remake the Bible in a singular form—to reaffirm one God, one Truth, one interpretation, one story. To give, in other words a scripture not open to Gnostic and other heretical rereadings. But reading through the lens of the ancient Gnostic gospels, the modernist *Finnegans Wake*, and the postmodern Altizer and Derrrida, this singularity is multiplied into a "collideorscape" of flickering and competing truths (*FW* 143.28). For Altizer, *Finnegans Wake*, like the death of God, represents an ending and a beginning—an apocalyptic event necessary for a sacred experience:

> Writing or scripture finally ends in *Finnegans Wake*, for this is a text in which a written or writable language has wholly disappeared as such, and disappeared to make way for or to awake that primal and immediate speech which is on the other side of writing or text, and on the infinitely other side of that writing which is Scripture or sacred text.
>
> (1985: 237)

This presence, though, is not one of immanence and materialism like the Book of Mormon, but is instead asserted through its fragility. Like destroyed but remembered devotional art, buried and rediscovered codices and plates, and fading, decaying notebooks, the sacred truth is always hinted at but unattainable.

Uncovered Writing

In this section, I will read two of the better-known passages from the two books alongside each other: the opening chapters of the Book of Mormon and section I.5 of *Finnegans Wake*, known as the "Mamafesta," a section that we looked at in chapter three. *Finnegans Wake* 1.5 describes the discovery of a letter, dug up from a trash heap by a hen, and then presents various methods of looking at, reading, and interpreting this found manuscript. The opening line of this chapter conflates fragments of invocations from Islamic and Christian traditions, combining the opening surah of the Quran (*Al-Fatihah*) with the Lord's Prayer (Matthew 6:9-13):

> In the name of Annah the Allmaziful, the Everliving, the Bringer of Plurabilities, haloed be her eve, her singtime sung, her rill be run, unhemmed as it is uneven.
>
> (*FW* 104.1–3)

The discovery of the letter, the various religious framings of it, and the modes of interpretation that are explored in this section can easily be read as a commentary on the Book of Mormon, which was reportedly *also* lost and dug out of a hill. Like the Golden Plates (which were described as eight inches square and bound with three large rings), attention is paid to the materiality of the letter; it *is*—or looks anyway—like a "goodish-sized sheet of letterpaper," whose ancient origins are authenticated by a large "teastain" (*FW* 111.8–9, 20). The letter has been compromised by being buried in the ground, like a photographic negative of a horse that melts while drying, it becomes a "grotesquely distorted macromass of all sorts of horsehappy values" (*FW* 111.29), and the "farther back we manage to wiggle," the more we need the "loan of a lens" (or in Joseph Smith's case, transparent stone lenses) in order to see as much as the hen saw (*FW* 112.1–2). As we look closer at the manuscript, we are able to locate multiple levels of distortion, repeating a theme of *Finnegans Wake* that suggests the more you look at history, the more it blurs and bends and multiplies in front of your eyes.

The opening invocation, through the use of the word "plurabilities," suggests the multiple possible meanings of sacred texts. We might especially think here of the Christian Gospels, the same stories told over and over again with variations, which certainly describes the *Wake*'s repetitive structure. The terms "maziful" (combining "merciful" and "amazing," but also "maze") and "unhemmed" also suggest and resemble postmodern descriptions of scripture as wandering, unframed, unraveling; this "unending search for presence" as Mark C. Taylor writes, comes "when God and self are dead and history is over" (1984: 157). Taylor expands the death-of-God theology to include the impossibility of imagining a single history or a coherent self—a reading that adapts well to reading the *Wake*. The description of ALP's letter as a "polyhedron of scripture" points to how it exists—like the Book of Mormon, like all scripture—in multiple spaces and times and, despite the ongoing search for presence in scripture, it now necessarily exists beyond a "time when naif alphabetters would have written it down" (*FW* 107.9–10). We are now far beyond this kind of naïve writing. We know that the act of writing changes a text; writing, translating, even copying are no longer, if they ever were, innocent acts.

The most common question surrounding the Book of Mormon is still of its origins, or, as an interrupting voice asks of the letter in the *Wake*: "Who in hallhagal wrote the durn thing anyhow? ... by the use of quill or style ... interrupted by visit of seer to scribe or of scribe to site ... laden with the loot of learning?" (*FW* 107.36, 108.1–7). As Margot Norris writes, "whatever the Letter may be, it is not a document that clarifies anything, proves anything, renders any verdict, or pardons anyone" (1976: 70). The letter, *Finnegans Wake*, and the Book of Mormon all force us to ask if scripture is *written* like any other piece of writing, or if it is somehow ontologically different. The "loot of learning" is a particularly apt phrase for *Finnegans Wake* and the Book of Mormon; both which quote, borrow, imitate, and plagiarize freely. The word "loot" can suggest riches, but also stolen goods—and scripture is always both.

Even the original title page of the Book of Mormon, meant to establish authority, opens up questions of its ontological foundation:

An Account Written by the Hand of Mormon
Upon Plates Taken from the
Plates of Nephi

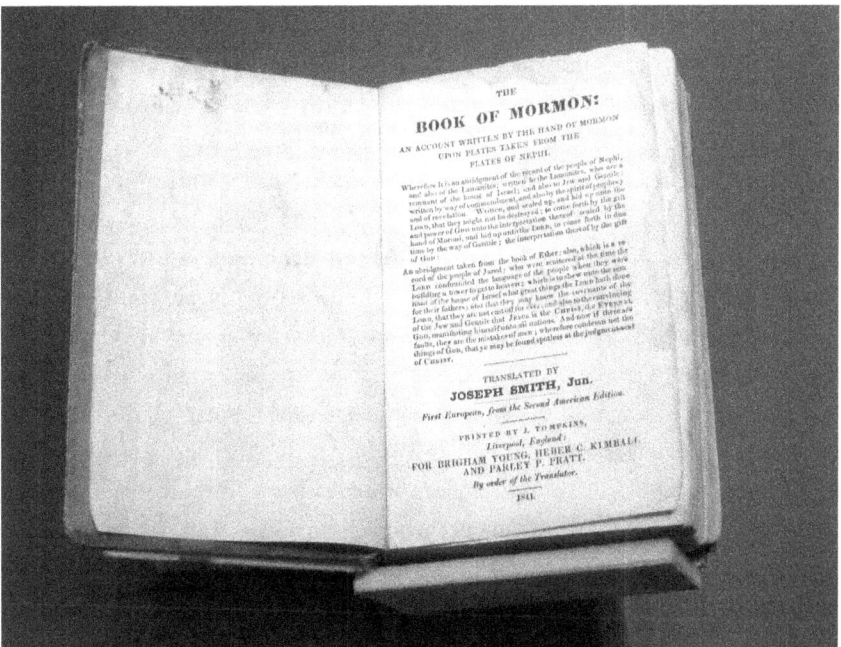

Figure 7 Original cover page of the Book of Mormon.

There is doubt written into this security. The phrase "an account" suggests that there may be other accounts, and a hand can make mistakes. There are also multiple and various shadings of the word "taken." And an account that is "taken" suggests that it is an imperfect copy of a lost original. All of these doubts play out in the internal plot of the Book of Mormon, as well as in the stories of how it came into print.

The opening book of Nephi is a first-person narrative beginning around 600 BCE, told from the point of view of Nephi, son of the patriarch Lehi. Living in Jerusalem, both characters have visions of God, Christ, and the twelve apostles, are warned of the coming Babylonian destruction, and are advised to flee to the wilderness. The chapter tells of their comings and goings, various other repeated visions, and describes in some detail the beginnings of writing, collecting, copying, and collating what will become the Book of Mormon. The opening obsessively reaffirms that the story we are reading was personally narrated by a historical—and very human—character, who wrote this down in order for it to be read:

"I, Nephi ... make a record of my proceedings in my days." (1 Nephi 1:1)
"I make a record in the language of my father." (1 Nephi 1:2)
"I make it with my own hand." (1 Nephi 1:3)
"I make it according to my knowledge." (1 Nephi 1:3)

The opening insists on the relationship between autonomous individual, pure origin, truth, history, and document—a relationship that we have come to associate with reading scripture (although one that is not so easily found in a scripture as ambiguous and plural as the Hebrew Bible). However, these same passages can be read against the grain. From the beginning, of course, the Book of Mormon forces us to think about and question its origin. Not only is there a slippage between Joseph Smith in the 1820s and Nephi in 600 BCE, and all the ancient and modern editors and editions in between, but Nephi himself retells, re-experiences, and even re-dreams the words of his father, he kills someone in order to gain part of the text, and other passages are borrowed word for word from the book of Isaiah in the Hebrew Bible. One way of reading the emphasis on process and materiality—although it *seems* to support ideas of continuity and presence—is to see how it suggests absence, through the revealing of the wandering process of writing, the permeable nature of a material text that can be stolen or lost, and the admission of incompleteness, gaps, misunderstandings, and omissions, as we see in the following examples:

Heretical and Sacred Reading Strategies   183

"Behold, I make **an abridgment** of the record of my father, upon plates which I have made with mine own hands" (1 Nephi 1:17)

" ... the things which are pleasing unto the world **I do not write**, but the things which are pleasing unto God" (1 Nephi 6:6)

" ... also a great many more things, which **cannot be written** upon these plates" (1 Nephi 1:9)

" ... **behold they are not the plates** upon which I make a full account of the history of my people" (1 Nephi 1:9)

"I, Nephi, am forbidden that I should write **the remainder** of the things which I saw and heard" (1 Nephi 14:28)

"If **all the things which I saw are not written**, the things which I have written are true" (1 Nephi 14:30)

Each of these statements points to the unsaid, the partial truth, the remainder, and to what falls outside the frame. Furthermore, in its own way the Book of Mormon, like *Finnegans Wake*, collapses past, present, and future into one. The Book of Mormon's Christ-centered opening chapter, apparently written 600 years before Christ, and its King James language "translation" originally written in languages such as "reformed Egyptian" 2,000 years before Tudor England, make a kind of theoretical sense if we accept the idea that the book's complex, contradictory portrayals of the concepts of book, historical narrative, narrator, individual personal revelation, and monotheism seem to be based upon a Christian world and later Christian traditions. Of course, this all makes another type of sense if we believe—as most non-Mormons and some Mormons do—that the book was imagined and written in the first half of the nineteenth century in upstate New York. We can also see its nineteenth-century incarnation, as Givens described it, as just "one more stage, one more version of prophetic utterance that can never be permanently fixed or final" (2009: 39). This is not the Book of Mormon as Joseph Smith (or Nephi) wrote it, but it is a Book of Mormon that we—post-*Finnegans Wake*—can read today.

* * *

When I presented some of this material at a Joyce conference, one of the questions, unsurprisingly, was about specific references to Mormonism in *Finnegans Wake*. There are very few obvious ones, and the one that I prepared to quote was "Brimgem young, bringem young, bringem young!" (*FW* 542.27)—a reference to HCE's desire for young girls. I was off the hook, and I could go back to my somewhat un-Joycean speculations.[1]

But Joyce does, at one point, seem to place Adam in the role of a Latter-Day Saint, in a sort of sermon delivered by Shaun to a group of female students: "You will hardly reconnoitre the old wife in the new bustle and the farmer shinner in his latterday paint" (*FW* 455.3–5).[2] Joyce's description of Adam (also HCE) as "a farmer shinner in his latterday paint"—where "farmer shinner" is "former sinner" (in a slightly drunk Irish accent) and "latterday paint" is also Latter-Day Saint—acknowledges the Mormon re-telling, even whitewashing, of biblical origin stories by painting over the old ones. It also suggests the rural status of Smith and his Americanization of the biblical myth. Both *Finnegans Wake* and the Book of Mormon are books where beginnings become endings and endings become beginnings, where cause and effect slip outside of history, where Christ's death is the end of God and not the beginning of salvation, where Adam and Eve become Eve and Adam, and where the Garden of Eden is Phoenix Park, Dublin or in Jackson, Missouri.[3] Although radically different in form, intent, and their reading communities, both texts form a tension between ancient and modern conceptions of God/book/history, and it is in this tension that something new and heretical is created. These new books challenge us at the level of the word, as well as the narratives of our own identity. They are in line with Derrida when he writes that "the end of linear writing is indeed the end of the book even if ... it is within the form of the book" (1976: 86). The Book of Mormon, like *Finnegans Wake*, helps us to imagine a type of scripture writing its way out of linear history or presence not by escaping it, but by demonstrating the unstable and imaginary foundations on which it has been built.

This unstable foundation, or its "manner of origins" is—as Mormon scholars such as Grant Hardy and Terryl Givens have pointed out—in many ways, the *message* of the Book of Mormon (Givens 2009: 84; Hardy 2010: 268). Their point is often that we should spend more time on the content of the whole book, rather than its miraculous origins, but because much of the book itself and its material remnants tend to be *about* the claims and confusions surrounding its origins, this is a difficult quest. So although the text itself is an understudied

---

1 Another example can be found in footnote one on page 262: "Yussive smirte and ye mermon answerth from his beelyingplace."
2 Shaun's sermon also resonates with Jesus speaking to the women of Jerusalem in the Gospel of Luke (23:28).
3 The location of the Garden in Missouri is not actually from the Book of Mormon but from Smith's later writings.

and important work of American religion, its positionality as an ontologically unstable heretical and spiritual event that materially bleeds into the twenty-first century should also not be under emphasized. The book is simultaneously literal, material, ancient, modern, heretical, and metaphorical. My time spent reading the Book of Mormon alongside *Finnegans Wake*—both impenetrable books that I still cannot claim to have "read"—feels somehow like similar explorations of wandering meaning.

In working our way back through texts and language to issues of origin, translation, interior and exterior, totality and fragment, and reading the body and/as text, another perspective—more specifically on themes of reversing time, and the sending and nonarrival of texts and ideas—is offered by Jacques Derrida's *The Post Card: From Socrates to Freud and Beyond*, published in 1980 and translated into English in 1987. The cover of the book and much of the written text is based on or inspired by a card Derrida found in the Bodleian Library at Oxford, which depicts a medieval Socrates taking dictation from Plato—an image which interested Derrida due to its reversal of the relationship: it is, of course, Plato who wrote down what Socrates said. As Derrida writes, "Socrates comes *before* Plato, there is between them— and in general—an order of generations, an irreversible sequence of inheritance" (1987: 20), and yet the postcard, like *Finnegans Wake*, like the Book of Mormon, plays with this sense of reversing time. On the first page of *The Postcard*, Derrida writes that one of the book's major concerns is the "possible subversion of what is usually taken as a fixed sequence—e.g. Socrates before Plato … the death of the old before the young" (1987: ix). The whole section returns time and again to questions of who writes, who dictates, where do the words come from, and how do they travel. This "postality" is, for Derrida not just traveling letters and ideas, but is also a matter of being, as he claims to compose a "post card ontology" (1987: 22). To exist is to be sent, to be an idea or text in transit. These are ideas we can bring to the scriptural nature of the Book of Mormon as we read it through *Finnegans Wake*: What happens to the idea of the original if the translation came first? How do we receive misplaced or lost scripture?

The first half of Derrida's book, titled *Envois*, is essentially half epistolary novel and half preface, and contains a sequence of letters addressed to an unnamed lover written by what seems to be a pseudo-fictional, pseudo-autobiographical Derrida. This series or sequence of letters, without clear origin, are not necessarily meant to be read, with Derrida himself confessing in the beginning: "I do not know if their reading is bearable" (1987: 3). Derrida used the motif of postcards to suggest that communication is not what philosophers often idealistically imagine it to be, but is instead a "wandering outcast" that is both open for all to read and, at the same time, only makes sense to one. Derrida's point is that all formative texts need to be read without an authorized source or a specific destination. He uses the trope of the postcard here, and these cryptic notes and messages, to emphasize the idea that origins and intentions are always unknown—letters often arrive late, already read, damaged, or in the wrong inbox—and that no form of communication, from Bibles to prayers to poems to love letters, are ever closed or direct routes of exchange.

By pointing to style and language as a type of postmodern scripture, we have circled back to certain ways of looking at the writing and language in *Finnegans Wake*, where the theme of the postal service is woven in the traveling of ideas in writing and scripture. "Bring us this days our maily bag!" it proclaims (*FW* 603.7–8), linking the post with the Eucharist. The movement and relationship between God and texts is a main theme in the work of theologians, for whom the postmodern God *is* writing, as opposed to a God of presence and speech. For Taylor, "writing inscribes the disappearance of the Transcendental Signified" (1984: 105), and if the "disappearance of the Transcendental Signified creates the possibility of writing" (1984: 108), then "God" *becomes* writing at the moment he ceases to be a determinate. This kind of God after God, this kind of writing after writing, is a scripture of indeterminacy, of endings, and of new possibilities. Read this way, the Book of Mormon's material and immanent depictions of the divine can do exactly the opposite of what they are intended to do. Just as Joyce's language can at once suggest both a loss of and surplus of meanings, so the language in the Book of Mormon and its surrounding discourses and practices establishes an immanence that subverts itself.

American Scripture

In the summer of 2015, I took a break from writing in upstate New York to take a bike ride along the Erie Canal with my partner. We planned to rent bicycles and start the ride in Palmyra, New York, but after an afternoon of Finger Lakes area wine tasting, we arrived to the town late and tired; just time enough to rent our bikes and check into our hotel. After a short rest, we went out for a twilight walk. The first thing we noticed was a little stone path curving away from the door of the hotel. We followed it around to the back of the hotel where it led to the Palmyra LDS Temple, standing impressively with its gleaming white granite, tall spire, and perfectly manicured lawn, looking a little too big and grand in the silent small-town evening. I had somehow forgotten that Palmyra was near the childhood farm of Joseph Smith and is considered a spiritual home to the Church of Latter-Day Saints. The Temple stands on a hill overlooking the Sacred Grove, the site of Smith's "First Vision" which, depending on the version, is where a fourteen-year-old Smith saw one or two physical divine figures or "personages" usually identified as God the Father and the Son. We wandered around the grove and the site of Smith's family farm, alone except for one other couple from Utah. The next day, to my partner's disappointment, we postponed our bike ride for a day of Mormon tourism and research. I visited the Hill Cumorah & Visitors' Center, an LDS museum and the site of the hill where Smith claimed to have dug up the golden tablets that would become the Book of Mormon. It is also the site of a huge, high-tech, yearly festival that I would attend later that summer, with 600 actors on the hill re-enacting the stories of LDS scripture for thousands of spectators.

Back in the town, I visited the Grandin Building, the former print shop where the first Book of Mormon was published. In printing the book, owner Egbert Grandin used a recently invented printing press available for small printers of the time. On March 26, 1830, the printed Book of Mormon was first offered for sale in Grandin's Palmyra Bookstore. I had read accounts of the early production and reception history of the book, but I was struck by the humble physical structure of the building in front of me. It was the opposite of the Temple in the way it comfortably fit with the surrounding town, the closed shops around it, and the churches on the nearby street corners. I later found out that in 1998, on the anniversary of the first printing, the Church had restored part of the original Grandin establishment, which the LDS Church now maintains for tours and as a Mormon pilgrimage site. My discovery, though, was quiet, private, and without commentary or explication. I was the only one on the street and the shop was closed—all I could do was stand outside and look in the windows, pondering the significance of the place. It is an obvious point, but what struck me was that a major global branch of Christianity has such a recent and immanent history. The actual material origins for arguably the most influential text of scripture since the Quran, is just a small building on a quiet street in upstate New York. In its unassuming materiality it seemed to physically enact the heretical processes that I have written about in the discovered Gnostic documents and in the destroyed art of the English Reformation. It is Mormon doctrine that the Book itself comes from texts that are already abridged, translated, lost, and retranslated, all by human hands. We have no access to an original. It is also a common observation that, while the Bible is divine in origin but was transmitted by humans, the Book

Figure 8 Grandin building in Palmyra, New York: Print shop where the Book of Mormon was first printed.

of Mormon is just the opposite: it claims to be written by fallible human hands, but reaches modern-day readers through divine intervention. And yet here I stood in front of the print shop, thinking about scripture and the idea of origin. Still and quiet, it felt both frozen in time and like heresy in action.

One of my main points has been that Joyce's references to heretics and heresy are ways of indirectly challenging traditional ideas about literature, narrative, and the creation of art. The Book of Mormon, in different ways, provides the same challenge. Making the unusual move of putting *Finnegans Wake* and the Book of Mormon into dialogue helps us to reframe questions of heresy and the readings of texts, sacred texts, and scripture. In juxtaposing these two dissimilar and rarely compared books, we can explore how texts read each other, are read *through* each other, and write each other; each text functions, in Derrida's words, as "a machine with multiple reading heads for other texts" (1979: 107). If—as I have been claiming—reading Joyce helps us understand ways in which heresy has been about constant re-readings of the already read, then the juxtaposition of the *Wake* and the Book of Mormon dramatizes the process for the modern world. *Finnegans Wake* here, works, as Jonathan Culler writes, as a way of "using the structures of one work to reveal a radical energy in apparently stultifying passages of another" (1982: 260). Comparing these two works brings us back to some of the themes of writing and history in chapter three, but instead of recreating a modernist version of ancient Gnostic texts, we instead find ourselves with modern texts re-imagining themselves as ancient. On the surface, the Book of Mormon and *Finnegans Wake* share a challenging and outsider status, an interest in alternative religious history and mythology, as well as a reputation for being famously unread or unreadable. Both books conflate Old and New Testaments and subvert linear chronology in narration and authorship; in neither book is history communicated as singular, but rather as uncertain and full of alternative paths. Looking deeper, we see that they also share an emphasis on the importance of reading, interpreting, translating, and copying; the importance of textual history, of historiography, and the constructed-ness of historical narrative; questions of authority of interpretation and origin; and the ontology and autonomy of texts—all themes that place them in the lineage of Christian heresy and debates over orthodoxy and heresy.

Joseph Smith's biggest accomplishment, as biographer Fawn Brodie famously wrote, was that he "dared to found a new religion in the age of printing." This fact results in a complex relationship between Mormonism and the material history of its sacred documents that is both like and unlike other Abrahamic religions. The story *of* the Book of Mormon, the stories *in* the Book of Mormon, and the perception of it by outsiders is dominated by questions and stories of origins: real, forgotten, mythical, and misinterpreted. Yet material evidence of the origin story is spread across the United States. While it was pretty clear that the buildings, from the frame house to the printing shop, had been renovated, they were still verifiably—supported by photographic proof—the actual building where Joseph

Smith had conceived, written, and published his scripture. Although the Book of Mormon comes out of a culture of fierce religious innovation, it was still presented to the world in an age of science—an age of proof and evidence—and both sides have continued to read this strange and fascinating book within this context of true or false, authentic or fraud, orthodox or heretical. As I was writing about how reading the twentieth-century works of Joyce can help us think about distant debates over Christian heresy, I realized that the Book of Mormon (heretical to many Christians) and the spaces that it came from, might play much the same role. The Book of Mormon and its reception are models for how literature becomes scripture and for how a modern text accrues multiple meanings. Our heretical history of the present has often come back to the ideas of the book and of writing, so we can start by paying particular attention to specific ways in which both *Finnegans Wake* and the Book of Mormon acknowledge the role of writing, remembering, forgetting, and transmitting of narrative as a creative force in what we think of as history, religious discourse, and concepts of divinity.

Fin Again: Writing and the Practice of Heresy

[Bloomsday: June 16, 2015, Cappadocia, Turkey]

Sightseeing and hiking in Turkey on Bloomsday is not a particularly Joycean activity, but is certainly an apt place to think through questions of orthodoxy and heresy.[1] Paul established the first Christian colony in this region, and, by the second century, Cappadocia had a large Christian community. As the home of the "Cappadocian Fathers"—including Basil ("the Great") and his brother, Gregory of Nyssa—in the fourth century, it was the birthplace of an early and influential theory of the Trinity. The Cappadocian Fathers created a Trinity that offered a balance between oneness and threeness that would be the basis for orthodoxy, although in the following centuries it would also lead to, as Joyce writes, the "fetter, the summe, and the haul it cost" (*FW* 153.31–2)—a dark transition from Father, Son, and Holy Ghost to chains, prisons, holocausts, and the crosses we all bear. As I walked through valleys, hills, and open-air museums, my main focus was on the many cave churches that date from early Christianity into the thirteenth century. The churches vary in size but are, for the most part, small, single nave structures built into cliffs and caves. The interiors feature colorful fresco paintings of saints, biblical scenes, and devotional images covering the curved walls, domes, and ceilings. I was aware, as I walked from one cave church to another, that I was seeing early medieval images that were essentially unknown in the West until the early-eighteenth century and that were also inaccessible between the First World War and 1950. This shifting sense of time, creation, and erasure shaped my viewing—I imagined seeing these images

---

1 Though, of course, with *Finnegans Wake*, there are always connections: "Turkish References in Finnegans Wake," Kevin M. McCarthy, *James Joyce Quarterly*, Vol. 9, No. 2 (Winter, 1972), pp. 250–8.

of Christ, Mary, John the Baptist, Basil, and St. George as they would have looked in the twelfth century, bright deep colors, shapes, and figures covering the soft rock of the cave walls.

But, as I discussed in chapter four, a work of devotional art does not just belong to its imagined point of origin; it lives, it changes, and it interacts with people, weather, and events. Looking closely at individual pieces of medieval stained glass in Yorkshire's Beverly Minster, for example, one finds carefully etched images of fighter planes honoring fallen pilots of the Second World War. In interacting with a work of art, we see the stages of construction, the imperfections, the damages, the alterations, and the restorations as a conversation and journey over time rather than as an idealized, clear window to a single imagined point in the past. Like so many intersections of religion and art, the experience is about understanding the desire for an impossible pure presence. A fresco that looks pristine does so only due to restoration, and, in its denial of the passage of time and effects of humans and nature, it is a fiction. It also mirrors iconoclastic defacement in that it represents one culture's view of what the image should look like in the present. It is a modern fantasy; only one version of the story that can be told. To see art this way is to break the frame; it is the opposite of Stephen's aesthetic theory in *Portrait*, which claims that you should apprehend art as *one* thing, as *one* whole (P 230). It is, instead, to view a text the way we must learn to read *Finnegans Wake*, where times intersect, collide, and blur together, where the boundaries of the book cannot contain the network of associations.

Once we start to notice these interplays of history, we see them everywhere: images representing different cultures, styles, and ideas and offering harmony and discord, orthodoxy and heresy. Some of the more striking cave church walls in Cappadocia revealed more nonrepresentational, simple images in faded earth colors: decorative geometric shapes, crosses, and floral patterns, later echoes of the aniconic images from a ninth-century Eastern Christianity that found the representation of religious scenes and figures heretical. One of the walls showed Islamic images painted into Christian scenes, decorating the shields of the soldiers at the crucifixion. Centuries, theologies, heresies, and religions blur together here: East and West, Christianity and Islam, medieval and modern.

In the Ihlara Valley, standing alone in Saint George's Church (Kirkdamalti), I found what the guidebooks describe as "damaged" and "vandalized" images of saints, the birth of Jesus, angels, the death of Mary, and the crucifixion. Faces and eyes were scratched out or removed, dark shadows of discoloration obscured details (smoke stains from the former location of lamps and candles, perhaps), and layers of graffiti were written over and around the various scenes. The sometimes carefully, sometimes aggressively scratched out faces of saints and removed images of Jesus suggest intentional acts of disfiguration, yet remain ambiguous in motivation. Like the paintings, windows, and medieval rood screens in chapter five, these damaged images (whether Protestant, Byzantine, or Islamic) can be seen as acts of devotion and creation as well as destruction—the afterlife and legacy of the images contain both the original artist and the defacement. The more I looked around the walls of the cave, the more words—painted, drawn, and etched—became my focus. I first noticed the original Greek names, inscriptions, and invocations, some probably painted at the same time as the original images. But, unlike the more recently restored churches, in this space the images were coved with a web of painted and scratched words: Greek, Arabic, Turkish, and even English. Some were faded, only visible by flashlight; others sharp and fresh. The words wrapped around the images, inscriptions, and scriptural quotations, augmenting them with names, curses, dates, drawings, and declarations of love. Without the appropriate language skills, I could not even guess at most of what was written, but the growing impression was that these walls represented an 800-year-old dialogue across faiths, cultures, practice, and beliefs—existing somewhere between institutions, theology, lived religion, and everyday life.

My experience of looking at and thinking about church graffiti had been sharpened the previous summer when I spent a day with archeologist Matthew J. Champion, hunting for medieval graffiti in York Minster Cathedral. Looking at

Figure 9 Images and graffiti on church wall in Saint George's in Cappadocia.

the oldest stones and bricks in the building, peering behind walls and tombs, we found charms, curses, mason marks, musical notations, crosses, ritual markings, word puzzles, ships, and heraldic designs. And while these faded lines are almost invisible today, if one remembers that the inside walls of churches and cathedrals were brightly colored surfaces, these markings would have stood out for all to see. They would have been, as Champion remarked to me, "as much a part of medieval church as the mass." Indeed, graffiti patterns indicate that their creators were often drawn to areas of religious importance: the back of rood screens, baptismal fonts, chapter houses, and funerary sculpture. For Champion, the importance of church graffiti is that it helps us glimpse beliefs of the average parishioner that are not to be found within mainstream areas of medieval studies. Lived religious experience, like theological heresy, exists on the fringes of official doctrine and practice, not always visible, but always present. Categories—like orthodoxy, Catholic, sacred, or scripture—always leave remainders and traces. Heresy, hidden in the margins, tucked into the hesitations and ambiguities of orthodox doctrine, and speaking to us from both the distant past and the future, is another way to get at these remainders and to question how we continue to organize knowledge.

It was partly in reaction to these experiences of early Christian sites that I began to reshape this book to acknowledge the practices involved—the social and physical acts of reading, writing, looking, and teaching that were all part of connecting my own experiences to the texts of Joyce and my understanding of the history of Christianity. Standing alone in a silent cave in Central Turkey, thinking about a cathedral in Northern England and their possible connections to my disorganized Joyce and heresy manuscript waiting for me back in New York, I arrived at a useful metaphor for revision. Church graffiti—these palimpsests in stone—capture the relationship between word, image, theology, practice, and people. In our study of religious spaces and words, we should not be content to just look, analyze, or dismiss, but we should allow ourselves the desire to *participate*. Whether Christian, atheist, Muslim, Jew, pagan, other, or none, we—like those before us—should not be willing to view religious writing as read-only documents. We instead leave our already fading words there to interact with the surrounding words, images, and natural elements, to become part of the conversation, and to be found, read, and reinscribed or blasphemed about again. In Northern England and Central Turkey, as centuries-old markings become visible, they transform church walls into interactive surfaces and into spaces for alternative expressions of belief—a gray area, outside the orthodox. Heretical writing and study—like this graffiti, like Joyce's works—are attracted to religious images and language. Written over, through, and intersecting with scriptural writing, they can be celebratory, antagonistic, blasphemous, and worshipful—but always in relation to religious signification, part of Joyce's multi-sided "polyhedron of scripture" (*FW* 107.8).

[*February 13, 2019, Buffalo, New York*]
It was late in my process of writing this book that I felt obligated to turn more to ideas of practice—not only to weave my own experience of art, literature, and travel into the chapters, but to actually think about the *doing* of scholarship and the *practice* of reading Joyce as it connects to ideas of lived religion, both orthodox and heretical. The process of trying to write with and through these new ideas had many starts and stops, but started to cohere around some specific texts and practices during the weeks I spent in the Joyce archives at the University of Buffalo.

On a random afternoon fighting my post-cafeteria lunch bleariness, looking at Joyce's indecipherable handwriting in the *Wake* Notebooks, I found myself staring at these lines:

> continent of Big Things
> floods reveal
>   history
> why bridge things
> winding roads
> avoid fallen trees (VI. B. 6)

As remarked before, the norm has been for Joyce scholars to trace the words in the Notebook back to the sources (books, places, people) Joyce was using, and to then trace the words forward as they grow, develop, change (and often disappear) through the subsequent drafts of *Finnegans Wake*. While, as far as I know, none of these lines have been definitively traced to a source text or connected to any of the manuscripts or published versions of *Finnegans Wake*, they suddenly began to work for me as a visual poem on the randomness of trying to write about or construct a version of history that is stable. More specifically, they seemed to speak to my own project. Writing for publication is, by nature, an arrogant act, and to write about such broad histories—to claim a sliver of permanence—in the face of a reality that is about lack of connection, decay and destruction, can seem like an imaginary "continent of Big Things." The word "big"—especially in Joyce's handwriting, but also in the context of the *Wake*—also looks like "bog" and "bug": suggesting both the wet, muddy layers of peat in which thousands of years of Irish history (and Irish bodies) are buried and preserved, and words that Joyce often uses instead of "god." The next lines "Floods reveal/history" point to how destruction reveals the past: accidents unearth long-buried scriptures, decay exposes medieval paintings under Reformation whitewash. As Stephen suggests in chapter two of *Ulysses*, there is no way to "bridge things" when we are talking about history, no true connection to a stable past. Here again, we see the role of time and the role of destruction—both natural and human—in understanding heresy and literature. This instability is what modernism brings to the study of heresy and what the study of heresy brings to modernism. In the early-twentieth century, they both provided the background for the other, as modernism introduced to a reading public the gaps and incoherence that heresy had already implanted in its religious subconscious.

In 1923, the year after *Ulysses* was published, Joyce began keeping a notebook (VI. B. 3) just as he was beginning to compose episodes for what would become *Finnegans Wake*. On page 11 are notes and drawings that were made as Joyce read J.M. Flood's *Ireland: Its Saints and Scholars*, a book that is not a work of original scholarship, but organizes information from other existing books. On this page of notes, Joyce uncharacteristically turned to the visual as he drew (or perhaps copied) five crosses in the middle of the page: three large and two smaller Irish or "Celtic" crosses (with a ring surrounding the intersection), and one next to the word "Irish." As Joyce would have known, the ring, or nimbus, on the Irish cross is usually dated back to the monumental high crosses of the ninth century and, while the ring may have merely been a practical way to support the cross arms, it may also date from earlier "cosmological crosses" that represent the celestial sphere. Joyce's depictions in the Notebook are simple line drawings without any obvious defining details. What are these crosses representing? Are they symbolic, mimetic, metonymic? Taken (it seems) from images in Flood's book, they could serve as copies, reminders, symbols, or metaphors. Scholars point to a specific image in Flood's book and then also to the Irish cross at Monasterboice, featured in the book as a source for Joyce's sketches and notes. Yet Joyce's drawings show no attempt at specific detail and it is only the few surrounding words like "shaft," "shrine," and "crozier" that point to details from Flood's book that are visually not in Joyce's sketches. They may remind us of an actual object, but are not attempts to represent. We have here something like the absence of the Catholic object in a Protestant church where the original detail is only remembered, or hinted at, by people crossing themselves as they pass an empty space. Intended or not, there is a revealing overlap between surviving remnants of medieval Christian Ireland, Flood's book, Joyce's sketches, and our reading of *Finnegans Wake*.

Scholars as different as the formalist Clive Hart and the postmodern psychoanalyst Jacques Lacan have identified circles and crosses as central to *Finnegans Wake*. In Hart's 1962 *Structure and Motif in Finnegans Wake*, he locates circles (or cycles) and crosses as the two structuring symbols or archetypal forms of the *Wake* as a whole as well as multiple mini-structures and themes throughout the novel. Hart maps the whole structure of *Finnegans Wake* onto these two shapes. The cross, for example, represents the "radically opposed orbits of Shem and Shaun," and also, the four old men (one evangelist on each point and a donkey in the middle that they all ride on). For Hart, "just as the minor cycles of *Finnegans Wake* are typified in and defined by the great cycle of the whole book, so the many cross-symbols are all variants of a pair of great archetypal crosses stretching across the total structure" (1962: 129). While Hart is mostly interested in a stable spatial organization of the book, Lacan takes the same two symbols and makes them into an anti-structure, where, "signifiers collapse into each other, are recomposed and mixed up" (qtd in Rabaté, 2014: 161). Lacan explained that:

> if Joyce is completely caught up in the sphere and the cross, it is not only because he read a lot of Aquinas thanks to his education with the Jesuits. You are all as caught in the sphere and the cross. Here is a circle, the section of a sphere, and within the cross … But no-one has perceived that this is already a Borromean knot.
>
> (qtd in Rabaté, 2014: 165)

Lacan's "Joyce seminar" was titled *Le sinthome*. According to Lacan, *sinthome* is the Latin way of spelling the Greek origin of the French word *symptôme*, meaning symptom. For Lacan, *sinthome* also functioned as a pun, standing for both symptom (*sinthome*) and holy man (*saint homme*), as they are both pronounced the same. And, as Colette Soler writes, "Lacan's play with writing can evoke not only 'saint' and 'sin' in English, but also 'Sinn' (sense) in German, and in French 'Saint Thomas' of the Summa and—why not—the French word 'somme' (sleep), from which *Finnegans Wake* is supposed to wake us!" (2018: 22). Lacan's Joyce seminar followed his famous R.S.I. seminar, in which he developed the idea of the three circles of the Borromean knot as a way to understand the interrelation of the layers of the Real, the Symbolic, and the Imaginary. The Borromean knot consists of three rings or circles which are linked together, but where removing any one ring leaves the other two unconnected. Often used in mathematics, they were also a common medieval visual representation of the Trinity.

Perhaps building on the obvious Trinitarian logic to this schema, Lacan also appreciated, that pronouncing the letters R, S, and I, sounds like *hérésie* in French. For Lacan, the three circles of the Real, the Symbolic, and the Imaginary had not been properly tied together, and needed, as Jean-Michel Rabaté writes a "re-plotting, a re-knotting." Rabaté uses the Lacan seminar to think about what he called the "untranslatable joy migrating between texts, bodies, and languages" (2014: 164–6). He finds that Lacan's adaption of Hart's forms of the circle and the cross allowed him to add to his logic of Borromean knots. What Lacan seemed to learn from Joyce and *Finnegans Wake* was how to add a fourth element to his Borromean knots—a fourth thread that was linguistic, psychological, and holy and, in the process, created a modernist heretical reframing of the cross itself.

Lacan's reading of Joyce has been criticized for its somewhat reductive biographical basis, but it is instructive to think about how Lacan sees Joyce's choice of an artistic career as compensating for an absent father. This absent father makes his reading more than just psychoanalytic—if we see the cross as his subject rather than Joyce, it is also scriptural and theological. If the absent father is an absent God, and the crosses represent the death of God, then Joyce's Irish crosses are—as symbols of the *Wake* and of reimagining the Father and the Son—a heretical, and radically theological way of imagining the Son. Lacan's idiosyncratic reading of the *Wake* allows him to bring a heretical version of Catholicism into his psychoanalyses. Lacan here creates a topological schema and a psychoanalysis of the shape, and allows us to appreciate the iconicity of the notebook. Created within the imaginary space between these representations of circles and crosses—the weather-worn medieval crosses standing quietly in a cemetery next to a cow field at Monasterboice, Hart and Lacan finding structures and cures within the crosses *Finnegans Wake,* and the drawing in the Notebooks—we find another heretical answer to the questions we keep returning to: What happened on the cross? What does a cross mean to us today? The answer, like everything else in this book, is plural: it is a material object, a fading drawing, an absent father, an anxious author, a cure, a salvation, and a dying god.

So, are these crosses in the Notebooks real, imaginary, symbolic, Christian, or heretical? In *Finnegans Wake*, as a scholar looks at the discovered letter he remarks "Such crossing is antechristian of course" (*FW* 114.11). Perhaps we can also read Joyce's crosses as anti-Christian—as symbols of disagreement and of death rather than resurrection and unity. Or, perhaps just the ones that Joyce draws—literally and symbolically in the Notebooks and the *Wake*, a redrafting of the cross through circles—suggest a history that is not a linear Christian one, not shaped by a single beginning and a promised end, but cyclical pagan one. We might think here about Adam's skull resting at the base of the cross at the crucifixion in a Renaissance painting. For Christians, this represents a linear success in which Christ's death forever overcomes Adam's fall. Add a circle and a Wakean interpretation to that image, however, and the fall returns, again and again—it becomes part of the cross—cycles blend with and overcome the right angles and directional history of the crucifixion. The Irish cross turns into a symbol that means the opposite: a "cruel fiction" indeed.

[June 12, 2018, Antwerp, Belgium]
Joyce readers love to quote Marshall McLuhan, who said, "LSD is the lazy man's *Finnegans Wake*." The line has always made me and my students laugh, but I never really took the content of it seriously. Although I was not a serious scholar of *Finnegans Wake* until writing the last chapters of this book, I have been reading, teaching, and writing about sections of it for quite a few years. I have also attended *Wake* reading groups in Philadelphia, New York City, London, and at almost every Joyce symposium since 2012. Throughout all of these experiences, I found the *Wake* to help me think about language, difficulty, experimentation, philosophy, artistic representations, scripture, music, and communal reading. But I never got the "trippy" part of it—until one summer night in 2018.

I was in Antwerp for the International Joyce Symposium—although I could only stay for the first two days because I had to go to London for a conference of the International Society of Heresy Studies. I was presenting related papers at both conferences on the relationship between Christian Gnosticism and *Finnegans Wake*, early versions of what eventually became chapter three in this book. I was also at the symposium to catch up with old friends and former students. The second night of the conference, I went out for drinks with two former students, Catie Piwinski and Tess Brewer. We first went to a tapas bar where we drank and ate, and my phone died while I was sending a text to another former student to tell him what we were up to. Derek Pyle, whom I knew from previous conferences and from having him visit my classes to talk about his *Finnegans Wake* music projects, had invited us to participate in a filming and recording project of reading the *Wake* later that night with filmmaker Gavan Kennedy, but none of us were feeling quite brave enough yet.

We headed out, more or less randomly, to find more drinks. I was drawn to the historical center of the city and the cathedral, which I had not yet had a chance to see. On a narrow street in the shadow of the cathedral we found a place called *Elfde Gebod*, a bar in an obviously four or five hundred-year-old building. At first, I thought it was perhaps a store or museum connected to the cathedral, as the window was filled with images and statues of religious figures and saints. A German couple smoking at the entrance enthusiastically gestured us in and brought us to a large center table. The bar was filled floor to ceiling with icons, religious images, statues, paintings, and a few more blasphemous or heretical modern images. Paintings and sculptures of saints, Mary, Jesus, and various angels lined the walls and hung from the ceiling. A few other curious Joyceans wandered in and sat around us. We ordered Belgian beers and engaged in an odd, rambling three or four-way tri-lingual conversations. A performer on stage sang Ed Sheeran songs and the German man got up on the stage and danced with a chair. I looked at the religious objects surrounding us, which became increasingly hallucinogenic-appearing the more we drank. It felt like a David Lynch film. We left the bar, convincing ourselves to go watch and support—but not participate—in Gavan's filming.

We were kind of lost and turned around—with no GPS from my dead phone—but we walked right into the mostly abandoned plaza where Gavan was filming. Gavan was full of good energy and Derek was sitting happily and Buddha-like under a tree and they convinced me to read. I was asked to choose a page of the *Wake* and a piece of music to listen to while I read. I chose the section of the *Wake* that I would be talking about in my paper, which focuses on various heretical figures and uses the word "gnawstick." For my piece of music, I choose an avant garde, unaccompanied trombone piece by Luciano Berio that I used to perform in my previous life as a professional trombone player. The piece, *Sequenza V*, is a tribute to the famous Swiss clown, Grock, and requires the trombone player to sing and play at the same time, inhale loudly through the horn, rattle a mute against the bell, and at one point turn to the audience and ask, "Why?" I also appreciated the fact that Berio had been a Joyce reader and had written a vocal work—*Omaggio a Joyce*—based on the Sirens chapter of *Ulysses*. They set the proper levels and I sat on a bench next to Catie and Tess and started to read: "would we now for annas and annas?" (*FW* 170.1). (Annas and annas is usually taken to mean years and years, but Annas was also a high priest before whom Jesus was brought for judgment.)

As I sat on a bench, next to two former students, looking out over the deserted streets of Antwerp, reading *Finnegan Wake*, listening to the blurps and blats of a trombone piece that I used to perform dressed in clown costume, thinking about Catholic saints and medieval cathedrals and Belgian beer bars and a man dancing with a chair, I realized what McLuhan meant. After I finished reading, Catie and Tess also read. Finn Fordham showed up and we talked about Deleuze, and then I talked to Derek about—I don't know—"life," and then we all headed off to our different hotels in an elated, but somewhat quiet mood. As Catie said later, the reading felt simultaneously "very lonely and very familial." I agreed. One felt simultaneously totally immersed in the page and the music, but then also aware of the camera, a few staring passersby, and the surrounding community.

I close with this anecdote for several reasons. First, I wanted to capture some of the joy this world and this project have brought to me. But more than that, this intersection of the social, the spiritual, the literary, and the intellectual as a way that both engages with and also challenges the way we live with our surrounding texts and histories is one of the reasons I wrote this book. As I write this epilogue—in the middle of a global pandemic, protests over police brutality, and some very serious challenges to American democracy—and as I look back on that night, it occurs to me that it is not just "trippy" but that it is *the* trip. It's all there. From Joyce's "gnawstick" to the actual Gnostics; from the funky saint-filled religiously saturated and beer-soaked bar and the man dancing with the chair to the medieval cathedral next door; from a trombone player dressed as a clown to my love for former students, this night, like *Ulysses* and *Finnegans Wake* itself, was orthodoxy and heresy, was both religion and the mockery of it—this was to live life and to laugh at it; to be alone with the words on the page and the music in your ears and the thoughts in your head, but to be fully connected at the same time.

They lived und laughed ant loved end left.

(*FW* 18.20–1)

Bibliography

Altizer, T. J. J. (1985), *History as Apocalypse*, Albany: SUNY Press.
Altizer, T. J. J. and W. Hamilton. (1966), *Radical Theology and the Death of God*, Indianapolis: Bobbs-Merrill Co.
Anidjar, G. (2002), "Introduction: 'Once More, Once More': Derrida, Arab, the Jew," in G. Anidjar (ed), *Jacques Derrida: Acts of Religion*, 1–39, New York: Routledge.
Aston, M. (1988), *England Iconoclasts: Volume I: Laws against Images*, Oxford: Oxford University Press.
Atherton, J. S. ([1959] 2009), *The Books at the Wake: A Study of Literary Allusions in James Joyce's Finnegans Wake*, Carbondale: Southern Illinois University Press.
Attridge, D., ed. (2004), *The Cambridge Companion to Joyce*. 2nd edn, Cambridge: Cambridge University Press.
Attridge, D. (2003), "The Finnegans Wake Notebooks at Buffalo," *Modernism/Modernity*, 10 (3): 571–3.
Atrridge, D. (2000), *Joyce Effects: On Language, Theory, and History*, Cambridge: Cambridge University Press.
Auerbach, E. ([1946] 2003), *Mimesis: The Representation of Reality in Western Literature, Fiftieth-Anniversary Edition*, trans. W. R. Trask, Princeton: Princeton University Press.
Auerbach, N. (1995), *Our Vampires, Ourselves*, Chicago: Chicago University Press.
Badiou, A. (2005), *Being and Event*, London: Continuum International Publishing Group.
Barber, T. (2013), "Idolatry, Iconoclasm and the Reformation's Long Legacy," in T. Barber and S. Boldrick (eds), *Art under Attack: Histories of British Iconoclasm*, 22–9, London: Tate Publishing.
Barber, T. and S. Boldrick, eds. (2013), *Art under Attack: Histories of British Iconoclasm*, London: Tate Publishing.
Barkan, L. (1999), *Unearthing the Past: Archaeology and Aesthetics in the Making of Renaissance Culture*, New Haven: Yale University Press.
Bauer, W. ([1934] 1971), *Orthodoxy and Heresy in Earliest Christianity*, Philadelphia: Fortress Press.
Beckett, S. (2009), *Letters of Samuel Beckett, Volume I: 1929–1940*, eds. M. Dow Fehsenfeld and L. More Overbeck, Cambridge: Cambridge University Press.
Bennett, G. (2013), "'Stomp on Jesus' Creator Says Exercise Often Reaffirms Faith," *The Ledger*, March 28, 2013. Available online: https://www.theledger.com/

news/20130328/stomp-on-jesus-creator-says-exercise-often-reaffirms-faith (accessed January 24, 2021).

Bennett, J. (2010), *Vibrant Matter: A Political Ecology of Things*, Durham: Duke University Press.

Bennington, G. and J. Derrida (1993), *Jacques Derrida*, Chicago: University of Chicago Press.

Berger, P. L. (1979), *The Heretical Imperative: Contemporary Possibilities of Religious Affirmation*, New York: Anchor Press.

Birmingham, K. (2014), *The Most Dangerous Book: The Battle for James Joyce's Ulysses*, New York: Penguin Books.

Blair, A. (2010), *Too Much to Know: Managing Scholarly Information before the Modern Age*, New Haven: Yale University Press.

Blick, S. and L. D. Gelfand, eds. (2011), *Push Me, Pull You: Imaginative, Emotional, Physical, and Spatial Interaction in Late Medieval and Renaissance Art, Volumes 1–2*, Leiden: Brill Publishers.

Boldrick, S. (2013), "Iconoclasms Past and Present: Conflict and Art," in T. Barber and S. Boldrick (eds), *Art under Attack: Histories of British Iconoclasm*, 14–21, London: Tate Publishing.

Boldrini, L., ed. (2002), *Medieval Joyce: European Joyce Studies 13*, Leiden: Brill Publishers.

Bollettieri Bosinelli, R. M., C. Marengo, and C. Van Boheemen, eds. (1992), *The Languages of Joyce: Selected Papers from the 11th International James Joyce Symposium, Venice 1988*, Amsterdam: John Benjamins Publishing Company.

Borg, R. (2007), *The Measureless Time of Joyce, Deleuze and Derrida*, London: Bloomsbury Publishing.

Bossy, J. (1983), "The Mass as a Social Institution 1200–1700," *Past & Present* (100): 29–61.

Boyle, R. (1972), "Miracle in Black Ink: A Glance at Joyce's Use of His Eucharistic Image," *James Joyce Quarterly*, 10 (1): 47–60.

Boyle, R. (1966), "*Finnegans Wake*, Page 185: An Explication," *James Joyce Quarterly*, 4 (1): 3–16.

Bradley, A. C. ([1904] 1991), *Shakespearean Tragedy: Lectures on Hamlet, Othello, King Lear and Macbeth*, New York: Penguin Books.

Brandes, G. (1898), *William Shakespeare: A Critical Study in Two Volumes*, London: William Heinemann.

Brick, M. (2012), "Joyce's Overlisting Eshtree: A Genetic Approach to Sacred Trees in *Finnegans Wake*," *Genetic Joyce Studies*, 12. Available online: https://www.geneticjoycestudies.org/articles/GJS12/GJS12_Brick (accessed January 24, 2021).

Brivic, S. (2008), *Joyce through Lacan and Žižek: Explorations*, London: Palgrave.

Brodie, F. M. ([1945] 1995), *No Man Knows My History: The Life of Joseph Smith*, New York: Vintage Books.

Brooke, C. (1971), "Religious Sentiment and Church Design in the Later Middle Ages," in C. Brooke (ed), *Medieval Church and Society: Collected Essays*, 162–82, London: Sidgwick and Jackson.

Brown, S. (2003), *"Our Magnificent Fabrick," York Minster: An Architectural History, c. 1220-1500*, Swindon: English Heritage.

Budgen, F. ([1934] 1972), *James Joyce and the Making of Ulysses: and Other Writings*, Oxford: Oxford University.

Campbell, J. and H. M. Robinson (1944), *A Skeleton Key to Finnegans Wake*, New York City: Harcourt Brace.

Caputo, J. D. and G. Vattimo (2007), *After the Death of God*, ed. J. W. Robbins, New York City: Columbia University Press.

Carlson, T. A. (2008), *The Indiscrete Image: Infinitude and Creation of the Human*, Chicago: University of Chicago Press.

Carlson, T. A. (2001), "And Maker Mates with Made: World and Self-Creation in Eriugena and Joyce," in C. Crocket (ed), *Secular Theology: American Radical Theological Thought*, 141–66, London: Routledge.

Carnes, N. (2018), *Image and Presence: A Christological Reflection on Iconoclasm and Iconophilia*, Stanford: Stanford University Press.

Catholic Encyclopedia, Volume 3 (1909), New York: Robert Appleton Company.

Cheng, V. J. (2015), *Amnesia and the Nation: History, Forgetting, and James Joyce*, London: Palgrave Macmillan.

Cheng, V. J. (1992), "'Goddinpotty': James Joyce and the Language of Excrement," in R.M. Bollettieri Bosinelli, C. Marengo, and C. Van Boheemen (eds), *The Languages of Joyce: Selected Papers from the 11th International James Joyce Symposium, Venice 1988*, 85–99, Amsterdam: John Benjamins Publishing Company.

Cheng, V. J. (1987), "Stephen Dedalus and the Black Panther Vampire," *James Joyce Quarterly*, 24 (2): 161–76.

Cheng, V. J. (1984), *Shakespeare and Joyce: A Study of Finnegans Wake*, University Park and London: Pennsylvania State University Press.

Cheng, V.J. (1995), *Joyce, Race, and Empire*, Cambridge: Cambridge University Press.

Chesterton, G. K. ([1908] 2010), *The Man Who Was Thursday*, London: Bibliolis Books.

Christie-Murray, D. (1989), *A History of Heresy*, Oxford: Oxford University Press.

Clark, S. (2007), *Vanities of the Eye: Vision in Early Modern European Culture*, Oxford: Oxford University Press.

Cliett, B. C. (2011), *Riverrun to Livvy: Lots of Fun Reading the First Page of James Joyce's Finnegans Wake*, Scotts Valley: CreateSpace Independent Publishing Platform.

"Conboy Recites from 'Ulysses' and Girl Flees" (1934), *New York Daily News*. 18 May.

Conley, T. (2018), "Revision Revisited," in G. Sartor, *James Joyce and Genetic Criticism: Genesic Fields*, Leiden: Brill Publishers.

Connolly, T. E. (1955), *The Personal Library of James Joyce, University of Buffalo Studies, Monographs in English, No. 6*, Buffalo: Buffalo University Press.

Crispi, L. and S. Slote, eds. (2007), *How Joyce Wrote Finnegans Wake: A Chapter-by-Chapter Genetic Guide*, Madison: Wisconsin University Press.
Cummings, B. (2002a), *The Literary Culture of the Reformation: Grammar and Grace*, Oxford: Oxford University Press.
Cummings, B. (2002b), "Iconoclasm and Bibliophobia in the English Reformations, 1521–1558," in J. Dimmick, J. Simpson, and N. Zeeman (eds), *Images, Idolatry, and Iconoclasm in Late Medieval England: Textually and the Visual Image*, 185–207, Oxford: Oxford University Press.
Culler, J. (1982), *On Deconstruction: Theory and Criticism after Structuralism*, Ithaca: Cornell University Press.
Day, R. A. (1980), "How Stephen Wrote His Vampire Poem," *James Joyce Quarterly*, 17 (2): 183–97.
De Vries, H. (1999), *Philosophy and the Turn to Religion*, Baltimore: Johns Hopkins University Press.
De Vries, H. and S. Weber, eds. (2001), *Religion & Media*, Stanford: Stanford University Press.
Derrida, J. (1992), *Acts of Literature*, ed. Derek Attridge, New York: Routledge.
Derrida, J. (1992), "Ulysses Gramophone: Hear Say Yes in Joyce," in D. Attridge (ed), *Acts of Literature*, 253–309, New York: Routledge.
Derrida, J. ([1980] 1987), *The Postcard: From Socrates to Freud and Beyond*, trans. A. Bass, Chicago: Chicago University Press.
Derrida, J. (1979), "Living On," in H. Bloom (ed), *Deconstruction and Criticism*, trans. J. Hulbert, 75–176, New York: The Seabury Press.
Derrida, J. ([1967] 1978), *Writing and Difference*, trans. A. Bass, London: Routledge.
Derrida, J. ([1967] 1976), *Of Grammatology*, trans. G. C. Spivak, Baltimore: Johns Hopkins University Press.
Devlin, K. J. and C. Smedley, eds. (2015), *Joyce's Allmaziful Plurabilities: Polyvocal Explorations of Finnegans Wake*, Gainesville: University Press of Florida.
Dimmick, J., J. Simpson, and N. Zeeman, eds. (2002), *Images, Idolatry, and Iconoclasm in Late Medieval England: Textually and the Visual Image*, Oxford: Oxford University Press.
Dinshaw, C. (1999), *Getting Medieval: Sexualities and Communities, Pre- and Postmodern*, Durham: Duke University Press.
Downes, G. (2002), "James Joyce, Catholicism and Heresy: With Specific Reference to Giordano Bruno," PhD diss., University of Saint Andrews.
Duffy, E. (1992), *The Stripping of the Altars: Traditional Religion in England, 1400–1580*, New Haven: Yale University Press.
Dworkin, C. (2003), *Reading the Illegible*, Evanston: Northwestern University Press.
Eagleton, T. (2004), *After Theory*, New York: Basic Books.
Eco, U. (1989), *The Aesthetics of Chaosmos: The Middle Ages of James Joyce*, trans. E. Esrock, Cambridge: Harvard University Press.
Ehrman, B. D. (2003), *Lost Christianities: The Battles for Scripture and the Faiths We Never Knew*, Oxford: Oxford University Press.

Eliade, M. (1959), *The Sacred and the Profane: The Nature of Religion*, trans. W. R. Trask, San Diego: Harcourt, Inc.

Eliot, T. S. ([1935] 1964), *Murder in the Cathedral*, New York: Harcourt Brace & Company.

Eliot, T. S. (1923), "Ulysses, Order, and Myth." Available online: http://people.virginia.edu/~jdk3t/eliotulysses.htm (accessed January 28, 2021).

Ellmann, M. (2004), "The Ghosts of Ulysses," in D. Attridge (ed), James *Joyce's Ulysses: A Casebook*, 83–101, Oxford: Oxford University Press.

Ellmann, R. ([1959] 1983), *James Joyce: New and Revised Edition*, Oxford: Oxford University Press.

Ellmann, R. (1975), "Pieces of Ulysses," *Times Literary Supplement*, October 3, 1975: 1118

Ellmann, R. (1972), *Ulysses on the Liffey*, Oxford: Oxford University Press.

Epstein, E. L. (2009), *A Guide through Finnegans Wake*, Gainesville: University Press of Florida.

Epstein, E. L. (1977), "Nestor," in C. Hart and D. Hayman (eds), *James Joyce Ulysses: Critical Essays*, 17–28, Berkeley: University of California Press.

Erickson, G. (2007), *The Absence of God in Modernist Literature*, New York: Palgrave Macmillan.

Erickson, G. (2016), "Arius and the Vampire: Figures of Heresy and Disruption in James Joyce's *Ulysses*," in *Religion and the Arts*, 20 (4): 442–58.

Erickson, G. (2018), "James Joyce's *Ulysses* and the Medieval Eucharist: Fragmented Narratives of Doubt and Creation," in E. A. Foster, J. Perratore, and S. Rozenski (eds), *Devotional Interaction in Medieval Britain and Its Afterlives*, 347–71, Leiden: Brill Publishers.

Erickson, G. and B. Schweizer, eds. (2017), *Reading Heresy: Religion and Dissent in Literature and Art: Selected Essays from the 2014 Conference of the International Society for Heresy Studies*, Berlin: De Gruyter.

Farmer, P. J. (1979), *Jesus on Mars*, New York City: Pinnacle Books.

Flaubert, G. (1997), *Selected Letters*, trans. Geoffrey Wall, New York: Penguin Books.

Fleming, J. (2016), *Cultural Graphology: Writing after Derrida*, Chicago: University of Chicago Press.

Fordham, F. (2013), "Between Theological and Cultural Modernism: The Vatican's *Oath against Modernism*, September 1910," *Literature & History*, 22 (1): 8–24.

Fordham, F. (2007), *Lots of Fun at Finnegans Wake: Unravelling Universals*, Oxford: Oxford University Press.

Frassetto, M. (2007), *The Great Medieval Heretics: Five Centuries of Religious Dissent*, New York: BlueBridge.

Frei, H. (1980), *Eclipse of Biblical Narrative: A Study in Eighteenth and Nineteenth-Century Hermeneutics*, New Haven: Yale University Press.

Garrison, J. (2017), *Challenging Communion: The Eucharist and Middle English Literature*, Columbus: Ohio State University Press.

Gerstel, S. E. J., ed. (2006), *Thresholds of the Sacred: Architectural, Art Historical, Liturgical, and Theological Perspectives in Religious Screens, East and West*, Washington, DC: Dumbarton Oaks Research Library and Collection, Harvard University.
Gifford, D. (2008), *Ulysses Annotated: Notes for James Joyce's Ulysses: 20th Anniversary Edition*, Berkeley: University of California Press.
Gilbert, S. (1952), *James Joyce's Ulysses: A Study*, New York: Vintage.
Giles, K. (2007), "Seeing and Believing: Visuality and Space in Pre-Modern England," *World Archaeology*, 39 (1): 105–21.
Gillespie, M. A. (2008), *The Theological Origins of Modernity*, Chicago: University of Chicago Press.
Gilman, E. B. (1986), *Iconoclasm and Poetry in the English Reformation: Down Went Dagon*, Chicago: University of Chicago Press.
Givens, T. L. (2009), *The Book of Mormon: A Very Short Introduction*, Oxford: Oxford University Press.
Givens, T. L. (2002), *By the Hand of Mormon: The American Scripture That Launched a New World Religion*, Oxford: Oxford University Press.
Givens, T. L. (1997), The *Viper on the Hearth: Mormons, Myths, and the Construction of Heresy*, Oxford: Oxford University Press.
Glieck, J. (2016), *Time Travel: A History*, New York: Vintage.
Gordon, J. (2020), *John Gordon's Finnegans Wake Blog*. Available online: https://johngordonfinnegan.weebly.com/ (accessed July 4, 2021).
Gottfried, R. (2008), *Joyce's Misbelief*, Gainesville: University Press of Florida.
Grafton, A, and M. Williams (2009), *Christianity and the Transformation of the Book: Origen, Eusebius, and the Library of Caesarea*, Cambridge: Harvard University Press.
Graham, E. (2002), *Representations of the Post/Human: Monsters, Aliens and Others in Popular Culture*, New Brunswick: Rutgers University Press.
Gregory, B. S. (2012), *The Unintended Reformation: How a Religious Revolution Secularized Society*, Cambridge: Belknap Press.
Greenblatt, S. (2004), *Will in the World: How Shakespeare Became Shakespeare*, New York: W. W. Norton & Company.
Greenblatt, S. (2001), *Hamlet in Purgatory*, Princeton: Princeton University Press.
Greenblatt, S. (1980), *Renaissance Self-Fashioning: From More to Shakespeare*, Chicago: University of Chicago Press.
Greenblatt, S. and Gallagher, S. (2000) *Practicing New Historicism*, Chicago: University of Chicago Press.
Gross, K. (1985), *Spenserian Poetics: Idolatry, Iconoclasm, and Magic*, Ithaca: Cornell University Press.
Haeckel, E. ([1900] 2009), *The Riddle of the Universe: At the Close of the Nineteenth Century*, trans. J. McCabe, Cambridge: Cambridge University Press.
Hall, E. H. (1891), *Ten Lectures on Orthodoxy and Heresy in the Christian Church*, Boston: American Unitarian Association.

Hanson, R. P. C. (2006), *The Search for the Christian Doctrine of God: The Arian Controversy, 318–381*, Ada: Baker Academic.

Hardison, O. B. (1965), *Christian Rite and Christian Drama in the Middle Ages: Essays on the Origin and Early History of Modern Drama*, Baltimore: Johns Hopkins University Press.

Hardy, G., ed. (2003), *The Book of Mormon: A Reader's Edition*, Urbana: Illinois University Press.

Hardy, G. (2010), *Understanding the Book of Mormon: A Reader's Guide*, Oxford: Oxford University Press.

Harris, F. (1909), *The Man Shakespeare and His Tragic Life-Story*, New York: Mitchell Kennerly.

Hart, C. (1962), *Structure and Motif in Finnegans Wake*, Evanston: Northwestern University Press.

Hart, C. and D. Hayman, eds. (1977), *James Joyce's Ulysses: Critical Essays*, Berkeley: University of California Press.

Hart, K. ([1985] 2000), *The Trespass of the Sign: Deconstruction, Theology and Philosophy*, New York: Fordham University Press.

Hatch, N. O. (1991), *The Democratization of American Christianity*, New Haven: Yale University Press.

Heidegger, M. (2008), *Basic Writings*, ed. D. Farrell Krell, London: Harper Perennial.

Herbert, S., D. Rose, and J. O'Hanlon, eds. (2018), "James Joyce Digital Archive: Ulysses & Finnegans Wake." Available Online: http://jjda.ie/main/JJDA/JJDAhome.htm (accessed January 28, 2021).

Hobson, S. (2011), *Angels of Modernism: Religion, Culture, Aesthetics, 1910–1960*, London: Palgrave Macmillan.

Holsinger, B. (2004), *The Premodern Condition: Medievalism and the Making of Theory*, Chicago: University of Chicago Press.

Ireneaus (1995), "Against Heresies," in L. S. Owens (ed), *The Gnostic Society Library in The Gnosis Archive*. Available online: http://www.gnosis.org/naghamm/gthlamb.html (accessed January 28, 2021).

Jaurretche, C. (2015), "Joyce's Common Reader: A Primer for Sensory Consciousness in I.5," in K. J. Devlin and C. Smedley (eds), *Joyce's Allmaziful Pluralities: Polyvocal Explorations of Finnegans Wake*, 75–89, Oxford: Oxford University Press.

Jaurretche, C. (2020), *Language as Prayer in Finnegans Wake*, Gainesville: University of Florida Press.

Jenkins, P. (2010), *Jesus Wars: How Four Patriarchs, Three Queens, and Two Emperors Decided What Christians Would Believe for the Next 1,500 Years*, New York: HarperCollins.

Jonas, H. (1958), *The Gnostic Religion: The Message of the Alien God and the Beginnings of Christianity*, Boston: Beacon Press.

Joyce, J. ([1959] 1989), *The Critical Writings*, eds. E. Mason and R. Ellmann, Ithaca: Cornell University Press.

Joyce, J. ([1914] 1967), *Dubliners*, eds. R. Scholes and R. Ellmann, New York: Viking Press.
Joyce, J. ([1939] 1999), *Finnegans Wake*, New York: Penguin Books.
Joyce, J. (2001), *The Finnegans Wake Notebooks at Buffalo: VI.B.3*, eds. V. Deane, D. Ferrerr, and G. Lernout, Turnhout: Brepolis Publishers.
Joyce, J. (2002), *The Finnegans Wake Notebooks at Buffalo: VI.B.6*, eds. V. Deane, D. Ferrerr, and G. Lernout, Turnhout: Brepolis Publishers.
Joyce, J. (2002), *The Finnegans Wake Notebooks at Buffalo: VI.B.14*, eds. V. Deane, D. Ferrerr, and G. Lernout, Turnhout: Brepolis Publishers.
Joyce, J. ([1957] 1966), *Letters of James Joyce, Vol. I*, ed. S. Gilbert, New York: Viking Press.
Joyce, J. (1966), *Letters of James Joyce, Vol. II, III*, ed. R. Ellmann, New York: Viking Press.
Joyce, J. (1991), *Poems and Shorter Writings*, eds. R. Ellmann, A. Walton Litz and J. Whittier Ferguson, London: Faber & Faber.
Joyce, J. ([1916] 1993), *A Portrait of the Artist as a Yong Man*, ed. S. Deane, London: Penguin Classics.
Joyce, J. ([1944] 1963), *Stephen Hero*, eds. J. J. Slocum and H. Cahoon, New York: New Directions.
Joyce, J. ([1922] 1986), *Ulysses*, ed. Hans Walter Gabler, New York: Vintage.
Joyce, S. (1958), *My Brother's Keeper: James Joyce's Early Years*, ed. Richard Ellmann, Cambridge: Da Capo Press.
Jung, J. E. (2013), *The Gothic Screen: Space, Sculpture, and Community in the Cathedrals of France and Germany, ca. 1200–1400*, Cambridge: Cambridge University Press.
Kazantzakis, N. (1960), *Last Temptation of Christ*, trans. P. A. Bien, New York: Simon & Schuster, Inc.
Kearney, R. (1984), *Dialogues with Contemporary Continental Thinkers: The Phenomenological Heritage*, Manchester: Manchester University Press.
Kearney, R. and B. Treanor (2015), *Carnal Hermeneutics: From Head to Foot*, New York: Fordham University Press.
Kessler, H. L. (1988), "On the State of Medieval Art History," *The Art Bulletin*, 70 (2): 166–87.
Kieckhefer, R. (2004), *Theology in Stone: Church Architecture from Byzantium to Berkeley*, Oxford: Oxford University Press.
King, K. L. (2003), *What Is Gnosticism?* Cambridge: Harvard University Press.
Kitcher, P. (2009), *Joyce's Kaleidoscope: An Invitation to Finnegans Wake*, New York: Oxford University Press.
Lang, F. K. (1993), *Ulysses and the Irish God*, Lewisburg: Bucknell University Press.
Larsen, M. D. C. (2018), *Gospels before the Book*, Oxford: Oxford University Press.
Lawrence, D. H. ([1915] 1995), *The Rainbow*, London: Penguin Books.
Lawrence, K. (1981), *The Odyssey of Style in Ulysses*, Princeton: Princeton University Press.

Laws, C. D. (2017), "James Joyce and His Early Church: The Art of Schism and Heresy," PhD diss., University of York, York,
Lee, S. (1898), *A Life of William Shakespeare*, New York: The Macmillan Company.
Leonard, G. (2015), "Soul Survivor: Stephen Dedalus as the Priest of the Eternal Imagination," *Joyce Studies Annual*: 3–27.
Lernout, G. (2010), *Help My Unbelief: James Joyce and Religion*, London: Bloomsbury Press.
Lewis, P. (2010), *Religious Experience and the Modernist Novel*, Cambridge: Cambridge University Press.
Lieu, J. M. (2015), *Marcion and the Making of a Heretic: God and Scripture in the Second Century*, Cambridge: Cambridge University Press.
Lowe-Evans, M. (2008), *Catholic Nostalgia in Joyce and Company*, Gainesville: University Press of Florida.
McDannell, C. (1995), *Material Christianity: Religion and Popular Culture in America*, New Haven: Yale University Press.
McCarthy, K. M. (1972), "Turkish References in Finnegans Wake," *James Joyce Quarterly*, 9 (2): 250–8.
McCoy, R.C. (2002), *Alterations of State: Sacred Kingship in the English Reformation*, New York: Columbia University Press.
MacCulloch, D. (2011), *Christianity: The First Three Thousand Years*, London: Penguin Books.
MacCulloch, D. (2005), *The Reformation: A History*, London: Penguin Books.
Mann, T. ([1947] 1997), *Doctor Faustus*, New York: Knopf.
Marquardt, J. T. (2011), "Introduction," in J. T. Marquardt and A. A. Jordan (eds), *Medieval Art and Architecture after the Middle Ages*, 1–17, Newcastle upon Tyne: Cambridge Scholars Publishing.
Marshall, P. (2018), *Heretics and Believers: A History of the English Reformation*, New Haven: Yale University Press.
Meyer, M. W., ed. (2007), *The Nag Hammadi Scriptures: The Revised and Updated Translation of Sacred Gnostic Texts Complete in One Volume*, San Francisco: HarperOne.
Mitchell, A. J. (2013), "Meaning Postponed: *The Post Card* and *Finnegans Wake*," in A. J. Mitchell and S. Slote (eds), *Derrida and Joyce: Texts and Contexts*, Albany: State University of New York Press.
Mitchell, A. J. and S. Slote, eds. (2013), *Derrida and Joyce: Texts and Contexts*, Albany: State University of New York Press.
Michalski, S. (1993), *Reformation and the Visual Arts: The Protestant Image Question in Western and Eastern Europe*, London: Routledge.
Millbank, J., G. Ward, and C. Pickstock, eds. (1998), *Radical Orthodoxy: A New Theology*, London: Routledge.
Mitchell, W. J. T. (1986), *Iconology: Image, Text, Ideology*, Chicago: Chicago University Press.

Morrison, S. (2000), "Heresy, Heretics and Heresiarchs in the Works of James Joyce," PhD diss., Royal Holloway, University of London, London.

Morrow, J.K. (1995), *Towing Jehovah*, Boston: Mariner Books.

Moses und Aron (1932), comp. A. Schoenberg, Zurich: Zürich Opera House.

Muehlberger, E. (2015), "The Legend of Arius' Death: Imagination, Space and Filth in Late Ancient Historiography," *Past and Present*, 227 (1): 3–29.

Mutter, M. (2017), *Restless Secularism: Modernism and the Religious Inheritance*, New Haven: Yale University Press.

Nagel, A. (2012), *Medieval Modern: Art Out of Time*, London: Thames & Hudson.

Nancy, J. L. (2001), "The Deconstruction of Christianity," trans. S. Sparks, in H. De Vries and S. Weber (eds), *Religion & Media*, 112–30, Stanford: Stanford University Press.

Newman, J. H. ([1833] 1897), *The Arians of the Fourth Century*, London: Longmans, Green, and Co.

Noon, W. T. (1957), *Joyce and Aquinas*, New Haven: Yale University Press.

Norris, M. (1976), *The Decentered Universe of Finnegans Wake: A Structuralist Analysis*, Baltimore: Johns Hopkins University Press.

Norris, M. (2004), "Finnegans Wake," in D. Attridge (ed), *The Cambridge Companion to Joyce*, 2nd edn, 149–71, Cambridge: Cambridge University Press.

Norris, M. (2011), *Virgin and Veteran Readings of Ulysses*, New York: Palgrave Macmillan.

Oberman, H. A. (1989), *Luther: Man between God and Devil*, trans. E. Walliser-Schwarzbart, New Haven: Yale University Press.

Orr, J. (1923) *New Testament Apocryphal Writings*, London: J. M. Dent & Sons.

Orwell, G. ([1946] 1981), "Inside the Whale," in *Collected Essays*, New York: Houghton Mifflin Harcourt Publishing.

Owens, L. S., ed. (1995), *The Gnosis Archive*. Available online: http://gnosis.org/welcome.html (accessed January 28, 2021).

Owens, L. S., ed. (1995), "Gospel of Thomas," in T. O. Lambdin (trans.), *The Nag Hammadi Library in The Gnosis Archive*. Available online: http://gnosis.org/library/advh1.htm (accessed January 28, 2021).

Parfit, D. (1984), *Reasons and Persons*, Oxford: Oxford University Press.

Pagels, E. (1979), *The Gnostic Gospels*, New York: Vintage Books.

Pelikan, J. (1971), *The Christian Tradition: A History of the Development of Doctrine, Vol. 1: The Emergence of the Catholic Tradition (100–600)*, Chicago: University of Chicago Press.

Pelikan, J. (1977), *The Christian Tradition: A History of the Development of Doctrine, Vol 2: The Spirit of Eastern Christendom (600–1700)*, Chicago: University of Chicago Press.

Pelikan, J. (1978), *The Christian Tradition: A History of the Development of Doctrine, Vol 3: The Growth of Medieval Theology (600–1300)*, Chicago: University of Chicago Press.

Pelikan, J. (1985), *The Christian Tradition: A History of the Development of Doctrine, Vol 4: Reformation of Church and Dogma (1300–1700)*, Chicago: University of Chicago Press.
Pickstock, C. (1998), *After Writing: On the Liturgical Cosummation of Philosophy*, Hoboken: Wiley-Blackwell.
Pinkerton, S. (2017), *Blasphemous Modernism: The 20th-Century Word Made Flesh*, Oxford: Oxford University Press.
Pratt, O. (1851), *Divine Authenticity of the Book of Mormon*. Available online: http://www.boap.org/LDS/Early-Saints/OP-BOM.html (accessed January 28, 2021).
Pratt, O. (1991), *The Essential Orson Pratt*. Available online: http://signaturebookslibrary.org/the-essential-orson-pratt/ (accessed January 28, 2021).
Rabaté, J. M. (2014), *Cambridge Introduction to Literature and Psychoanalysis*, Cambridge: Cambridge University Press.
Renan, E. (1864), *Life of Jesus*, New York: Carleton Publisher.
Roberts, T. (2013), *Encountering Religion: Responsibility and Criticism after Secularism*, New York: Columbia University Press.
Roe H. M. (1972), "A Medieval Alabaster Figure, Black Abbey, Kilkenny," *Old Kilkenny Review* (24): 33–6.
Roffey, S. (2006), "Constructing a Vision of Salvation: Chantries and the Social Dimension of Religious Experience in the Medieval Parish Church," *Archaeological Journal*, 163 (1): 122–46.
Rubin, M. (1991), *Corpus Christi: The Eucharist in Late Medieval Culture*, Cambridge: Cambridge University Press.
Rubin, M. (1999), *Gentile Tales: The Narrative Assault on Late-Medieval Jews*, Philadelphia: University of Pennsylvania Press.
Santana, R. (2005), *Language and the Decline of Magic: Epistemological Shifts in English Literature from Medieval to Modernist*, Lewiston: Edwin Meller Press.
Sauer, M. M. (2013), "Architecture of Desire: Mediating the Female Gaze in the Medieval English Anchorhold," *Gender & History*, 25 (3): 545–64.
Schneidau, H. (1976), *Sacred Discontent: The Bible and Western Tradition*, Berkeley: University of California Press.
Schutte, W. M. (1971), *Joyce and Shakespeare: A Study in the Meaning of Ulysses*, Hamden: Archon Books.
Schweitzer, A. (1910), *The Quest of the Historical Jesus: A Critical Study of Its Progress From Reimarus to Wrede*, London: Adam and Charles Black.
Scott, W. A. (1971), *Sources of Protestant Theology*, Milwaukee: The Bruce Publishing Company.
Seeger, S. (2017), *Nonlinear Temporality in Joyce and Walcott: History Repeating Itself with a Difference*, London: Routledge.
Seidel, M. (1976) "'Ulysses' Black Panther Vampire," *James Joyce Quarterly*, 13 (4): 415–27.
Shaw, G. B. ([1923] 2001), *Saint Joan*, New York: Penguin Books.

Simmons, T. F., ed. (1879), *The Lay Folks' Mass Book: or, Manner of Hearing Mass: with Rubric and Devotions for the People; in Four Texts; and, Offices in English according to the Use of York: from MSS. of the Xth to the XVth century*, London: Early English Text Society.

Simpson, J. (2010), *Under the Hammer: Iconoclasm in the Anglo-American Tradition*, Oxford: Oxford University Press.

Smith, J. (2013), *The Doctrine and Covenants of the Church of Jesus Christ to Latter-Day Saints*, Salt Lake City: The Church of Jesus Christ of Latter-Day Saints. Available online: https://www.churchofjesuschrist.org/study/scriptures/dc-testament?lang=eng (accessed January 28, 2021).

Smith, J. ([1844] 1971), "King Follett Sermon," *Ensign*, 1 (4). Available online: https://www.churchofjesuschrist.org/study/ensign/1971/04/the-king-follett-sermon?lang=eng (accessed January 28, 2021).

Socrates Scholasticus (4th/5th century), *Church History*.

Soler, C. (2018), *Lacan Reading Joyce*, trans. D. Simiu, London: Routledge.

Spenser, E. ([1590; 1596] 1978), *The Faerie Queene*, New York: Penguin Classics.

Spenser, E. (1633), "A View of the Present State of Ireland," *CELT: Corpus of Electronic Texts*. Available online: https://celt.ucc.ie//published/E500000-001/ (accessed January 28, 2021).

Spivak, G. C. (1976), "Translator's Preface," in G. C. Spivak (trans.), *Of Grammatology*, ix–lxxxvi, Baltimore: Johns Hopkins University Press.

Spoo, R. (1994), *James Joyce and the Language of History: Dedalus's Nightmare*, Oxford: Oxford University Press.

Sternberg, M. (1984), *The Poetics of Biblical Narrative: Ideological Literature and the Drama of Reading*, Bloomington: Indiana University Press.

Stevens, W. (1990), *Opus Posthumous*, ed. Milton Bates, New York: Vintage Books.

Stoker, B. ([1897] 2008), *The New Annotated Dracula*, ed. L. S. Klinger, New York: W. W. Norton & Company.

Strauss, D. ([1835] 1860), *The Life of Jesus Critically Examined*, trans. M. Evans, New York: Calvin Blanchard.

Sullivan, S. E. ([1920] 1993), *The Book of Kells*, London: Studio Editions.

Taylor, M. C. (1984), *Erring: A Postmodern A/theology*, Chicago: University of Chicago Press.

Taylor, M. C. (2007), *After God*, Chicago: University of Chicago Press.

"The Dream of the Rood." Available online: https://oldenglishpoetry.camden.rutgers.edu/dream-of-the-rood/ (accessed January 28, 2021).

Thomas, S. (1991), *Newman and Heresy: The Anglican Years*, Cambridge: Cambridge University Press.

Tillich, P. (1952), *The Courage to Be*, New Haven: Yale University Press.

Tonning, E. (2014), *Modernism and Christianity*, London: Palgrave Macmillan.

Topping, M. (2013), "Religion," in A. Watt (ed), *Marcel Proust in Context*, 137–44, Cambridge: Cambridge University Press.

Tracy, D. (1999), "Fragments: The Spiritual Situation of Our Times," in J. D. Caputo and M. Scanlon (eds), *God, the Gift, and Postmodernism*, 170–81, Bloomington: Indiana University Press.

Tuggle, B. (2016), "*The Faerie Queene* at *Finnegans Wake*," *The Explicator*, 74 (2): 129–32.

Twitchell, J. (1981), *The Living Dead: A Study of Vampires in Romantic Literature*, Durham: Duke University Press.

University at Buffalo, The Poetry Collection, The James Joyce Collection.

van Boheeman-Saaf, C. (1999), *Joyce, Derrida, Lacan, and the Trauma of History: Reading, Narrative, and Postcolonialism*, Cambridge: Cambridge University Press.

van Hulle, D. (2009), "Genetic Joyce Criticism," in J. McCourt (ed), *James Joyce in Context*, Cambridge: Cambridge University Press.

Van Mierlo, C. (2017), *James Joyce and Catholicism: The Apostate's Wake*, London: Bloomsbury.

von Harnack, A. ([1920] 1990), *Marcion: The Gospel of the Alien God*, trans. J. Steeley and L. Bierma, Jamestown: Labyrinth Press.

von Ranke L. (1847), *The History of the Popes, Their Church and State, in the Sixteenth and Seventeenth Centuries*, trans. W. Keating Kelley, New York: William H. Colyer.

Wagner, R. (2011), *Godwired: Religion, Ritual, and Virtual Reality*, London: Routledge.

Walsh, R. (1969), "In the Name of the Father and the Son: Joyce's Use of the Mass in *Ulysses*," *James Joyce Quarterly*, 6 (3): 321–47.

West End Presbyterian Church. Available online: https://westendchurchnyc.org (accessed July 5, 2021).

Williams, R. (1987), *Arius: Heresy and Tradition*, London: Darton, Longman and Todd Ltd.

Williams, R. (2013), "Reformation," in T. Barber and S. Boldricks (eds), *Art under Attack: Histories of British Iconoclasm*, 48–73, London: Tate Publishing.

Wilson, C. (1990), *The Gothic Cathedral: The Architecture of the Great Church, 1130–1530*, London: W. W. Norton & Company.

Wright, J. (2011), *Heretics: The Creation of Christianity from the Gnostics to the Modern Church*, Boston: Houghton Mifflin Harcourt.

Yee, C. D. K. (1997), *The Word according to James Joyce: Reconstructing Representation*, Lewisburg: Bucknell University Press.

York Minster Guidebook (2014), York: York Minster.

Žižek, S. and J. Milbank (2009), *The Monstrosity of Christ: Paradox or Dialectic?*, ed. C. Davis, Cambridge: MIT Press.

Index

Age of Faith 42–3
Altizer, Thomas J. J. 7, 22, 77–8,
    111–12, 153, 169, 172, 178–9
Ambrose of Milan 129
Apostles' Creed 109
Aquinas, Thomas 16, 129, 151, 158–9
Aristotle 103
Arius xii, 3–4, 6, 12–13, 20, 26, 36–42,
    87–112, 151
Aston, Margaret 48, 140
atheism xi, 10, 12–13, 123, 141, 153
Atherton, James 151, 174
Attridge, Derek 80, 84, 166
Auerbach, Eric 85
Auerbach, Nina 96

Barber, Tabitha 146
Barkan, Leonard 150
Bataille, George 111
Baudrillard, Jean 22
Bauer, Walter 33–4, 36
Beckett, Samuel 7, 172
Bennett, Jane 117, 141
Best, Richard 102
Bible 6, 22–3, 25, 38, 49, 50, 67, 97,
    142, 149, 151, 160, 163, 167,
    176, 178, 188
  Acts 39
  Exodus 154
  Genesis 5, 9–10, 73, 85, 156, 159
  history of 26, 47–8, 56, 62–3, 66–7
  interpretation of 29, 75, 84–5,
    155–6
  John 8–10, 61–2, 78, 156
  Luke 184
  Matthew 30, 152, 154, 180
  Mark 65
  Philippians 37
  Proverbs 39, 77
  Revelations 73, 159
  Romans 64
Blair, Ann 46
Blake, William 52, 111–12

Blick, Sarah 113, 117, 127
blindness 42, 170–2
Bloomsday xiii–xvi, 191–5
Bogomils 43
Boldrick, Stacy 140, 148
Boldrini, Lucia 125–6, 135
book history 8, 47, 66–7, 142
Book of Mormon xi, xii, xiii, 26, 50–2,
    142, 151, 173–9, 180–2, 184–6,
    187–90
  1 Nephi 176–7, 182–3
  2 Nephi 174
Borges, Jorge Luis 111
Borromean knot 197–8
Boyle, Robert 158–9
Brivic, Sheldon 17
Brodie, Fawn M. 51, 189
Brown, Dan x
Bucer, Martin 148–9
Budgen, Frank 78–9

Calvin, Jean 46, 49
Cappadocian Fathers 191
Carlson, Thomas 7, 153
Cathedrals 114–16, 117, 121, 127,
    130–1, 134–5, 200–1
  Black Abbey 161–2
  York Minster 114, 127, 130–1,
    192–4
  St. Canice's 161
Champion, Matthew J. 193–4
Cheng, Vincent 17–18, 72, 99, 150
Chesterton, G. K. 10, 26, 139–40
christology xii, 3–4, 41–2, 43, 88, 91–3,
    98–9, 100, 102, 103, 107, 110–11,
    111–12, 135–6, 163
Church of Latter-Day Saints (the
    Mormons) 6, 50–2, 62, 155,
    174–90
Clark, Stuart 46
Clement of Alexandria 79, 156
Cliett, Bill Cole 82–3
Conley, Tim 57

Covid xiv
Cranmer, Thomas 143, 149
Cromwell, Oliver 163, 168
Croxton Play of the Sacrament 129
crucifixion 4, 11, 12, 16, 32, 44
Cummings, Brian 147, 149, 160
Curtis, Penelope 143

Dante 68, 155, 169
Day, Robert Adams 94–5
de Vries, Hent 14–15, 22
death of God 13, 22, 77–8, 103, 111, 153, 172, 179, 180, 198
Derrida, Jacques 12, 22, 40, 52, 67, 122, 171, 177–9, 184, 185–6, 189
Dettmar, Kevin ix
Dickens, Charles 115
Dinshaw, Carolyn 121
Dostoyevsky, Fyodor 7, 112
Dublin ix, 3, 59
  as a character 4, 127–8, 131
  Literary culture of 102, 104–5
Dubliners
  "Grace," 70–1
  "The Sisters," 123
Duffy, Eamon 43, 45, 119–21, 129, 143, 145
Dworkin, Craig 171

Eco, Umberto 125, 127
Eglington, John 102, 109–10
Ehrman, Bart D. 21, 27–8, 52, 55, 62, 65, 74
Einstein, Albert 77
Eliade, Mircea 6, 115, 127
Eliot, T. S. x, 34, 75, 84
  Murder in the Cathedral 5
  "*Ulysses*, Order, and Myth," 69
  Waste Land 145
Ellmann, Maud 108
Ellmann, Richard 2, 13, 81, 88, 110, 114, 132, 152, 177
Epstein, Edmund 73, 82–3
Eucharist xii–xiii, 43–5, 116–18, 122–3, 135
  elevation of the Host, 118–21
  in *Finnegans Wake*, 150, 158–9, 186
  gnostic depictions of 32
  historic development of, 48, 115, 132–3, 142–3
  in *Portrait of the Artist* 19
  in *Ulysses* 113–14, 124–7, 128–30, 131
Eusebius 68
evil 80, 96, 99

Farmer, Philip José 11
Finnegans Wake 7, 22–3, 41, 52, 70, 71, 89, 163
  the cross, 198–9
  deconstruction of language 19–20, 67, 143–6
  the Fall 81, 152
  and Ireland 168, 195–6
  identity 184
  linearity of history 23, 28–9, 60, 62, 81–3, 139–41, 165, 183
  materiality 9–10, 136, 142, 159–60
  Mamafesta 53–5, 57, 62, 179–81, 195
  "Mookse and the Gripes," xv
  reading 68–9, 171–2, 184–5, 189–90, 192, 197, 198–9, 199–201
  and scripture 154–7, 169
  and The Book of Mormon 173–9, 186
  creation 116
  god 56, 77–8
  trinity 191
  Shem and Shaun 64–6, 157–9, 160, 197
  word and image 121–2, 149–51, 170
Finnegans Wake Notebooks xvii, 55, 141, 163–6, 167–8, 172, 197–9
  Book 1 82, 171
  Book 3 196
  Book 6 195
  Book 7 167
First World War 60, 191
Flaubert, Gustave 18–19
Fleming, Juliet 68
Flood, J. M. 196–7
Fordham, Finn 57–8, 150, 159–60, 164, 201
Frei, Hans 67

Garrison, Jennifer 116, 132
Gelfand, Laura xiii, 113, 117, 127
genetic criticism 57, 159–60, 165
Gifford, Don 17

Gilbert, Stuart 84, 104
Giles, Kate 133
Gilman, Ernest B. 140–1
Ginnungagap 84
Givens, Terryl 174–5 177, 183–4
gnosticism xi, xii, 4, 5–6, 16, 21, 26,
    55–9, 69–70, 71–2, 83
    Acts of John 63, 100
    and Christianity 36–7
    beliefs 32–3, 35, 73–4, 77, 79, 105
    definition 30–1, 33–5, 72
    gnostic Christ 63–6, 79–80
    gospel of Mary 80
    gospel of Philip 80, 171
    gospel of Thomas 31–2, 37, 58
    gospel of Truth 32, 65–6
Goethe, Johann Wolfgang von 102, 103
    Faust 156
gospel of Peter 62, 65
Gottfried, Roy x, 2, 4–5, 17–18, 58, 71
graffiti 46, 117, 121, 166, 193–4
Graham, Elaine 96
Greenblatt, Stephen 50, 106, 153, 169
Gregory, Brad 142–3
Gross, Kenneth 147, 168–70

Haigh, Christopher 43, 49
Hall, Edward 36
Hardy, Grant 175–6, 184–5
Hart, Clive 53–4, 197–8
Hatch, Nathan O. 50
Hegel, Georg Wilhelm Friedrich 38, 52
Heidegger, Martin 22, 91–2, 171
Hippolytus 56
Hobson, Suzanne xiv, 15
Hollywood, Amy xv, 7
Homer 68, 84
    Odyssey 70, 85, 103, 126
Howe, Susan 166
Hus, Jan 46
Hussites 43, 46, 116
hypostasis 41–2

iconoclasm xii–xiii, 48, 121–3, 140, 141,
    142–3, 143–7, 148–50, 152–3,
    157–8, 161, 165–6, 168–70, 172,
    192
Irenaeus 11–2, 26, 39, 77
    Against Heresies 35–6, 56, 64
Islam 53, 64, 179, 192, 193

James, Henry ix
Jaurretche, Colleen 55, 149–50
Jonas, Hans 33, 34–6, 58, 74
Joyce, Stanislaus 123
Jung, Carl 58, 60
Jung, Jaqueline 120

Kabbalah 74, 175
Kafka, Franz 7, 111
Kazantzakis, Nikos 11
Kearney, Richard 22
Kermode, Frank 68
Kieckhefer, Richard 118, 130–1
King, Karen L. 33, 35, 55, 68–70
Kitcher, Philip 84

*La civilization et les grandes fleuves
    historiques* 82
Lacan, Jaques 197–8
Lang, Frederick K. 1, 2, 92, 109–10,
    124–5
Larsen, Matthew 56–7, 68
Laws, Christopher David 4
Lawrence, D. H. 114–16
Lawrence, Karen 93, 104
Le Fanu, J. Sheridan 96
Leonard, Gary 19
Lernout, Geert xiv, 1, 71, 109, 164
Letters of James Joyce 1, 51, 132
Levering, Miriam 174–5
Lewis, Pericles xiv
Luther, Martin 22, 46, 129, 147
    95 theses 46
Lyster, Thomas 102, 103

MacCulloch, Diarmaid 9, 16, 47–8, 51,
    149
Mann, Thomas 5
Mantel, Hilary 115
Marquardt, Janet T. 136
Marriott, McKim 158
Marshall, Peter 45, 49–50, 146–8
Martello Tower 3, 124
Mass
    experience of 115–16, 120–1
    imagery 19, 122
    and Joyce 123, 132, 134–5, 143
    performance of 32, 44–5, 118–19,
        127
    reformation impacts 46, 49, 140

in *Ulysses* xvii, 3, 28, 61, 68, 79, 87, 98, 113, 122, 123, 124–7, 128–30, 131–2, 134, 135–7, 152
Marcion 20–2, 31
McCoy, Richard C. 49
McLuhan, Marshall 80, 199
Milton 150, 156, 163, 169
  Paradise Lost 28, 29
Mitchell, W. J. T. 170–1
Morrison, Stephen 17–18, 71, 89, 110
Morrow, James K. 11
Muehlberger, Ellen 100
Muhammad, Ali 59
Mutter, Matthew 5

National Endowment for the Humanities (NEH) ix, 113
Nag Hammadi 31, 32, 51, 59–60, 62, 63, 66, 83, 85
new materialism 117
Newman, Cardinal John Henry 40, 88–9
Newton, Isaac 77
Nicaean Creed 3, 6, 38, 41, 93, 109, 110
Nietzsche, Friedrich 72, 77–8
Noon, William T. 103
Norris, Margot 54, 71, 90, 181
nothing (nothingness) 87–92, 172

Origen 26
Orr, James 65
Orwell, George 123

Pagels, Elaine x, 36, 59–60
Parfit, Derek 107
Pater, Walter 102
Pelikan, Jaroslav 25–6, 27, 29, 31, 36–40, 43–5, 68, 77, 92, 118, 145
Photius 3–4, 151
Pickstock, Catherine 122
Pinkerton, Steve xiv, 1
Plato 74, 103, 104, 185
Polidori, John William 96
A Portrait of the Artist as a Young Man 3, 12, 13–19, 22, 28, 37, 40, 63, 65, 76, 89, 92, 107, 123, 151, 192
Pound, Ezra 34
Pratt, Orson 175

Proust, Marcel xiii, 60–1, 115
pun xiii, 10, 14–15, 22, 52, 65, 151–3, 154–7, 161, 170, 197
Pyrrhus 73

Rabaté, Jean-Michel 197–8
radical theology 7, 10, 22, 78, 122, 151, 158, 159, 172
radical orthodoxy 122
Reformation xii, xiii, 26, 32, 43, 165, 196
  art and literature 139–41, 143, 145–6, 164, 167, 187
  catalysts of 47–8, 116, 142
  defining 45–7,146–9
  effects of 48–50, 92, 142–3, 160, 167
  and *Finnegans Wake* 149–51, 151–3, 161
Renan, Ernest 88–9
Roberts, Tyler xi, 6
Roffey, Simon 133–4
rood screen 44, 46, 117, 120–1, 123, 133–5, 143, 159, 172
Rubin, Miri 44, 116–17, 118, 124
Russel, George (AE) 72, 102, 104–5, 107, 168

Sabellius 3–4, 12, 90, 91–2, 99, 103, 105, 109–10
Saint Augustine 5, 26, 68, 152, 156
  Confessions 28
Saint Joan 5
Saint Michan's Church 95
Santana, Richard 125–6
Sartre, Jean-Paul 91–2
Schneidau, Herbert 85
Schoenberg, Arnold ix, 5
Schutte, William M. 104, 110
Schweitzer, Albert 88–9
Scott, William A. 147–8
scripture xiv, 48, 66, 68, 142, 149, 153–65, 180, 186
  expansion of 60
  Hebrew 5, 6–7, 22–3, 34, 36, 39, 45, 56, 66, 77, 173, 182
  interpreting 6–7, 8–9, 20–1, 26, 27–30, 41, 67
  recreating 29, 50, 52, 145, 151–3, 174–9

Sola scriptura 46
  as text 8, 12, 25, 27, 30, 142, 166, 167
Second World War 192
Shakespeare, William 50, 68, 77, 98, 102, 104, 115, 139, 153
  Hamlet 42, 90, 92, 93, 102–3, 105–11
Shelley, Mary 96–7
Simpson, James 48, 140, 148–9, 172
Sistine Chapel 33
Smith, Joseph xi, 6, 50–2, 176, 180, 182–3, 187, 189
  Doctrine & Covenants 51
  Golden Tablets 55, 62, 180, 187
  King Follett Sermon 51
Socrates 103, 99–100, 185
Soler, Colette 197–8
Spenser, Edmund 50, 139–40, 147, 149, 168
  The Faerie Queene 74, 168–71
Spivak, Gayatri xiv, 12, 67, 171
Spoo, Robert 69–70, 72, 75
squint 132–4
Stephen Hero 10, 63, 64, 79–80, 123–4
Sternberg, Meir 85
Stevens, Hugh 7
Stoker, Bram 95, 139–40
  Dracula 96–7, 97–8
Strauss, David 88–9
Sullivan, Edward
  The Book of Kells 55, 83

Taylor, Mark C. 7, 22, 78, 111, 180, 186
Tertullian 21, 25, 36, 56
theosophy 31, 50, 56, 71–2, 105
Thomas, Stephen 89
Tonning, Erik xv
Topping, Margaret 115
transubstantiation 3, 44, 79, 93–4, 98, 120, 124, 132, 134, 158–9
Trinity xvi, 41–2, 50, 90–4, 106–10, 149, 161–3, 191–2, 197–9
Tuggle, Brad 168
Turkey 41, 191–5
typology 21, 28–9, 75, 177

Ulysses ix, 7, 10, 19–20, 22, 41, 42, 51, 56, 60, 67–70, 71, 77–8, 78–9, 81, 84, 95, 113, 115, 124–7, 142, 151, 158, 163, 174

history of 34
Episode 1, Telemachus 3, 79, 87–8, 90, 98, 102, 124
Episode 2, Nestor 72–6, 196
Episode 3, Proteus 61, 92, 93, 102, 135–6
Episode 4, Calypso 100
Episode 5, Lotus Eaters 128
Episode 6, Hade 99
Episode 7, Aeolus 80–1
Episode 8, Lestrygonians 92, 97–8
Episode 9, Scylla and Charybdis 20, 72, 77, 90, 102–5, 105–11
Episode 11, Sirens xv–xvi
Episode 13, Nausicaa 61–2
Episode 14, Oxen of the Sun 98–9
Episode 15, Circe 9, 28, 94–5, 98, 131–2, 136
Episode 17, Ithaca 56
Episode 18, Penelope 136–7

Valentinus 4, 11–2, 32, 53, 56, 79, 109, 151
vampires 52, 88, 92, 93–5, 96–8, 98–9, 100, 102
van Boheemen-Saff, Christine 10, 15, 57, 85, 111, 152–3
van Hulle, Dirk 165
Van Mierlo, Chrissie x, 2, 64, 164
Van Mierlo, Wim 164
von Harnack, Adolf 21–2
von Ranke, Leopold xv
Vernon Manuscript 129

Wagner, Rachel 142
Waldrop, Rosemarie 166
Wells, H. G. 60–1
Wilde, Oscar 102
Wilson, Christopher 114
Woolf, Virginia, 44, 111
Wright, Jonathan 147–8
Wycliffe, John 46
  Lollards 46, 47, 48, 102, 129

Yee, Cordell D. K. 125
Yeats, William Butler 168
York, 113, 114–5, 120–2, 125, 127, 130, 134–5, 149, 192–3

Žižek, Slavoj 7, 10–11, 12–13, 38, 96

www.ingramcontent.com/pod-product-compliance
Lightning Source LLC
Chambersburg PA
CBHW062215300426
44115CB00012BA/2074